MONETARY POLICY

Advanced Studies in Theoretical and Applied Econometrics

Volume 19

For a list of volumes in this series see final page.

Monetary Policy

A Theoretical and Econometric Approach

edited by

P. Artus and Y. Barroux

SPRINGER-SCIENCE+BUSINESS MEDIA, B.V.

Library of Congress Cataloging in Publication Data

Monetary policy : a theoretical and econometric approach / edited by
P. Artus and Y. Barroux.
p. cm. -- (Advanced studies in theoretical and applied
econometrics ; v. 19)
Selected papers from a Jan. 1987 international conference
organised by the Applied Econometric Association.
ISBN 978-90-481-4062-6 ISBN 978-94-015-7852-3 (eBook)
DOI 10.1007/978-94-015-7852-3
1. Monetary policy. 2. Monetary policy--Econometric models.
I. Artus, Patrick. II. Barroux, Y. (Yves), 1945- . III. Applied
Econometric Association. IV. Series.
HG230.3.M636 1990
332.4'6--dc20 89-26856

ISBN 978-90-481-4062-6

Printed on acid-free paper

TABLE OF CONTENTS

Introduction vii
P. Artus and Y. Barroux

PART I: OPTIMAL MONETARY POLICY AND REACTION FUNCTION OF THE MONETARY AUTHORITIES

1. Optimal Monetary Policy and the Revealed Preference Function of the Swiss National Bank 3
U. Camen, H. Genberg and M. Salemi
2. Optimal Monetary Policies in a Small Open Economy 15
T. Chauveau

PART II: CREDIBILITY AND REPUTATION

3. Credibility, Reputation and the Indeterminacy of Macroeconomics 63
C. Carraro
4. Policy Credibility and the Lucas Critique – Some New Tests with an Application to Denmark 79
M. Christensen

PART III: THE DEMAND FOR MONEY

5. Dynamics of the Demand for Money and Uncertainty: The US Demand for Money Revisited 99
E. Koskela and M. Viren
6. Analysis of the Relationship between Money Stock and Monetary Base: The French Experience during the Period of Quantitative Controls on Credit (1973–1985) 117
Y. Barroux and N. Dagognet

PART IV: CAUSALITY ANALYSIS AND THE EFFECTS OF MONETARY POLICY

7. Causal Relationships between Money and Income in the Spanish Economy 133
A. Aznar and F.J. Trivez

8. Interest Rates and Inflation in Italy during the Seventies 163
E. D'Elia

9. A Short–Term Disequilibrium Model with Carry–Over, for US Business Loans 179
M.G. Dagenais

PART V: ECONOMETRIC MODELS OF THE FINANCIAL MARKETS: THEIR USE IN ASSESSING THE CROWDING–OUT EFFECTS

10. Real and Financial Linkages in the UK Economy 203
G.W. McKenzie and S.H. Thomas

11. Crowding–Out, Reagonomics and Monetary Policy 233
J.C. Siebrand and J. Swank

INTRODUCTION

Patrick Artus and Yves Barroux

The Applied Econometric Association organised an international conference on "*Monetary and Financial Models*" in Geneva in January 1987. The purpose of this book is to make available to the public a choice of the papers that were presented at the conference. The selected papers all deal with the setting of monetary targets and the effects of monetary policy on the economy as well as with the analysis of the financial behaviours of economic agents. Other papers presented at the same conference but dealing with the external aspects of monetary policy (exchange rate policy, international coordination of economic policies, international transmission of business cycles, ...) are the matter of a distinct publication.

The papers put together to make up this book either are theoretical research contributions or consist of applied statistical or econometric work. It seemed to be more logical to start with the more theoretical papers. The topics tackled in the first two parts of the book have in common the fact that they appeared just recently in the field of economic research and deal with the analysis of the behaviour of Central Banks. They analyse this behaviour so as to be able to exhibit its major determinants as well as revealed preferences of Central Banks: this topic comes under the caption "optimal monetary policy and reaction function of the monetary authorities". The second topic has a different purpose and, in analysing the implementation of monetary policy and its consequences, is mainly interested in the problems of time consistency that confront monetary authorities: it is usually referred to as the problem of Central Bank credibility and reputation.

The last three parts of the book give more room to empirical approaches. Dealing with more traditional topics and often already widely explored fields of economic research, the selected papers aim at giving sort of a comprehensive view of the theoretical knowledge and econometric findings in any of the particular fields. Sometimes, the purpose is to take into account the changes that have materialised in the financial system, to suggest interpretation of recent breaks and to try to guess their significance both in terms of the changing of the behaviour of economic agents and in relationship with the efficiency of monetary policy. Such topics are money demand and the analysis of the effects of monetary policy appraised through the use of either a reduced form equation or a complete model of the economy describing both the real and the financial sectors.

All these papers tend to bring out new ways of thinking that might be useful to Central Banks in dealing with problems as important to them as the choice of instruments of monetary policy, the setting of strategies able to enlarge the credibility of the implemented monetary policy, the explanation for the recent movements in the velocity of money, the estimation of the respective effects on prices and output of changes in the money supply, the understanding of the determination of interest rates and the evaluation of the size of crowding–out effects.

PART I
OPTIMAL MONETARY POLICY AND REACTION FUNCTION OF THE MONETARY AUTHORITIES

U. Camen, H. Genberg and M. Salemi seek to reveal the preferences of the Swiss National Bank. To this end, they use a vector autoregression (*VAR*) model of the Swiss economy, which includes an equation determining the monetary base. They try to characterise the preference or loss function that would allow for the correspondingly determined monetary base to be as close as possible to the observed data. They conclude that reducing inflation appears to be the major objective of the Swiss monetary authorities.

Th. Chauveau, using a traditional model with rational expectations, seeks to specify optimal rules for either setting the money market rate or controlling the monetary base. He assumes that the objective of the authorities might consist either in lowering the variance of the foreign exchange reserves or in reducing the fluctuations of output and inflation. Solving his model in the two cases of fixed and flexible exchange rates leads him to the two conclusions that:

- Whenever the money multiplier is instable, controlling the money market rate appears to be preferable to controlling the monetary base;
- whatever the exchange rates system might be, optimal monetary policies exhibit very similar features and the exogenous variables entering the reaction functions are the same as those showing in most of the empirical studies (foreign interest rate, foreign exchange reserves, expected exchange rate, ...).

PART II
CREDIBILITY AND REPUTATION

C. Carraro is interested in the definition of an economic policy strategy that would be optimal from the point of view of the policy maker. We know that pure optimal economic policies are time inconsistent and time–consistent policies are sub–optimal. Barro and Gordon have shown that, when the private sector threatens the policy maker to adopt a non–cooperative behaviour if the latter does not stick to its announced policy, a better outcome than the one achieved in a non–cooperative environment can be obtained. Carraro underlined the fact that there might be a large number of such outcomes and it looks very unlikely that the private sector will threaten the policy maker in such a way that it would allow the latter to implement the policy it precisely wants to. He then suggests that the policy maker might be the leader of the game and, in a Stackelberg trigger strategy, threatens the private sector. Under these assumptions, he shows that the policy maker can achieve a multiplicity of outcomes, any of them being better than the non–cooperative one, and, of course, the one it thinks is optimal; the time consistency problem is thus solved.

M. Christensen analyses empirically the consequences of a change of policy regime that took place in Denmark in 1982: in October, the monetary authorities let it be known that the system of recurrent devaluations of the exchange rate would not be pursued. He wonders if, in so doing, the authorities have acquired a better reputation. In order to find out whether they actually did, an equation for the long term interest rate is estimated, in which the exchange rate variability comes in both directly and as a parameter influencing other explanatory variables. Observing that the exchange rate variability has been reduced because of the policy change, he concludes to its credibility and underlines that the use of a varying parameter model allows for taking into account the Lucas critique, stating that the decisions and actions of the private sector depends on expectations on the policy to be implemented.

PART III
THE DEMAND FOR MONEY

E. Koskela and M. Viren estimate various money demand functions for the United States using different specifications: the usual partial adjustment model, the so–called threshold model (where the parameters take different values depending on whether any particular driving variable is below or above the "*threshold*"), error correction models. They finally turn to a specification which looks closer to the theoretical model of portfolio choice, where variances and covariances of interest rates and inflation rate intervene explicitly. This model shows the most satisfactory results.

Y. Barroux and N. Dagognet analyse the evolution of the monetary base (B) over the last fifteen years in France compared to the one of the money stock (M). As a matter of fact, they analyse the changes in the ratio B/M and seek to uncover major explanatory factors. The method used consists in pairing a traditional money demand function with a divisor–type relation and in deriving from these an equation for B/M whose specification is very close to the error correction model. Estimating this model, they obtain rather satisfactory results that yields long term elasticities relative to interest rates that are weak and appear to be consistent with the so–called credit divisor framework , which was governing the working of the French monetary system for at least the last fifteen years.

PART IV
CAUSALITY ANALYSIS AND THE EFFECTS OF MONETARY POLICY

A. Aznar and F.J. Trivez consider the causal relationship between the money stock and the gross domestic product at constant prices in Spain. The statistical method they use consist in stationarising the series, determining the optimal auto–correlation coefficient of the variables and measuring the degree of predicting performance of each equation, which allows for performing a causality test "a la Granger". Applying this procedure to the Spanish data leads to the conclusion that the money stock and the real output are independent.

E. d'Elia analyses the causal relationship between nominal interest rates and inflation. Economic theory shows that the direction of this relationship might be different depending on the nature of the shocks affecting the economy. However, similar movements in the rate of inflation and in nominal interest rates may be caused simultaneously by other variables, for instance domestic demand, the rate of exchange or the trade deficit. Causality tests realised using Granger's method show that, in Italy, the rate of inflation and the nominal interest rates were influenced simultaneously by the evolution of other variables without being indexed on one another.

M. Dagenais estimates a disequilibrium model of the U.S. credit market. The specification of the model has two original features: on one hand, part of the unsatisfied demand may spill over into the next period; on the other hand, the interest rate varies in response to market disequilibrium. Using monthly data, the study suggests that the U.S. business loan market does behave like a market in disequilibrium since interest rate variations do not succeed in balancing supply and demand within the monthly period. Furthermore, the empirical results show that about one third of the unsatisfied demand carries over to the next month and the complete equilibrium is reached by the end of the quarter.

PART V
ECONOMETRIC MODELS OF THE FINANCIAL MARKETS: THEIR USE IN ASSESSING THE CROWDING–OUT EFFECTS

G. Mackenzie and S. Thomas seek to evaluate the ability of monetary authorities to control the money stock and the amount of bank credit and eventually to affect economic activity. They argue that classical models do not allow for answering this question accurately as it would require the use of a highly disaggregated model which would only make visible and measurable the substitutability between the financial assets included in the controlled monetary aggregate and other financial and real assets (or goods). Accordingly they propose a model determining simultaneously prices, wages, the exchange rate, the various financial assets and their rates of return and finally the domestic expenditure. Estimating this model, they draw the conclusion that it is both theory and data consistent and will provide a suitable vehicle for subsequent policy simulations, particularly for quantification of the impact of monetary policy.

J.C. Siebrand and J. Swank seek to assess the consequences of fiscal and monetary policies implemented in the U.S. in the early eighties by using an econometric model in which the crowding–out effects play a major role. The model describes both demand and supply sides, puts a special emphasis on portfolio structure considerations and has an endogenous determination of the exchange rate. Simulations realised with the model exhibit large crowding–out effects and suggest that, for a tax cut policy to be effective, it must go along with a parallel reduction of public spending.

PART I

OPTIMAL MONETARY POLICY AND REACTION FUNCTION OF THE MONETARY AUTHORITIES

CHAPTER 1

OPTIMAL MONETARY POLICY AND THE REVEALED PREFERENCE FUNCTION OF THE SWISS NATIONAL BANK

Ulrich Camen and Hans Genberg, *Graduate Institute of International Studies, Geneva, Switzerland*
Michael Salemi, *University of North Carolina, USA*

1. INTRODUCTION

This paper applies the inverse control problem to characterise Swiss National Bank (SNB) policy during both periods of fixed foreign exchange rates and of floating. It asks how well, for reasonable specifications of SNB objectives, actually observed policy can be reconciled to policy that would have been optimal given preferences and an estimate of the economic environment. By optimal policy is meant the optimal, steady state settings of parameters of a feedback equation. A detailed discussion of optimal policy in this context is provided by Chow (1975). Discussion of the inverse control problem is contained in Chow (1981).

This paper grows out of our earlier work on the Swiss economy. It characterises the Swiss economic environment as a vector autoregression (VAR). One equation of the VAR system explains the Swiss Money Base as a function of lagged variables in the VAR system and is therefore a feedback equation. Béguelin and Rich (1985) make it clear that the SNB regarded the monetary base as its control variable at least during the flexible rate period.

In our view, the approach of this paper is not susceptible to the Lucas critique. We do not assume that the SNB behaves as if the VAR equations were invariant to changes in policy. We simply ask whether the estimated reduced form and the estimated policy are compatible in the sense that, for reasonable policy objectives, they imply good agreement between optimal and observed

P. Artus and Y. Barroux (eds.), Monetary Policy, 3–14.

policy. The SNB may well recognise that our reduced form equations for Swiss variables would not hold if it altered policy dramatically.

The paper consists of three parts. In section 2, we explain our methodology in detail. In section 3, we apply that methodology to our Swiss data. In section 4, we draw conclusions and indicate directions for further research. We consider our conclusions interesting but tentative for reasons we shall explain in what follows.

2. METHODOLOGY

The goal of this paper is to characterise the monetary policy of the Swiss National Bank during both the fixed rate and the flexible rate periods and to discover whether the advent of flexible rates produced a change in SNB policy objectives. Our answer is based on what the engineering literature calls the "inverse control problem". We begin with estimates of the SNB's feedback equations for the money base and the reduced form equations for the variables entering the SNB's loss function and with an assumption about the contemporaneous effects of policy. We then compute the loss function parameter values that best reconcile optimal policy with observed policy. Those parameter estimates are the basis of our characterisation.

2.1 The Model for the Endogenous Variables

Collect the endogenous variables of interest into an (nx1) vector, y_t. Let x_t be the monetary base and let u_t be a white noise vector of dimension (nx1). Suppose that m is the highest order dynamic appearing in the equation system explaining y_t and let d = (nx1) x m. Equation (1) is a model for y_t

$$Y_t = AY_{t-1} + CX_t + B + U_t \tag{1}$$

where the (dx1) vectors, Y_t, U_t, C and B and the (dx1) matrix A are defined by comparing (1) and (1′).

$$\begin{bmatrix} y_t \\ y_{t-1} \\ \vdots \\ y_{t-m+1} \\ x_t \\ x_{t-1} \\ \vdots \\ x_{t-m+1} \end{bmatrix} = \begin{bmatrix} A_1 & A_2 \ldots\ldots A_m & C_1 \ldots\ldots C_m \\ I & 0 \ldots\ldots 0 & 0 \ldots\ldots 0 \\ \vdots & & \\ 0 & \ldots I \;\; 0 & 0 \ldots\ldots 0 \\ 0 & \ldots 0 \;\; 0 & 0 \ldots\ldots 0 \\ 0 & \ldots 0 \;\; 0 & I \ldots\ldots 0 \\ \vdots & & \\ 0 & \ldots 0 \;\; 0 & 0 \ldots I \;\; 0 \end{bmatrix} \begin{bmatrix} y_{t-1} \\ y_{t-2} \\ \vdots \\ y_{t-m} \\ x_{t-1} \\ x_{t-2} \\ \vdots \\ x_{t-m} \end{bmatrix} + \begin{bmatrix} C_0 \\ 0 \\ \vdots \\ 0 \\ I \\ 0 \\ \vdots \\ 0 \end{bmatrix} x_t + \begin{bmatrix} b \\ 0 \\ \vdots \\ \vdots \\ \vdots \\ \vdots \\ \vdots \\ 0 \end{bmatrix} + \begin{bmatrix} u_t \\ 0 \\ \vdots \\ \vdots \\ \vdots \\ \vdots \\ \vdots \\ 0 \end{bmatrix} \tag{1′}$$

In (1′) A_j and C_j are the (nxn) and (nx1) parameter matrices that record the relationship between y_t and, respectively, y_{t-j} and x_{t-j} while b is an (nx1) vector of constants. The pattern of I's and 0's in (1′) is chosen to permit an mth order system to be written as an equivalent first order system.

The feedback equation for the monetary base, x_t, is given by equation (2)

$$x_t = G_t Y_{t-1} + g_t + v_t \tag{2}$$

where G_t is a (1xd) vector of feedback parameters, g_t is a (1x1) function of t, and v_t is a serially uncorrelated stochastic variable. In general, the optimal policy plan implies time dependent settings for feedback parameters. In many cases, however, variation in G_t required by an optimal plan occurs at the end of the planning period so that for most of the planning period the optimal G is constant.

Together (1) and the steady–state version of (2) imply the following reduced form for Y_t.

$$Y_t = (A+CG)Y_{t-1} + (b+Cg_t) + (U_t+Cv_t) \tag{3}$$

By estimating a VAR system comprising X and Y we obtain estimates of A + CG, G, and the covariance matrix of G. These estimates are used to characterise actual SNB policy and the policy environment.

2.2 The General Bank Policy Problem

The Swiss National Bank is presumed to minimise

$$L = E_0[\sum_{t=0}^{T} \delta^t (Y_t - a_t)' K (Y_t - a_t)] \tag{4}$$

where $E_0[\cdot]$ is the expectation operator conditional on time zero information. Three parameters in (4) characterise SNB preferences: a_t is the target path for Y_t, K is the matrix of weights which describe the relative importance to the SNB of stabilising various elements of Y_t, and δ is the rate at which the SNB discounts future "instability". That is, δ determines the relative value of future and current stability. A larger value of δ would indicate, ceteris paribus, that the SNB gave greater weight to the future implications of policy.

Given K and δ, it is straightforward to show that the optimal G_t for t=0,1,...,T satisfy a recursion commonly called the Matrix Ricatti equation (5b) with an initial condition given by (5a).

$$H_t = (\delta)^T K \tag{5a}$$

$$G_t = -(C' H_t C)^{-1} C' H_t A \qquad t = T, T-1, ..., 0 \tag{5b}$$

$$H_{t-1} = (\delta)^{t-1}K + A'H_t(A+CG_t) \qquad t = T-1, T-2, \ldots, 0$$

Chow discusses conditions under which G_t converges to a constant matrix. For the empirical example in this paper convergence generally occurred within very few iterations.

Note that the solutions for G_t and for its steady state value do not depend upon either a_t, the target path for y_t, or upon g_t, the deterministic component of policy. Since we are reluctant to specify a target path, we confine our attention to the feedback component of policy, G_t.

2.3 The Inverse Control Problem

Our strategy for characterising SNB policy turns the typical optimal policy problem on its head. Collect δ and the free parameters of the (dxd) matrix K into a (px1) vector k. Given estimates $\hat{G}$ and $\hat{R}$ of, respectively, G and R = (A+CG) and an assumption about the contemporaneous effects of policy, we compute the k that best reconciles optimal policy, G*, with our estimate of actual policy, $\hat{G}$. In particular, we compute the k that solves the following problem.

$$\min \phi(k) = (G^*-\hat{G})'(\mathrm{Cov}(G))^{-1}(G^*-\hat{G}) \qquad (6)$$

The algorithm used to solve the minimisation problem has several steps: First, choose an initial value for k. Second, iterate the Matrix Ricatti equations until either G_t converges or an iteration limit (30) is reached. The last value of G obtained in this manner is G*(k). Third, compute ϕ(k) according to (6). Fourth, test for convergence of k and either stop or update k and return to the second step. We implemented our algorithm numerically using the DFP hill climber from GQOPT, the Goldfeld–Quandt package.

3. AN EXAMPLE THAT CHARACTERISES SWISS MONETARY POLICY DURING FIXED AND FLEXIBLE EXCHANGE RATE REGIMES

At this preliminary stage in our work, we confine our attention to two questions. First, how closely do $\hat{G}$ and G* agree for reasonable, parsimonious specifications of K? Second, what appear to be the major differences in SNB policy objectives in the fixed rate and flexible rate periods.

3.1 A Characterisation of Actual Swiss National Bank Policy

To proceed we require estimates of G, R, and C_0, the nonzero component of C which contains the contemporaneous effect of changes in the money base on the components of Y_t. Our estimates of G and R were obtained by fitting vector autoregressions to a system of Swiss and foreign variables. Our previous research has shown a strong dependence of Swiss variables on foreign variables, particularly, the US Treasury Bill rate and the German wholesale price level. It has also shown that Swiss industrial production is remarkably independent of movements in both Swiss and foreign macrovariables including the Swiss monetary base.

Guided by our earlier findings we fit VARs to the following systems.

For the fixed rate sample (1964–1971),

TB3US the 3–month US Treasure Bill rate
WPIGE the German wholesale price index
MBCH the Swiss monetary base
WPICH the Swiss wholesale price index
E3LCH the interest rate on 3–month Euro–SFr deposits

For the flexible rate sample (1973–1981),

TB3US the 3–month US Treasury Bill rate
WPIGE the German wholesale price index
SCHUS the SFr/$ spot exchange rate
MBCH the Swiss monetary base
WPICH the Swiss wholesale price index
E3LCH the interest rate on 3–month Euro–SFr deposits

All variables except the interest rates were transformed to natural logarithms. Monthly data were employed. Each equation contained six lags of each variable in the system, a linear time trend, and a set of monthly dummy variables.

A striking feature of the VAR estimates is the strong endogeneity of the monetary base. In the fixed rate period, shocks in TB3US and WPIGE account respectively for 12% and 31% of the 48–month–ahead forecast error variance (FEV) of MBCH. In the flexible rate period, the comparable accounting is 49% for TB3US, 8% for WPIGE and an additional 6% for SCHUS. At shorter horizons, the picture is different. For the fixed period, surprises to MBCH itself account for the great majority of FEV for the first 12 months. Then, as the forecast horizon is increased, other shocks, and primarily foreign shocks, gain importance. For the flexible rate period, the importance of own shocks declines more rapidly. Swiss variables gain importance quickly. At a six month horizon WPICH,SCHUS and E3LCH account respectively for 12%, 11%, and 2% of FEV of the monetary base. As the forecast horizon increases, TB3US gains in importance.

The responses of MBCH to simulated surprises in foreign and domestic variables suggest that SNB policy is well characterised as a feedback rule. Figure 1 reports impulse response functions for MBCH which highlight similarities and differences between the feedback rule for the fixed rate period and that for the flexible rate period. For example, MBCH declines in both periods after an increase in either TB3US or WPICH. On the other hand, it falls in the fixed rate period but rises in the flexible rate period after a shock to German prices. Also, the initial reaction of MBCH to a shock in the Swiss interest rate is opposite in the two periods: a decrease in the fixed case but an increase in the flexible rate period.

3.2 Characterisation of the Swiss National Bank Objective Function

The chief objective of this paper is to determine whether our estimates of the SNB feedback equation can be reconciled to optimal policy. The next step in the analysis is to characterise the set of SNB objective functions that we consider. We assume throughout that the objective of the SNB is to minimise L given by (4). It remains to characterise the form of the K matrix, the matrix of weights that govern the relative importance of various stabilisation objectives.

One obvious, but important restriction placed on the K matrix is that the SNB has stabilisation objectives only for Swiss variables. This restriction implies that feedback from TB3US and WPIGE to the monetary base can be part of an optimal monetary policy only to the extent that the feedback is justified by the dependence of WPICH, E3LCH, and SCHUS on these same foreign variables.

To clarify matters, suppose momentarily that Y_t and K have dimension (2x1) and (2x2) respectively and that a_t=0. Then

$$(Y_t-a_t)'K(Y_t-a_t) = K_{11}Y_{1t}^2 + K_{22}Y_{2t}^2 + (K_{12}+K_{21})Y_{1t}Y_{2t}$$

Suppose the SNB dislikes instability in Y_1 and Y_2. Then the appropriate K matrix sets $K_{11} = w_1$, $K_{22} = w_2$ and $K_{12} = K_{21} = 0$ where w_1 and w_2 are the weights placed on each of the two stabilisation objectives. Suppose, alternatively, that the SNB attempts to stabilise the difference between Y_1 and Y_2. Then the

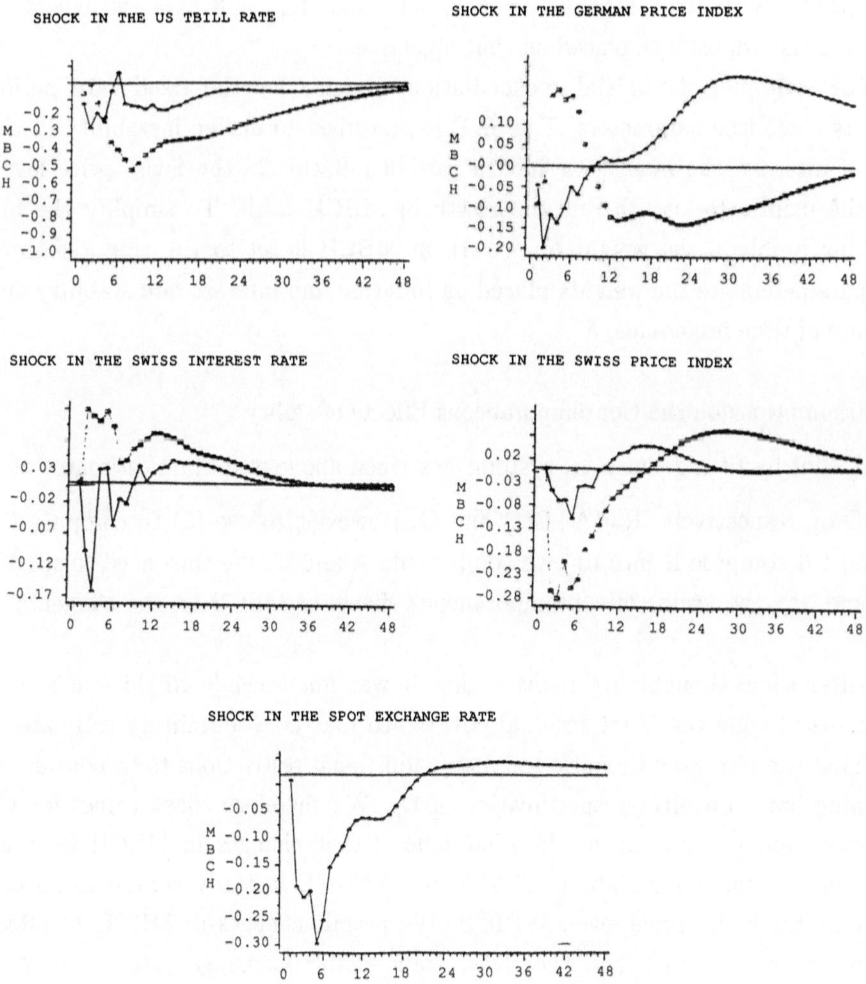

Figure 1. Responses of MBCH to various innovations
(Star (box) is fixed (flexible) rate period)

appropriate K matrix sets $K_{11} = K_{22} = w$ and $K_{12} = K_{21} = -w$ where w describes the importance placed on that objective.

For example, the initial reconciliation exercise for the fixed rate period permits three free parameters. The SNB is presumed to dislike instability in the rate of interest, the month–to–month rate of inflation in the Swiss price level, and the month–to–month rate of growth in MBCH itself. To simplify the hill climbing problem, the weight on growth in MBCH is set to 1.0. thus the three free parameters are the weights placed on inflation and interest rate stability and the rate of time preference, δ.

3.3 Assumptions on the Contemporaneous Effects of Policy

Recall that by fitting the VAR systems described above we obtain estimates of $\hat{R}$ and $\hat{G}$ of, respectively, R=(A+CG) and G. However, to use (5) to compute G* we must decompose R into its two components A and C. We thus need to specify in some way the vector of contemporaneous effects of MBCH on the elements of Y_t.

After some thought, we realised that it was not sensible to think that one could disentangle the VAR residual covariance matrix to obtain an estimate of C_0. That exercise would require too many additional restrictions to be considered anything but an arbitrary specification of C_0. We therefore chose values for C_0 on prior grounds. We assume in what follows that changes in MBCH have no effect on the foreign variables, TB3US and WPIGE nor any contemporaneous effect on the Swiss price level, WPICH. We permit changes in MBCH to affect the Swiss interest rate and the Swiss franc–dollar exchange rate contemporaneously. We chose small values for those effects but test our results for sensitivity to those choices.

In particular, we assume that a 1% increase in MBCH instantaneously lowers the Swiss interest rate, E3LCH, by one–tenth of a percentage point in both periods and raises the Swiss franc price of the dollar by .25 percent. We test our findings for robustness to these assumptions and intend, in future work, to use daily data to estimate C_0 directly.

3.4 Empirical Findings

Our preliminary empirical results are reported in Table 1. For the fixed rate period, the best reconciliation of G* to G suggests that the SNB was patient in the sense that it placed equal weight on future and current policy objectives. It

Table 1. Values of Swiss National Bank Objective Function.
Parameters that Best Reconcile Observed & Optimal Feedback Equations for the Monetary Base

	Fixed Rate Period				Flexible Rate Period			
	1	2	3	4	5	6	7	8
Contemporaneous Effects of a 1% Rise in MBCH								
Exchange Rate	-	-	-	-	.25	0	.25	1.00
Interest Rate	-.10	-.10	-.20	-.01	-.10	0	-.10	-.25
Number of Parameters	3	3	3	3	4	4	5	4
Estimated Weights								
Time Preference	1.0	1.0	1.0	1.0	.001	.091	.001	.001
$(P_t-P_{t-1})^2$	3262	-	3381	3158	6217	2.83	7.3 (+0.4)	7.51
$(P_t-P_t^*)^2$	-	561	-	-	-	-	-	-
$(R_t)^2$	.0005	-	.0005	.0005	0	.0004	.40 (-5)	0*
$(R_t-R_t^*)^2$	-	.0002	-	-	-	-	-	-
$(e_t-e_{t-1})^2$	-	-	-	-	1.07	22.3	.828	1.84
$(MB_t-MB_{t-1})(P_t-P_{t-1})$					-	-	-1.83	-
(MB_t-MB_{t-1})	1.0*	1.0*	1.0*	1.0*	1.0*	1.0*	1.0*	1.40
$\phi(k)$	84.3	81.9	84.4	84.4	80.6	85.1	75.0	39.3

* indicates that a parameter was constrained to equal the given value.

suggests too that the SNB greatly disliked instability in prices but cared relatively little about instability in interest rates. These three findings proved quite robust both with respect to the assumed value for contemporaneous policy effects and to variation in the permitted pattern of weights in the K matrix. Columns 1 and 2 make clear, however, that a model where the SNB minimises variation in the terms of trade (the difference between Swiss and German price levels) provides as good a reconciliation as a model in which the SNB minimises variation in the inflation rate.

Columns 3 and 4 contain results that check the sensitivity of our fixed rate period findings to our assumption about the initial impact on E3LCH of changes in MBCH. Column 3 shows that doubling the short run policy effect leaves the estimates of policy objective weights essentially unaltered. Column 4 reports a similar result when the contemporaneous effect is near zero.

We next consider how successful the reconciliation of G^* and $\hat{G}$ is for the fixed rate period. If we consider our computed G^* as a constant, then $\phi(k)$ is a test statistic for the hypothesis $\hat{G} = G^*$ which, under the null, is distributed as $x^2_{\cdot}(m \cdot n)$. The 95th and 99th percentiles of $x^2(30)$ are 43.8 and 59.9 indicating rejection of the null. However, it is likely that this statistic is biased toward s rejection since it ignores the fact that randomness in the reduced form parameters induces randomness in G^*. We intend in future work to readdress the question of the distribution of $\phi(k)$.

For the flexible rate period, the best reconciliations of G^* and $\hat{G}$ suggest, as in the fixed rate case, that the SNB was very concerned about stabilising inflation and unconcerned about stabilising the Swiss interest rate. But in this case the SNB appears to give much greater weight to current than to future stabilisation objectives. One feature of the results is very sensitive to the values chosen for the contemporaneous policy effects. When we make our normal assumption that a 1% increase in MBCH lowers E3LCH by –.10 and raises SCHUS by .25, the best reconciliation (columns 5 and 7 of Table 1) place a relatively small weight on stabilising the exchange rate. When we assume instead that a 1% increase in MBCH has no immediate effect on either E3LCH or SCHUS (column 6), we find that the best reconciliation places a greater weight on the exchange rate stabilisation objective than on the inflation stabilisation objective. Clearly, it will be important in future work to gather evidence on the contemporaneous effects of policy.

In column 7 of Table 1, we report the estimated weights when we permit an interaction between the objective of money base stability and inflation stability. The interaction term may be interpreted as permitting the weight placed by the SNB on money base stability to vary with inflation. If the interaction term is positive, the weight placed on money stability is greater when inflation is high and smaller when it is low. Our interaction term estimate is negative but very small relative to the own–weight on inflation.

Consider again our measure of success of the reconciliation between G* and Ĝ. For the flexible rate case, G contains 36 elements. The 95th and 99th percentiles of $x^2(36)$ are, respectively, 51.0 and 58.6 so that one would reject the null. But recall that this test is likely to be biased against the null.

We tried a number of additional specifications for both periods which proved less successful than the ones reported here. In particular, we tried specifications where the SNB sought to stabilise the six month average inflation rate, interest rate, and money growth rate. For the flexible rate period, we also permitted additional interaction terms. One additional specification is of interest and is reported in column 8 of Table 1. We found that when we assumed that policy had larger contemporaneous effects, the reconciliation improved dramatically. For example, when we assumed that a 1% increase in MBCH immediately raised SCHUS by 1% and lowered E3LCH by –.25 percentage points, we found as before that the largest weight was placed on inflation stabilisation. But we found as well that the value of $\phi(k)$ was cut in half reflecting a much improved match between G* and Ĝ*.

4. CONCLUSIONS

For several reasons our conclusions must be considered tentative. Chief among these is that some of the findings appear sensitive to our assumptions about the immediate effects on Swiss interest and exchange rates of changes in the money base. Nevertheless, we find solid consistent evidence that the SNB sought to stabilise Swiss prices but not Swiss interest rates. It is not clear yet what weight the SNB placed on exchange rate stability.

Overall, we find our results encouraging. Using few parameters to model SNB preferences, we are able to reconcile, to a reasonable degree, the policy that would have been optimal given the economic environment with the policy estimated to have actually been in place. In future work, we intend to use finer data to estimate contemporaneous policy effects, to think further about the distribution of $\phi(k)$, to experiment further with our specification of SNB preferences, and to test the hypothesis the SNB preferences changed within the flexible rate period.

REFERENCES

Béguelin, J.–P. and G. Rich (1985), "Swiss Monetary policy in the 1970's and 1980's" in K. Brunner et al., *Monetary Policy and Monetary Regimes, a Symposium Dedicated to R.E. Weintraub*, Centre Symposium Series, No. CS–17, Centre for Research in Government Policy and Business, University of Rochester.

Chow, G. (1975), *Analysis and Control of Dynamic Economic Systems*, John Wiley & Sons, New York.

Chow, G. (1981), *Econometric Analysis by Control Methods*, John Wiley & Sons, New York.

Genberg, H. and A.K. Swoboda (1985), *External Influences on the Swiss Economy Under Fixed and Flexible Exchange Rates*, Verlag Ruegger, Grusch.

Genberg, H. and M. Salemi (1987), "The Effects of Foreign Shocks on Prices of Swiss Goods and Credit: An Analysis Based on VAR Methods", *Annales d'Economie et de Statistique*, No. 6/7, pp.101–24.

Genberg, H., M. Salemi, and A.K. Swoboda (1987), "The Relative Importance of Foreign and Domestic Disturbances in the Open Economy: Switzerland 1964–81", *Journal of Monetary Economics*, 19, pp.45–67.

CHAPTER 2

OPTIMAL MONETARY POLICIES IN A SMALL OPEN ECONOMY

Thierry Chauveau, *University of Paris 1 and IPECODE, France*

1. MAIN RESULTS

This work deals with the determination of short term interest rates by central banks. Their behaviour is described as a reaction function linking the level of the short domestic interest rate to the values of variables characterising domestic and foreign conjunctures. It is suggested that for a "small open economy" three of them are of primary importance:

– the short term interest rate prevailing in the rest of the world,
– the domestic rate of inflation, and
– the foreign rate of inflation

An optimal monetary rule should exhibit the following features:

– any change of the foreign nominal short term interest rate must induce, almost instantly, a similar change of the domestic one.
– variations of the domestic inflation rate must be incorporated in the nominal domestic interest rate but more slowly. The rate to be selected is an expected one.
– foreign inflation plays a role strictly opposite to the one of domestic inflation.

Finally, monetary policy should *stabilise the difference between the real rates of interest* or, more precisely, modulate this gap as variables such as the real exchange rate vary[1]. The preceding results prevail in the case of *flexible exchange rates.*

Somewhat different conclusions are reached in the polar case of *fixed exchange rates.* The difference between *nominal rates of interest* should vary according to the fluctuations of *foreign exchange reserves.*

This paper is organised as follows: a comment of the main results is provided

P. Artus and Y. Barroux (eds.), Monetary Policy, 15–60.

in section 1; it focuses on French experience. As simplified model of a small open economy is detailed in section 2. Section 3 copes with the generalisation of the model used in section 2. Some empirical results are given in section 4.

There is, at least in this country, a divorce between monetary theory and effective practice of the central bank, as it is described in most empirical studies.

On the one hand, French econometric works usually emphasise the concern of stabilising the exchange rate, as a main determinant of the short term domestic interest rate by the Bank of France (see, for example, Metric, 1981, Artus et al, 1987, Barroux and Chauveau, 1985, Avouyi–Dovi et al, 1987, Coudert and Topol, 1987). This concern has undoubtedly increased since the creation of the European monetary system (EMS hereafter). From this point of view, the behaviour of the Bank of France exhibits the following features:

(i) the level of the domestic short term interest rate depends primarily on the value of foreign short term interest rates and, more precisely, on the German one.

(ii) the gap across short term interest rates depends on the difference between the desired and the observed capital movements. The desired movements, in their turn, depend essentially on the level of foreign exchange reserves.

(iii) this gap is fairly independent of domestic variables such as money supply, production, inflation, etc.

Such a point of view is illustrated in Figure 1 where French and German short term rates of interest are plotted together with the ratio 'Foreign exchange reserves/GDP'. The gap between those two rates obviously decreases (increases) when reserves increase (decrease).

On the other hand, there is little work about monetary theory agreeing with such results.

As a matter of fact, two points of views generally prevail as far as *monetary reaction functions* are concerned.

A *static* analysis can be undertaken: it is postulated that the Central Bank maximises a utility function depending on the values of its instruments and targets. The utility function is quadratic; instruments and targets are bound by linear constraints. This optimisation problem can be solved by the usual Lagrange method (see, e.g. Theil, 1964, Turnovsky, 1977). One can think of many targets ('domestic' targets such as the level of prices, money supply, GDP, etc. and 'foreign' targets such as exchange rate, balance of current account, level of foreign exchange reserves, etc.). Avouyi–Dovi et al (1987) suggest that econometricians should select among these variables those which are more likely to characterise the behaviour of Central Banks.

A *dynamic* analysis of the behaviour of a central bank can also be undertaken. Its major interest is to avoid 'ad hoc' specifications when the rational expectations hypothesis is taken into account. Unfortunately, most of the studies of this type deal with a closed economy. An exception is Aoki (1985).

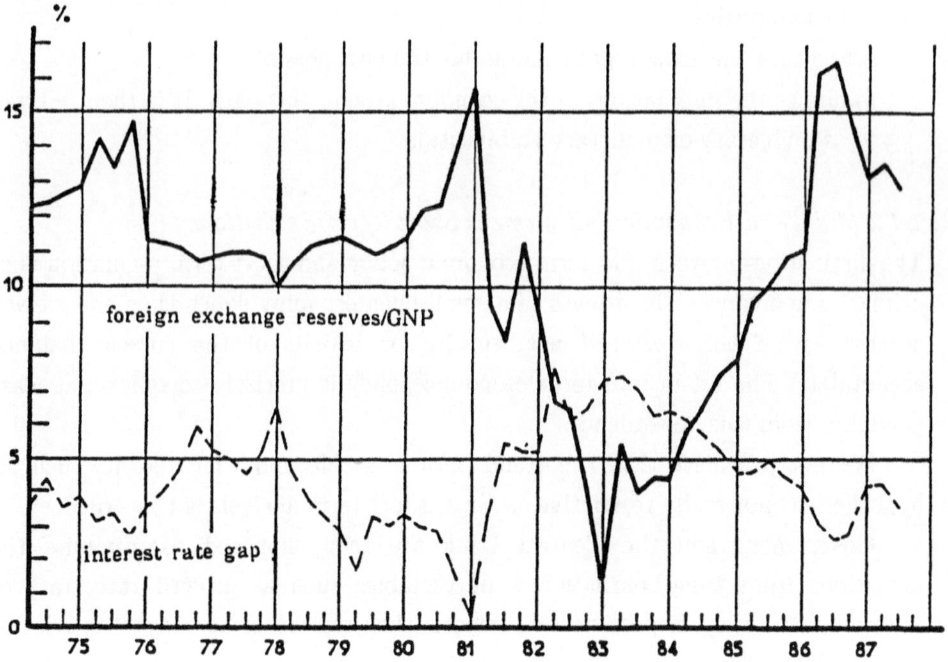

Figure 1

Our economy here is a 'small open' one; rational expectations are supposed to prevail.

1.1 We first recall some definitions

1.1.1 Short Term and Mid Term Equilibria

An economy is usually described as follows: a trend path can be defined and the values of the variables characterising the 'small open economy' fluctuate near those characterising the trend path. Of course the relevant path is not intangible but we can postulate that the values of its parameters change slowly.

Whatever the practical difficulties of valuing the parameters of this path, it is, at least theoretically, possible to split the values of the main variables describing the economy — rate of PNB, rate of inflation, etc. — into two components:

- the values corresponding to the trend path, characterising mid term equilibrium,
- deviations from these values; it is then referred to as short term equilibrium.

It is generally postulated that government and monetary authorities must carry out two duties:

- act so that the growth path should be 'the best possible'
- minimise the fluctuations of the economy around this path. It is then referred to as budgetary or monetary stabilisation.

1.1.2 Mid Term Economic Policy versus Short Term Regulations

The distinction between mid term economic policy and short term regulation is of primary importance. The growth of a small open economy depends on the growth of the rest of the world; if not, surplus or deficits of the current balance accumulate. The art of mid term economic policy is precisely to relieve, at least partially, from this dependence.

We not postulate that the trend path is stable and well known. Such an hypothesis is not really restrictive as far as short term analysis is concerned.

Government and the Central Bank are then supposed to minimise the deviations from trend path values of variables such as growth rate, rate of inflation, etc. They dispose of instruments; they can either act discretionarily or follow rules.

1.1.3 Final versus Intermediary Targets

Variables that government and the Central Bank seek to stabilise are called 'targets'. Their mid term equilibrium values (i.e. their trend path values) are also often called 'targets'. It may thus appear a confusion between a variable and its value. Whatever the exact nature of the target (variable or its level), they are referred to as '*final targets*'.

A general agreement prevails on the targets that should be selected: they are the growth rate of GDP, the rate of inflation and the level of exchange rate.

These three targets — or more precisely their trend path values — cannot be chosen independently. there is a well known trade–off implying the following propositions:

- inflation increases if the growth rate of GDP increases, the level of the exchange rate held constant (cf. Phillips curve)

- the level of the exchange rate decreases when the rate of inflation increases, the growth rate held constant
- the level of the exchange rate increases when the growth rate of GDP increases, the rate of inflation held constant.

As a matter of fact, there exist only two independent targets (e.g. the growth rate of GDP and the level of the exchange rate). The question is then to minimise deviations of these *two targets* from their trend path values.

Before answering this question, it should be remembered that neither Government nor the Central Bank know the trend path values of these targets. Moreover, the actual values of most of the economic variables are known lately. It can thus avert useful to substitute intermediary targets – generally growth rates of monetary aggregates – to final targets if their values are known better or earlier. If not, or if the relationship between an intermediary target and a final one is unstable, or if its trend path value is valued with difficulties, reasons for taking intermediary targets into account vanish.

In this paper, we do not take into account intermediary targets as most of the variables entering the monetary reaction functions are known exactly and instantly (e.g. exchange rates, foreign and domestic interest rates, foreign exchange reserves, et.). Others are known very soon and with negligible errors (foreign and domestic prices). GDP will play a very little role in those functions and therefore the use of intermediary targets is all the more questionable as the knowledge of the values of monetary aggregates is neither early nor precise.

1.1.4 Instruments

The instrument that Government can use is public expenditure and taxes. As far as short term regulation is concerned, we can reduce budgetary policy to the determination of *public deficit.* The Central Bank has to choose among two instruments:

- the short term domestic interest rate, or
- the amount of open market operations.

Indeed, the bank cannot fix discretionarily the values of both instruments for they are linked by a relationship. If such a relationship were perfectly known, it would be useless to distinguish between those two instruments. In fact, the link between the short term rate of interest and the amount of the sales or purchases of bills by the bank is stochastic. If one of the two variables is the instrument chosen by the bank, the other one is a random variable.

We now suppose that the rate of interest is the selected instrument; there are three reasons for this:

- It is easy to identify "the" rate of interest of a standard macroeconomic model and the rate chosen by the bank for its open–market operations. The link between short and long term interest rates is, indeed, very strong (see, e.g., the literature on the term structure of interest rates).
- If the amount of open market operations were the selected instrument the accounting framework should be considerably enlarged to take into account the behaviour of financial institutions unless a very questionable assumption is made: assimilate the control of open market operations and the one of a monetary aggregate. Of course the Central Bank cannot determine, in a discretionary way, the level of the stock of money.
- The rate of interest is the instrument usually selected by central banks (see, e.g., the case of France, Germany, United Kingdom, Italy, Japan, etc.).

1.1.5 Monetary and Budgetary Rules

We now postulate that Government and the Central Bank follow *rules* and that they cooperate. They have therefore the same targets: minimise the variances of deviations from trend path values of final targets.

As for trend path values, there appears to be a trade–off between the following deviations from trend path values:

- the minimum of the variance of the growth rate of GDP,
- the minimum of the variance of the rate of inflation, and
- the minimum of the variance of the level of the exchange rate.

We therefore suppose that two among those three targets are actually taken into account by Government and the Central Bank.

It is generally granted that the first target is always looked at because of its consequences on unemployment. The following choice is thus left between:

- minimising the variance of growth rate of GDP and of the rate of inflation,

or

- minimising the variance of growth rate of GDP and of the level of the exchange rate.

In this paper, those two points of view are successively followed.

Whatever the couple of targets, a budgetary and a monetary rule must be worked out, taking into account all the constraints describing the behaviour of private and public agents, market equilibria relationships, and postulating the existence of rational expectations.

1.1.6 Fixed and Flexible Exchange Rates

When fixed exchange rates prevail, the existence of a trade–off between targets implies that budgetary policy is sufficient to ensure the minimum of the variance of GDP is reached. What then can monetary policy be used for?

A first analysis can be undertaken along the following lines. The assumption of fixed exchange rates implies that monetary authorities fix the level of the short term domestic rate so as to *minimise the fluctuations of foreign exchange reserves.* This is easily understood if one remembers that a balance of payments crisis cannot be ruled out if the level of foreign reserves diminishes drastically. What is to happen if, on the contrary, a small open country accumulates foreign exchange reserves? Such a phenomenon is, at first sight, much less pregnant than the loss of foreign reserves. However, it can be guessed that the rest of the world will, sooner or later, anticipate a change of par.

Actually, a second analysis can be undertaken. The case of fixed exchange rates can be seen as a limit of the one of flexible exchange rates with the assumption of a central bank obeying the following "foreign exchange reserves reaction functions"; split the effect of the surplus (or deficit) of the payments into two components:

(i) a change in the foreign exchange reserves
(ii) a change in the foreign exchange rate

The case of flexible exchange rates corresponds to a null first component and the antagonistic case to a null second component. Moreover, it can be shown (see section 2) that the criterion of the minimum of the variance of the foreign exchange reserves must be substituted to the one of the minimum of the variance of the rate of growth of the exchange rate when we shift from one limiting case to the other. The first analysis is thus comforted.

When flexible exchange rates prevail the choice of the average domestic rate of inflation is left to the small open country. The average growth rate of the exchange rate obeys Purchasing Power Parity theory (elsewhere PPP). It can "isolate" from foreign inflation. On the contrary, it can stabilise the exchange rate and equalise the mid term equilibrium value of the domestic rate of inflation and the foreign one.

1.2 Characterisation of the Optimal Monetary Policy

We now comment on the main results of this study. We first recall the major assumptions:

- the short term domestic interest rate is the instrument used for monetary policy;
- no intermediary target is selected;
- two final targets are selected. The first one is the minimum of the variances of the growth rate of GDP, and the second one depends on them prevailing exchange rate system:
  - with fixed exchange rates it is the *minimum of the variance of the ratio "foreign exchange reserves/ GDP"*
  - with flexible exchange rates it is the *minimum variance of the rate of growth of the exchange rate.* The *minimum domestic inflation* can be substituted for the former criterion. If so, the results are slightly modified (see 1.2.4)

Other assumptions are made mainly for simplicity's sake:

- public expenditures are well controlled
- the portfolio choice of the agents is supposed to obey a marginal adjustment process

Moreover, stochastic assumptions and the lag structure of the model are supposed to be very simple (for further details see section 2). Most of these assumptions can be removed without questioning the correctness of the results (see section 3).

1.2.1 Fixed Exchange Rate

The optimal rules are as follows: budgetary policy should be assigned to the stabilisation of output and monetary policy to the stabilisation of foreign exchange reserves. The latter rule can be written as follows:

$$R = R' - \sum_j a_j FER(-j)/GDP(-j) + \sum_i b_i EXC(-i) + c \qquad (1)$$

with

R	= domestic interest rate
R′	= foreign interest rate
FER	= foreign exchange reserves (real exchange rate)
GDP	= gross domestic product
EXC	$= P/P' \cdot E$
P	= domestic implicit deflator of GDP

P′ = foreign implicit deflator of GDP

E = exchange rate

According to this formula a change of the foreign short term rate of interest involves, ceteris paribus, a similar change of the domestic one. Moreover, a decrease of the foreign exchange reserves implies an increase of the domestic rate. Both results are consistent with French practice. The foreign reserves need not be lagged when imports depend but on current values of prices and exchange rate. Similarly, a growth of the real exchange rate will bring about an increase of the domestic rate of interest. However, the short term effects of such a growth rate are, at first sight, ambiguous. This ambiguity is due to the existence of a "J–curve".

One can easily understand these results if one remembers that the difference between the return on a domestic investment and the one on a foreign investment just equals the gap across the two nominal short term rates of interest. The Central Bank can thus make this difference vary in order the induce capital movements which will oppose the autonomous fluctuations of the balance of payments. The smaller the foreign exchange reserves the higher the amplitude of interest rate movements.

If the real exchange rate increases, exports become less competitive and decrease whereas simultaneously imports will increase. There appears a deficit of the balance of payments. the Central Bank must increase its rate of interest in order to attract foreign funds. However, if the short term effects of a change of the real exchange rate are, as usual, perverse, the monetary authorities will first reduce the level of the domestic rate.

Finally, the main determinant of the domestic rate is the foreign one and the gap between those two rates depends on:

- the level of real exchange rate
- the ratio "foreign exchange reserves/GDP".

1.2.2 Flexible Exchange Rates

Of course, the preceding results do not hold when flexible exchange rates prevail. However, one can notice many similarities. The optimal monetary rule is now obtained under the assumption that the Central Bank minimises the fluctuations of the rate of growth of the exchange rate or of the consumer price index. We now assume that the first target is selected. Results with the antagonistic assumption are given below (see 1.2.4). Government is still supposed to minimise the variance of output. We can now write

$$R = R' + (R^* - R'^*) + b \cdot EXCL + c \tag{2}$$

with

R = domestic interest rate (current value)
R′ = foreign interest rate (current value)
R* = domestic interest rate (mid term equilibrium)
R′* = foreign interest rate (mid term equilibrium)
GDP = gross domestic product
FER = foreign exchange reserves
EXCL = $\Sigma_i b_i EXC(-i)$
EXC = $P/P' \cdot E$ (real exchange rate)
P = domestic implicit deflator of GDP
P′ = foreign implicit deflator of GDP
E = exchange rate

R*, R′* are mid term equilibrium values of domestic and foreign rate of interest, i.e. trend path values or final targets.

There are two main differences between formulas (1) and (2):

(i) Foreign exchange reserves do not intervene in the last formula; they do not vary any more.

(ii) The second difference is the inclusion of the gap across the mid term equilibrium values of the domestic and the foreign rate of interest. These values obey Fisher's law and we can therefore write for trend path values:

nominal rate of interest = rate of inflation + real rate of interest
(R^* or R'^*) = (p^* or p'^*) + (r^* or r'^*)

p* and p′* are both expected and effective rates of inflation as no difference between those two definitions can occur for trend values. Real interest rates in the small open country and in the rest of the world should be equal if mid term equilibrium is referred to. We can thus rewrite (2) as:

$$R = R' + (p^* - p'^*) + b \cdot EXCL + c \tag{2'}$$

with

R = domestic interest rate (current value
R′ = foreign interest rate (current value)
p* = domestic inflation rate (mid term equilibrium value)
p′* = foreign inflation rate (mid term equilibrium value)
EXCL = $\Sigma_i b_i EXC(-i)$
EXC = $P/P' \cdot E$ (real exchange rate)

P = domestic implicit deflator of GDP

P′ = foreign implicit deflator of GDP

E = exchange rate

Equation (2') states that the real domestic rate of interest (R–p*) equals the foreign one (R′–p′*) plus a residual expression depending on real exchange rate[3]. The Central Bank now acts so as to compensate the surplus or deficit of the current operations balance by inducing capital movements whose importance depend on two elements:

- the difference between the two short term nominal interest rates
- the expected growth rate of the exchange rate.

Using PPP's relationship, it can be equivalently stated that capital movements depend on

- the difference between the two short term real interest rates
- the deviation from the trend path value of the expected growth rate of the exchange rate.

1.2.3 A More Realistic Point of View

Of course, the two polar cases of fixed or flexible exchange rates are somewhat unrealistic as many central banks intervene on the exchange market. If so, variations of foreign exchange reserves should be, again, taken into account and equation (3) should be substituted into equation (2) or (2′). Such an equation holds whatever the nature – discretionary or rule –of sales and purchases on the foreign exchange market.

$$R = R' + (p^* - p'^*) - \sum_j a_j FER(-j)/GDP(-j) + \sum_i b_i EXC(-i) + c \qquad (3)$$

with

R = domestic interest rate (current value)

R′ = foreign interest rate (current value)

p* = domestic inflation rate

p′* = foreign inflation rate

GDP = gross domestic product

FER = foreign exchange reserves

EXC = P/P′·E

P = domestic implicit deflation of GDP

P′ = foreign implicit deflator of GDP

E = exchange rate

1.2.4 Concluding Remarks

Four remarks must be made:

(i) When the minimum of domestic inflation is a final target, equations (2), (3) and (3') must be slightly modified: the deviation between the actual rate of growth of the exchange rate and its expectation must be taken into account. (3') must now be written as follows

$$R = R' + (p^* - p'^*) + \epsilon^e - \sum_j a_j FER(-j)/GDP(-j) + \sum_i b_i EXC(-i) + c \quad (3')$$

with

R = domestic interest rate (current value)
R′ = foreign interest rate (current value)
p* = domestic inflation rate
p′* = foreign inflation rate
GDP = gross domestic product
FER = foreign exchange reserves
EXC = $P/P' \cdot E$ (real exchange rate)
ϵ^e = expected growth rate of exchange rate (deviation from equil. value)
P = domestic implicit deflator of GDP
P′ = foreign implicit deflator of GDP
E = exchange rate

(ii) With fixed though revisable exchange rates it appears more convenient to substitute equation (3") for (3'). In the new equation the expected exchange rate is explicitly taken into account and this allows for a step by step evolution.

$$R = R' + e^e - \sum_j a_j FER(-j) + \sum_i b_i EXC + c \quad (3'')$$

with

R = domestic interest rate (current value)
R′ = foreign interest rate (current value)
GDP = gross domestic product
FER = foreign exchange reserves
EXC = $P/P' \cdot E$ (real exchange rate)
e^e = expected growth rate of exchange rate
P = domestic implicit deflator of GDP
P′ = foreign implicit deflator of GDP
E = exchange rate

(iii) When fixed exchange rates prevail, i.e. when monetary agreements have been reached, equation (3") is still valid but must be carefully interpreted. If the domestic target of inflation is correct, it should not differ from the foreign one and the stability of the exchange rate should be postulated by economic agents. On the contrary, if the two targets do not coincide, agents will anticipate, sooner or later, a change of par. Obviously their behaviour will depend on current information and especially the values of three important variables: the gap between effective and PPP pars, the level of foreign exchange reserves and the difference between effective exchange rate and "central par".

(iv) The case of fixed exchange rates may be seen as the limit towards which a small open economy converges when a Central Bank intervenes more and more in the foreign exchange market when flexible exchange rates prevail. The target of this bank should now be the level of the exchange rate. More comments are made in sections 2.2.1 and 2.3.1.

2. A SIMPLIFIED MODEL

We now present a simplified model of a small open economy. First we comment on the main assumptions. Then we examine the two polar cases of flexible and fixed exchange rates.

2.1 Main Assumptions

This section deals with five questions: the accounting framework, behavioural assumptions, temporary equilibrium, mid term equilibrium and dynamics of the economy.

2.1.1 The Accounting Framework

Table 1 illustrates the accounting framework. There are five sectors: corporate sector (CS), household sector (HS), banking sector (BS), public sector (PS), and foreign sector (FS). There are two composite goods: the domestic one which is produced and invested by firms, consumed by households and administrations and exported. The foreign good is imported and consumed by households. Two exogenous parameters, (u) and (t), characterise the relative importance of taxes, households' net income and retained earnings. There are three financial assets: domestic money issued by the banking sector and held by households, domestic bonds issued by firms and administrations and held by households, banks and foreigners and one foreign asset exclusively held by the Central Bank.

Table 1. Accounting Framework

CS	HS	PS	BS	FS		CS	HS	PS	BS	FS
$P\mathcal{I}$	$P\mathcal{C}$	PG		PX	domestic goods	$P\mathcal{Y}$				
	$EP'\mathcal{M}$				foreign goods					$EP'\mathcal{M}$
$(u+t)P\mathcal{Y}$					transfers		$uP\mathcal{Y}$	$tP\mathcal{Y}$		
	$\Delta\mathcal{L}$				money				$\Delta\mathcal{L}$	
	ΔB_m		ΔB_b	ΔB_f	bonds	$\Delta_c B$		$\Delta_p B$		
			ΔF		foreign assets					ΔF

Abbreviations

CS = Corporate Sector
HS = Household Sector
FS = Foreign Sector
$\mathcal{I}$ = investment
$\mathcal{C}$ = consumption
$\mathcal{G}$ = public expenditures
$\mathcal{X}$ = exports
$\mathcal{M}$ = imports
$\mathcal{Y}$ = domestic output
B_m = bonds held by households
B_b = bonds held by banks
B_f = bonds held by foreigners
${}_cB$ = bonds issued by firms
${}_pB$ = bonds issued by the public sector

PS = Public Sector
BS = Banking Sector
W = nominal wage
P = domestic price
P′ = foreign price
P = consumer index of living
K = stock of productive capital
E = exchange rate
S = $P/P'E$ = terms of trade
R = domestic rate of interest
$\mathcal{L}$ = money supply
R′ = foreign rate of interest
F = foreign assets

N.B. $p = \Delta \text{Log } P$, $p' = \Delta \text{Log } P'$, $p^e = \text{Log } P^e/P(-1)$
$e = \Delta \text{Log } E$, $w = \Delta \text{Log } W$;
$\Delta X = X - X_{-1}$, X^e = expected value of X

Such an accounting framework is a compromise between the need for simplicity and the care of generality. It is very similar to those used in the literature. The interest payments are not taken into account explicitly. For a justification of this hypothesis see e.g. Turnovsky (1977).

2.1.2 Main Behavioural Assumptions

The main behavioural assumptions are as follows:

The price of the domestic good is set by firms according to a mark–up process. A richer specification would be of no interest here.

$P = W(1 + m)$

The nominal wage W is fixed, as in Villa (1986) by a contract signed at the beginning of the current period. It is fully indexed on cost of living expectations.

$w - \tilde{p}^e = \Delta \text{Log } W - \text{Log } p^e/p_{-1} = p_o + p_1(Y - \bar{Y})/\bar{Y}$

The gap between the rate of growth (w) of the nominal wage and cost of living expectations $\tilde{p}^e$ depends, as usual, on the difference between effective and potential output.

The index takes into account the domestic price P and the foreign price $P' \cdot E$ expressed in domestic currency. As in Turnovsky (1977) and for the same reasons, we postulate a constant elasticity of the index of cost of living towards foreign and domestic price. Thus we can write:

$$\tilde{p} = p^{p_2}(P'E)^{1-p_2}$$

hence

$$\tilde{p}^e = \text{Log } \tilde{P}^e/\tilde{P}_{-1} = p_2 p^e + (1 - p_2)(p'^e + e^e)$$

and

$$\tilde{p} = \Delta \text{Log } \tilde{P} = p_2 p + (1 - p_2)(p' + e^e)$$

According to a traditional procedure (see e.g. Turnovsky, 1977), we specify the behavioural equations in the following way: $\mathscr{C}$, $\mathscr{I}$, $\mathscr{Y}$, ... are divided by wealth (K^*), and we assume that we have to do with homogeneous functions with degree one. We can thus express $C = \mathscr{C}/K^*$, $I = \mathscr{I}/K^*$, ... as linear functions of other arguments. Wealth is identified by the stock of productive capital. Actually, permanent wealth is taken into account and identified by the long run equilibrium value K^* of this stock prevailing at the end of the previous period.

Consumption of the domestic good depends on current income, wealth and the relative price of the two goods, i.e. the term of trade S. S is lagged in the simplest way.

$$C = c_o + c_1 uY - c_2 LS$$

Imports depend on the same variables as consumption: the sign of the partial derivative of M against S is opposite to the one of C. S is lagged as in the consumption function.

$$M = m_o + m_1 uY + m_2 LS$$

Exports vary positively with foreign wealth and negatively with S. S is not lagged in the export function; this is the simpler way of allowing for a "J–curve". More general specifications are undertaken in section 3.

$$X = (x_o + x_2 S^{-1})k$$

Investment follows an 'accelerator–profit' scheme: it therefore depends on expected and current values of output, and on the real rate of interest. A more sophisticated specification is discussed in section 3.

$$I = i_o + i_1(Y^e - (1-d)Y) - i_2(R - p^e)$$

The demand for money is a standard one. Its main arguments are output, the level of price index and the rate of interest.

$$\mathscr{L}^d = (l_o^d + l_1^d uY - l_2^d R)S^{p_2}$$

Financial behaviour of foreigners is described in a usual way: the proportion (a) of their wealth invested in French bonds is fixed according to portfolio theory. The following equation prevails in the case of a logarithmic utility.

$$a = (R - R' - e^e)(1 - R')/(\sigma^2 + (R - R' - e^e)^2)$$

with

$$B = B_F/PK^* = (a(1 - L)K'^*) = a\xi k/S$$

2.1.3 Temporary Equilibrium

A temporary equilibrium of our economy can be described with four equations: (IS), (LM), (PH) and (BP).

Output, prices, money supply and foreign exchange reserves can be calculated given expectations, the exchange rate, policy variables (public expenditures and the domestic rate of interest), and foreign variables. Before studying the dynamics of the system when expectations are rational we must answer the two following questions: which targets should be selected? Which values must be given to those targets?

Table 2

$$Y = C + I + G + X - M \quad \text{(IS)}$$

$$\mathcal{L}^d = \mathcal{L} \quad \text{(LM)}$$

$$p - p^e = p_o + p_1(Y-\bar{Y})/\bar{Y} \quad \text{(PH)}$$

$$F = X - M + B \quad \text{(BP)}$$

or

$$Y = d_o + d_1Y^e - d_2(R-p^e) - d_3LS + d_3'S^{-1}$$

$$\mathcal{L} = (l_o^d + l_1^d uY - l_2^d R)S^{p_2}$$

$$p = p_2p^e + (1-p_2)(p'^e+e^e) + p_o + p_1(Y-\bar{Y})/\bar{Y}$$

$$F = (x_o + x_2)k - S^{-1}(m_o + m_1uY + m_2LS) + a\,\xi S^{-1}$$

2.1.4 Mid Term Equilibrium

As it has already been said, targets should coincide with the values of the variables ensuring the existence of a balanced growth. If a star refers to those values we can write:

Table 3

$$Y^* = C^* + I^* + G^* + X^* - M^* \quad \text{(IS')}$$

$$\mathcal{L}^d = \mathcal{L}^* \quad \text{(LM')}$$

$$p^* - p^{*e} = p_o^* + p_1^*(Y^*-\bar{Y})/\bar{Y} \quad \text{(PH')}$$

$$0 = X^* - M^* + B^* \quad \text{(BP')}$$

or

$$Y^*(1-d_y) = d_o - d_2(R^*-p^*) - d_3S^* + d_3'S^{*-1}$$

$$\mathcal{L}^* = (l_o^d + l_1^d uY^* - l_2^d R^*)S^{*p_2}$$

$$p^* = p_2p^* + (1-p_2)(p^{*\prime}+e^*) + p_o + p_1(Y^*-\bar{Y})/\bar{Y}$$

$$0 = (x_o + x_3)k - S^{*-1}(m_o + m_1uY^* + m_2S^*)$$

Moreover, in the case of *fixed exchange rates,* we obviously have the nullity of the rate of growth of the exchange rate and of its expectation. The terms of trade should be constant so that the rate of domestic inflation must equalise the foreign one. An analogous property prevails for price expectations. Hence,

$$e^* = e^{e^*} = 0, \quad p^{e^*} = p^* = p'^* = p'^{e^*}$$

We get G* from (IS′), L* from (LM′), Y* from (PH′) and S* from (BP′). We must add an equation which is but an accounting relation between investment and the stock of productive capital. If d′ is the rate of depreciation of physical capital, we can write:

$$d' = i_0 + i_1.d.Y^* - i_2.(R^* - p^*)$$

It is the condition ensuring the equality of rates of physical growth in both countries. As one can easily check, initial conditions generally do not fulfill the quasi–equilibrium requirements. However, there is an opportunity for modifying either the ratio reserves of foreign exchange/capital or the ratio public expenditures/capital so as to modify k until it reaches the required value k*.

The case of *flexible exchange rates* is very similar to the preceding one. However, there is one degree of freedom left; the nominal rate of interest. We have a Fisher relation linking the rate of inflation to this rate since equation (SF") remains unchanged when both rates vary in the same way.

$$e^* = e^{e^*} = p^* - p'^* = p^{e^*} - p'^{e^*}$$

We must emphasise the difference between the two quasi–equilibria. In the case of *fixed* exchange rates *public authorities cannot choose any of the values of the parameters* characterising the growth of the economy. On the contrary, they have to determine the right par, i.e. the value of the exchange rate ensuring the achievement of the quasi–equilibrium by the economy. When the L.R.E. hypothesis is made, perfect knowledge of the model describing the economy is taken for granted.

In the case of *flexible* exchange rates an option is left to the Central Bank: *isolate its country from foreign inflation (p*=0) and leave to the market the care of determining the exchange rate (according to PPP, i.e. e*=p′*) or stabilise the exchange rate (e*=0) and 'import' foreign inflation (p*=p′*).* Any combination of these two polar rules can also be retained. Those results are well known (see e.g. Turnovsky, 1977).

2.1.5 Dynamics of the Economy

As usual, we now linearise the relations characterising the temporary equilibrium, assuming the economy is close to the quasi–equilibrium. The results of such a calculation are produced in Table 4.

Table 4

$$y = d_1y^e - d_2(r-q^e) - (d_3'+d_3L)s + d_4g$$
$$q = b_1y + b_2q^e + b_3(q_o^e+\epsilon^e)$$
$$l = l_1y - l_2r + l_3s$$
$$f = -f_1y + f_2(r-r'-\epsilon^e) + (f_o-f_o'L)s$$

The values of the new coefficients (d_1, d_2, ...) are given in Appendix 1. The variables q, ϵ, and s are defined as follows:

$$q = p - p^*$$
$$\epsilon = e - e^*$$
$$s = S - S^*$$

And, for convenience, we impose $S^*=1$.

We now add stochastic disturbances v_y, v_l, v_p and v_f to equations (IS), (LM), (PH) and (BP) of Table 3, so that they are now written as shown in Table 5.

Table 5

$$(1-L)y = d_1(1-L)y^e - d_2(1-L)(r-q^e) - (d_3'+d_3L)(q-q'-\epsilon) + d_4(1-L)g + (1-L)v_y$$
$$(1-L)q = b_1(1-L)y + b_2(1-L)q^e + b_3(1-L)(q'^e+\epsilon^e) + (1-L)v_l$$
$$(1-L)l = l_1'(1-l)y - l_2'(1-L)r + l_3'(q-q'-\epsilon) + (1-L)v_p$$
$$(1-L)f = -f_1(1-L)y + f_2(1-L)(r-r'-\epsilon^e) + (f_o-f_o'L)(q-q'-\epsilon) + (1-L)v_f$$

Fuller information about stochastic assumptions must be given. As pointed out by Champsaur and Melitz (1982) there are *two ways* of taking lags into account: the simpler one is the neglect those lags when specifying behaviours of economic agents and to introduce autocorrelation or cross–correlations among shocks. this way is not the more general one. a main drawback is a very particular and somewhat unrealistic structure of lags.

The better way is to introduce explicit lags in the equations. If so, disturbances should lack autocorrelation.

However, *speculative bubbles* may occur on the foreign exchange market so that positive autocorrelation of residuals of the last equation cannot be ruled out. We therefore make the following stochastic assumptions.

Table 6. Stochastic Assumptions

$$v_y = \rho_y L v_y + w_y \qquad v_l = \rho_l L v_l + w_l$$

$$v_p = \rho_p L v_p + w_p \qquad v_f = \rho_f L v_f + w_f$$

$$v' = \rho' L v' + w'$$

$$\rho_f > 0 \quad \rho_y = \rho_l = \rho_p = 0$$

$$E(w_i w_j) = 0 \quad \text{if } i{=}j \quad (i,j = y,l,p,f,')$$

$$p' = \rho' L p' + w'$$

$$p'^e = \rho' L p'$$

More general specification, allowing for sophisticated lag structure will be examined in section 3. As usual, autoregressive processes are postulated for foreign parameters such as foreign inflation p', but we suppose that r' is instantly and perfectly known. A complete description of the economy can be achieved by taking into account the rational expectations hypothesis.

2.2 The Case of Flexible Exchange Rates

We now examine the case of flexible exchange rates. Some methodological comments must first be made.

2.2.1 Methodological Comments

Our paper is very similar to the work of Villa (1986) despite two main differences:

- Our economy is an open one whereas Villa's economy is closed.
- We do not impose any condition ensuring the boundedness of the asymptotical variance of the price index level.

This latter observation requires some more explanation.

The final target, in Villa's paper, is inflation so that specifying an optimal monetary policy is equivalent to writing the condition ensuring the minimum of the variance of inflation is reached. Such a condition can be written as

$$E(p_{t+1}/I_t) = 0$$

The minimum of the conditional variance of p_t is reached when its conditional expectation is null. (For proof see Villa, 1986, appendix 1).

Moreover, Villa presents a standard macroeconomic model including three usual equations (IS), (LM) and the augmented Phillips one (PH). After convenient elimination, he obtains an equation linking the rate of inflation, inflationary expectations and other variables depending on past values of stochastic disturbances. This equation is of the following form:

$$A_q(L)\cdot p_t = A_p(L)\cdot E(p_t/I_{t-1}) + \sum_i A_x^i(L)\cdot x_t^i \qquad \text{(LRE)}$$

where L is the lag operator, $A_q(L)$, $A_x^i(L)$ and $A_p(L)$ are polynoms in L, p_t is the rate of inflation and x_t^i are variables depending on past values of stochastic disturbances. All values are deviations from mid term equilibrium values.

Taking conditional expectations of both sides of the last equation, gives a relation between past values of variables and of the parameter to be set up. This relation defines the optimal policy. Such a method is used in this paper.

It should be noticed that *minimising the variance of inflation is not equivalent to minimising the variance of the level of price index P* and a question immediately arises: will the level of prices P (or Log P) be asymptotically distributed with finite variance? The answer to this question is generally negative unless a supplementary condition is fulfilled. To show this, we refer to the linear rational expectations model (LRE) as it is described in Broze, Gourieroux and Szafarz (1985). Let us define

$$z_t = p_t - E(p_t/I_{t-1})$$

This error can but depend on non expected shocks of the current period. Therefore it is not correlated with x_t. It is a linear combination of the current disturbances u_t^i so that we have:

$$z_t = \sum_i \psi_i \cdot u_t^i$$

where the ψ_i's characterise the expectation revision process. Equation (LRE) can be written as:

$$(A_p(L) - A_q(L))p_t = A_q(L)z_t - \sum_i A_x^i(L)LX_t^i \qquad \text{(LRE}')$$

with

$$x_t^i = \sum_k \psi_k^i u_t^k$$

As pointed out by Villa the boundedness of the asymptotic variance of the level of price cannot be taken for granted. Indeed a specific feature of Villa's model is that $(A_p(L)–A_q(L))$ reduces to $(1–L)$: this polynom has thus only one root which equals 1. Obviously, the solution will not exhibit bounded variance unless $(1–L)$ (or more generally $(A_p(L)–A_q(L))$) divides the second side of equation (LRE′). This divisibility property can be expressed as mathematical conditions binding the ψ^i's but the economic meaning of such equations remains questionable. The divisibility property should not be considered as a stability condition. We therefore do not follow Villa and allow for unbounded variance of prices. This is not a major drawback as, in the long run, the level of prices can be thought as indefinite.

2.2.2 Optimal Policies

We now characterise optimal policies in a small open economy with a flexible exchange rate. We first suppose that the two final targets are output and the exchange rate. We therefore write

$$y_t^e = E(y_{t+1}/I_t) = 0$$

$$\epsilon_t^e = E(\epsilon_{t+1}/I_t) = 0$$

And from (PH) we get:

$$E(q_t/I_{t-1}) = q_t^e = b_1E(y_t/I_{t-1}) + b_2q_t^e + (1-b_2)(q'^e_t+\epsilon_t^e) + E(v_t/I_{t-1})$$

hence

$$q^e = \rho' Lq' + b_3^{-1}\rho_p Lv_p$$

We must again trade off between the three variables, p, q, and ϵ. We cannot minimise simultaneously the variances of output inflation (or prices) and exchange rate. We must choose two targets among three (or a linear combination of those targets).

Moreover, we suppose that the Central Bank does not intervene in the foreign exchange market: the level of foreign exchange reserves thus remains unchanged (f=0).

Taking conditional expectations of both sides of the equations characterising our temporary equilibrium leads to writing

$$-Ly = -d_2(1-L)(r-q^e) - d_3L(q-q'-\epsilon) - d_3'(q^e-q^{e'}-\epsilon^e) + d_4(1-L)g - (1-\rho_y)Lv_y$$

$$q^e(1-b_2) = b_1y^e + b_3(q^e+\epsilon^e)$$

$$0 = -f_1Ly + f_2(1-L)(r-r'-\epsilon^e) + f_o(q^e-q'^e-\epsilon^e) - f_o'L(q-q'-\epsilon) - (1-\rho_f)Lv_f$$

The *optimal budgetary policy* is thus given by:

$$d_4(1-\rho_y)g = -\rho_yLy + d_2(1-\rho_y)L(r-q^e) + d_3'L(q-q'-\epsilon) + (d_3'+d_3L)(1-\rho_y)Ls + d_3b_3^{-1}Lv_p \qquad \text{(BO1)}$$

with

$$Lv_o = Lq - (b_2+b_3)Lq'^e - b_1Ly$$

and

$$q'^e = L\rho'q'$$

With the stochastic hypotheses of Table 6 this last equation simplifies drastically:

$$g = g_2L(r-q'^e) + g_3L(q-q'-\epsilon) + (g_3'+g_3L)Ls \qquad \text{(BO2)}$$

with

$$g_2 = d_2/d_4 \qquad g_3 = d_3/d_4 \qquad g_3' = d_3'/d_4$$

Similarly, we can define an *optimal monetary policy*:

$$(1-\rho_fL)f_2(r-r') = f_ob_3^{-1}\rho_pLv_p + f_o'L(q-q'-\epsilon) - f_o-f_o'L)(1-\rho_fL)Ls + f_1\rho_fLy \qquad \text{(MO1)}$$

which, again, simplifies drastically if the stochastic assumptions of Table 6 are made:

$$(1-\rho_fL)f_2(r-r') = f_o'L(q-q'-\epsilon) - (f_o-f_o'L)(1-\rho_fL)Ls - f_1\rho_fLy \qquad \text{(MO2)}$$

If ρ_f is null, the preceding equation reduces to:

$$r = r' + f_2^{-1}(f_o'L(q-q'-\epsilon) - (f_o-f_o'L)Ls) \qquad \text{(MO3)}$$

With the stochastic hypotheses of Table 6 and assuming that no intense speculation prevails (ρ_f=0), we have thus *shown that the optimal monetary policy can be specified as indicated in section 1.* Recall we have:

$$r = R - R^* \qquad r' = R' - R'^* \qquad EXC = S = S^* + s$$

Equation (MO3) is thus strictly equivalent to equation (2) of section 1, for it can also be written as follows:

$$R = R' + R^* - R'^* + f_2^{-1}(f_o'L(1-L)(S-S^*) - (f_o-f_o'L)(S-S^*)) \qquad \text{(MO'3)}$$

In particular, the *short term domestic rate depends on the foreign one with and unitary coefficient.* We can use once again the Fisher relation to change R^* and R'^* into mid term rate of inflation in this country and in the rest of the world. Those results are general as they hold for (MO1) and as well as (MO2).

Three remarks will conclude this section.

(i) If optimal budgetary and monetary policies prevail, it is easy to *calculate* y. (IS) can be written as:

$$(1-L)y = -d_2(1-L)(r-q^e) - (d_3'+d_3L)(q-q'-\epsilon) + d_4g + (1-L)v_y$$

Taking conditional expectations and subtracting gives

$$y = y - y^e = -d_3'((q-q^e) - (q'-q'^e))$$

Similarly, we obtain from (PH)

$$q - q^e = b_1(y-y^e) + w_p$$

Moreover, (BP) can be written as

$$0 = -f_1(1-L)y + f_2(1-L)(r-r'-\epsilon^e) + (f_o-f_o')(q-q'-\epsilon) + (1-L)v_f$$

Taking conditional expectations, recalling that ϵ^e and y^e are null and subtracting, leads to writing

$$0 = -f_1y + f_o((q-q^e) - (q'-q'^e) + \epsilon) + w_f$$

After convenient elimination we obtain:

$$y = (f_ow_y-d_3'w_f)/(f_o-d_3'f_1)$$

The fluctuations of output depend but on the current (IS) and (BP) shocks. Similarly we can calculate q

$$q = q^e + b_1y + w_p$$

with

$$q^e = b_3^{-1}\rho_pLv_p$$

(ii) If inflation were the selected target, the preceding results would be slightly different. Indeed, equations (BO1), (BO2), (MO1), (MO2) and (MO3) should be replaced by the following ones:

$$d_4(1-\rho_y)g = -\rho_yLy + d_2(1-\rho_y)L(r-q^e) + d_3'L(q-q'-\epsilon)$$
$$+ (d_3'+d_3L)(1-\rho_y)Ls + d_3b_3^{-1}Lv_p \qquad \text{(BO1')}$$

$$g = d_2Lr + d_3'L(q-q'-\epsilon) + (d_3'+d_3L)Ls \qquad \text{(BO2')}$$

$$(1-\rho_f L)f_2(r-r') = f_o b_3^{-1} \rho_p L v_p + f_o' L(q-q'-\epsilon) - (f_o - f_o' L)(1-\rho_f L)Ls - f_1 \rho_f Ly \qquad \text{(MO1')}$$

$$(1-\rho_f L)f_2(r-r'-\epsilon^e) = f_o' L(q-q'-\epsilon) - (f_o - f_o' L)(1-\rho_f L)Ls - f_1 \rho_f Ly \qquad \text{(MO2')}$$

$$r = r' + \epsilon^e + f_2^{-1}(f_o' L(q-q'-\epsilon) - (f_o - f_o' L)Ls) \qquad \text{(MO3')}$$

One can notice that equation (MO3') is equivalent to equation (3') of section 1. The calculation of y remains unchanged; q^e is now null.

(iii) If the Central Bank acts on the foreign exchange market, the optimal monetary policy should then be written as:

$$(1-\rho_f L)f_2(r-r') = -L(f+F(1+f_o/(f_o-f_o'))) + f_o b_3^{-1} \rho_p L v_p + f_o' L(q-q'-\epsilon)$$

$$- (f_o - f_o' L)(1-\rho_f L)Ls + f_1 \rho_f Ly \qquad \text{(MO1")}$$

or, with the assumptions of Table 6:

$$(1-\rho_f L)f_2(r-r') = -L(f+F(1+f_o/(f_o-f_o' L)) + f_o' L(q-q'-\epsilon)$$

$$- (f_o - f_o' L)(1-\rho_f L)Ls - f_1 \rho_f Ly \qquad \text{(MO2")}$$

We can write, if lags in the import function are neglected ($f_o'=0$):

$$r = r' - L(F+f) + f_2^{-1}(f_o' L(q-q'-\epsilon) - (f_o - f_o' L)Ls) + Lfy \qquad \text{(MO3")}$$

which is equivalent to equation (3) of section 1.

2.3 The Case of Fixed Exchange Rates

2.3.1 Fixed Exchange Rates as a Limit of Flexible Exchange Rates

We now examine the case of fixed exchange rates. A technical difficulty occurs. If the exchange rate is actually intangible, its current and expected rate of growth should equal zero. Simultaneously, its variance should become negligible. If so, we cannot make the assumption that foreigners behave according to portfolio theory. We must postulate that the domestic interest rate equals the foreign one ($R=R'$), which is obviously of little empirical interest.

If not, it can easily be guessed that economic agents will not believe the current exchange par will last long if the Central Bank does not show them it is willing to maintain such a par. Otherwise its credibility should be questioned. Such an argument is still somewhat heuristical; a more rigorous proof can be given as follows.

We can ask ourselves what would occur if a Central Bank sought to stabilise the *level* of the exchange rate instead of its *rate of growth.* If so, the Central Bank acts on the foreign exchange market: the amount f of its sales (or purchases) of foreign exchange reserves lies between f*, which corresponds to the case of fixed exchange rate, and 0 when flexible rates prevail. hence we write:

$$f = \lambda f^*$$

with

$$(1-L)f^* = -f_1(1-L)y + f_2(1-L)(r-r'-\epsilon^e) + (f_o-f_o')(q-q'-\epsilon) + (1-L)v_f$$

We must now substitute the criterion of the stabilisation of the level of the exchange rate for the one of its growth. Thus we write:

$$E(\epsilon_{t+1}/I_t) = -\epsilon_t/(1-L)$$

instead of

$$E(\epsilon_{t+1}/I_t) = 0$$

A straightforward calculation then leads to writing

$$(1-L)(1-\lambda)(f^{*e}-f^*) = f_o(\epsilon^e-\epsilon)$$

Hence

$$E(f_t/I_{t-1}) = -(L/(1-L))f_t(1-f_o'/(f_o-f_o'L)$$

$$= -LF_t(1-f_o'/(f_o-f_o'L))$$

When no lag is incorporated in the import equation ($f_o'=0$) this last equation reduces to:

$$E(f_t/I_{t-1}) = -Lf_t$$

which expresses that the *conditional variance of the foreign reserves is minimum,* which is the criterion we emphasised in section 1. indeed, we have

$$E(f_t/I_{t-1}) = 0$$

The case of fixed exchange rates can thus be seen as the limit of the one of flexible exchange rates when the variance of ϵ decreases and the one of F increases.

2.3.2 Optimal Policies

We now suppose that monetary authorities act as suggested in 2.3.1, i.e. they minimise the variance of current foreign reserves – or of distributed lags of these reserves. Government is still supposed to minimise the variance of output. It must first be recalled that there remains a trade–off between output and inflation as (PH) can now be written as:

$$q = b_1 y + b_2 q^e + (1-b_2)q'^e + v_1$$

Hence

$$q^e = \rho' Lq' + b_3^{-1} \rho_p Lv_p$$

Again, we cannot minimise simultaneously the variance of q and of y. one must choose between those two targets. As before, we choose output and can write

$$E(y_t/I_{t-1}) = y^e = 0$$

A calculation similar to those of section 2.2 gives the optimal budgetary and monetary rules. the first one can be written as

$$d_4(1-\rho_y)g = -\rho_y Ly + d_2(1-\rho_y)L(r-q^e) + d_3' L(q-q') + (d_3+d_3'L)(1-\rho_y)Ls + d_3 b_3^{-1} Lv_p$$

with

$$Lv_p = Lq - (b_2+b_3)Lq'^e - b_1 Ly$$

Again, this equation simplifies if the stochastic hypotheses of Table 6 are valid:

$$g = g_2 L(r-q'^e) + g_3 L(q-q') + (g_3'+g_3 L)Ls$$

The monetary rule can now be expressed as

$$(1-\rho_f L)f_2(r-r') = -L(f+F(1-f_o/(f_o-f_o'L))) + f_o b_3^{-1} \rho_p Lv_p + f_o' L(q-q'-\epsilon) - (f_o-f_o'L)(1-\rho_f L)Ls + f_1 \rho_f Ly \qquad \text{(MO4)}$$

or, with the stochastic assumptions of Table 6:

$$(1-\rho_f L)f_2(r-r') = -L(f+F(1-f_o/(f_o-f_o'L))) + f_o' L(q-q') - (f_o-f_o'L)(1-\rho_f L)Ls - f_1 \rho_f Ly \qquad \text{(MO5)}$$

or, in the case of negligible speculation:

$$r = r' + f_2^{-1}(-L(f+F(1-f_o/(f_o-f_o'L))) + f_o' L(q-q') - (f_o-f_o'L)Ls)$$

y and q can be calculated as for the flexible exchange rate case. We obtain:

$$y = (d_3'(w_p-w') + w_y)/(1-b_1 d_3')$$

$q = b_1 y + (1-\rho_p)Lv_p$

It must be pointed out the equation (MO4) is very close to the econometric specification of Barroux and Chauveau (1985). Some new empirical evidence can be found in Chauveau (1987). We have therefore found a way of reconciling monetary theory and effective practice of central banks or, at least, of the French bank. Before emphasising this point (see section 4 below), must must give further theoretical results.

3. FURTHER RESULTS

In this section we show that the preceding results remain valid, even if less restrictive assumptions are made.

3.1. The New Framework

3.1.1 Preliminary Remarks

Before describing the new framework, it may be useful to give notational conventions. L is the lag operator. B(L) refers to a polynom in L, i.e.

$$B(L) = \sum_i b_i L^i$$

Hence

$$B(L)X = \sum_i b_i X(-i)$$

We shall use many L–polynoms; $B_x(L)$, $B_m(L)$, $B_c(L)$, $B'_m(L)$, $B'_c(L)$, etc. Notice that $B((1+\xi)^{-1}L)$ can be written as:

$$b_o + b_1 L/(1+\xi) + \ldots + b_n (L/(1+\xi))^n$$

Moreover we shall, without loss of generality, impose the following conditions:

$$B_m(1) = 1 \qquad B'_m(1) = 1$$
$$B_c(1) = 1 \qquad B'_c(1) = 1$$
$$B_i(1) = 1 \qquad B'_i(1) = 1$$
$$B_1(1) = 1 \qquad B_2(1) = 1$$
$$B_x(1) = 1$$

An exception prevails for $B_y(L)$.

3.1.2 More Realistic Behaviour

We can generalise the simplified model of an open economy in the following way: assumptions about wages and prices are the same as in section 2 (see Table 7). we now allow for a sophisticated lag structure in the equations characterising the behaviour of economic agents. Moreover, we do not suppose any more that the portfolio choice of the agents obeys a marginal adjustment process. The temporary equilibrium is thus modified as indicated in Table 7. so is the mid term equilibrium.

Table 7. Main Assumptions

Wages and prices

$P = W(1+m)$

$\tilde{P} = P^{p^2}(p'E)^{1-p^2}$

$p = \Delta \text{Log } P \qquad p' = \Delta \text{Log } P'$

$\tilde{p} = \Delta \text{Log } \tilde{P} = p_2 p + (1-p_2)(p'+e)$

$\tilde{p}^e = \text{Log } \tilde{P}^e/p_{-1} = p_2 p^e + (1-p_2)(p'^e+e^e)$

$w - \tilde{p}^e = \Delta \text{Log } W - \text{Log } \tilde{P}^e/p_{-1} = p_o + p_1(Y-\bar{Y})/\bar{Y}$

Other behavioural assumptions

$C = c_o - c_2 B_c(L)S + c_1 u B_c'((1+\xi)^{-1}L)Y \qquad (7.6)$

$M = m_o - m_2 B_m(L)S + m_1 u B_m'((1+\xi)^{-1}L)Y \qquad (7.7)$

$I = i_o - i_2 B_i(L)(R-p^e) + i_1 u(Y^e-(1-d)Y) \qquad (7.8)$

$X = (x_o + x_2 B_x(L)S^{-1})k \qquad (7.9)$

$\mathscr{L}^d = (l_o^d + l_1^d uY - l_2^d R)S^{p_2}$

$B = B_F/PK^* = (a(1-L)K'^*)/SK^* = a\xi k/S$

$a = (R-R'-e^e)(1-R')/(\sigma^2+(R-R'-e^e)^2)$

Temporary equilibrium

$$B_y(L)Y = i_1 Y^e + y_o + x_o k + x_2 k B_x(L)S^{-1} - (m_2 B_m(L) + c_2 B_c(L)S - i_2 B_i(L))(R-p^e) + G \qquad \text{(IS)}$$

$$\mathscr{L} = (l_o^d + l_1^d uY - l_2^d R)S^{p_2} \qquad \text{(LM)}$$

$$p = p_2 p^e + (1-p_2)(p'^e+e^e) + p_o + p_1(Y-\bar{Y})/\bar{Y} \qquad \text{(PH)}$$

$$F = (x_2 k B_x(L) - (m_o + m_1 u B_m'((1+\xi)^{-1}L)Y + m_2 B_m(L)S)S^{-1} + x_o k + k(1-\Xi L)S^{-1}a \qquad \text{(BP)}$$

with

$$B_y(L) = 1 - u(c_1 B_c'((1+\xi^{-1})L) - u(m_1 B_m'((1+\xi^{-1})L) + i_1(1-d'')$$

$$y_o = c_o + x_o - m_o = (1+\xi')^{-1}(1+p')^{-1}$$

$$\Xi = (1+\xi')^{-1}(1+p')^{-1}$$

$$d'' = d' = \xi$$

<u>Mid term equilibrium (fixed exchange rates)</u>

$$p^{e^*} = p^* = p'^* = p'^e; \quad e^{e^*} = e^e = 0; \quad Y^e = Y^*$$

$$B_y(1)Y^* = y_o + x_o k + x_2 k S^{*-1} - (m_2+c_2)S^* - i_2(R^*-p^*) + G^* \qquad \text{(IS')}$$

$$\mathscr{L}^* = (l_o^d + l_1^d uY^* - l_2^d R^*)\ S^{*p_2} \qquad \text{(LM')}$$

$$p^* = p_2 p^* + (1-p_2)(p^{*\prime} + e^*) + p_o + p_1(Y^* - \bar{Y})/\bar{Y} \qquad \text{(PH')}$$

$$0 = x_o k + (x_2 k - (m_o + m_1 uY^* + m_2 S^*)S^{*-1} \qquad \text{(BP')}$$

$$d'' + \xi = i_o + i_1 d'' Y^* - i_2(R^* - p^*) \qquad \text{(SF')}$$

$$k = k_o \quad \text{or} \quad \xi = \xi' \qquad \text{(GE')}$$

<u>Quasi–equilibrium (flexible exchange rates)</u>

$$p^{e^*} = p^*; \quad p'^* = p'^e; \quad e^{e^*} = e^e = p^* - p'^*; \quad Y^e = Y^*$$

$$B_y(1)Y^* = y_o + x_o k + x_2 k S^{*-1} - (m_2+c_2)S^* - i_2(R^*-p^*) + G^* \qquad \text{(IS'')}$$

$$\mathscr{L}^* = (l_o^d + l_1^d uY^* - l_2^d R^*)S^{*p_2} \qquad \text{(LM'')}$$

$$p^* = p_2 p^* + (1-p_2)(p^{*\prime} + e^*) + p_o + p_1(Y^* - \bar{Y})/\bar{Y} \qquad \text{(PH'')}$$

$$0 = x_o k + (x_2 k - (m_o + m_1 uY^* + m_2 S^*)S^{*-1} \qquad \text{(BP'')}$$

$$d'' + \xi = i_o + i_1 d'' Y^* - i_2(R^* - p^*) \qquad \text{(SF'')}$$

$$k = k_o \quad \text{or} \quad \xi = \xi'$$

with

$$B(1) = 1 - u(C_1 B_c'((1+\xi)^{-1} - m_1 B_m'((1+\xi)^{-1})) - i_1 d''$$

N.B. The case of stationary equilibrium

$\xi' = \xi = d'' = 0$ and $B(1) = 1 - u(c_1 - m_1)$

3.2 New Results

3.2.1 Linearisation

Again, we linearise the four equations (IS), (LM), (PH) and (BP). A calculation similar to the one performed in section 2 leads us to write

Table 8. Linearisation: Temporary Equilibrium

$$B_y(L)(1-L)y = d_1(1-L)y^e - d_2B_i(1-L)(r-q^e) - B_1'(L)(q-q'-\epsilon)$$
$$+d_4(1-L)g + (1-L)v_y \qquad (8.1)$$
$$(1-L)q = b_1(1-L)y + b_2(1-L)q^e + b_3(1-L)(q'^e+\epsilon^e) + (1-L)v_1 \qquad (8.2)$$
$$(1-L)l = l_1'(1-L)y - l_2'(1-L)r + l_3'(q-q'-\epsilon) + (1-L)v_p \qquad (8.3)$$
$$(1-L)f = -f_1(1-L)y + B_2(L)(q-q'-\epsilon) + (1-L)v_f + f_2(1-\rho L)(1-L)(r-r'-\epsilon^e)$$
$$+ f_4(1-L)q' \qquad (8.4)$$

with

$$B_y(L) = 1 - u(c_1B_c'((1+\xi^{-1})L) - u(m_1B_m'((1+\xi^{-1})L)$$
$$B_1(L) = x_2kB_x(L) + m_2B_m(L) + c_2B_c(L)$$
$$B_2(L) = x_2kB_x(L) + m_2B_m(L) + m_o - m_1uY$$
$$B_y(L) = B_m'((1+\xi)^{-1}L)$$

and

$$f_2 = ka^*(R-R'-e^e)(\chi+(1-\chi)(p'^*+\xi'))(1-2a^*(R+R'+e^e)$$
$$f_3 = m_1u$$
$$f_4 = ka^*$$
$$\rho = \chi(1-(p'^*+\xi'))/(1-(1-\chi)(1-(p^*+\xi'))$$

3.2.2 Optimisation

The optimal policies are once more given by taking into account the equations of Table 8 and one of the couple of familiar conditions:

$y^e = 0;\ \epsilon^e = 0$ (flexible exchange rates with exchange rate as a target)

$y^e = 0;\ q^e = 0$ (flexible exchange rates with exchange rate as a target)

$y^e = 0;\ F^e = 0$ (fixed exchange rates with $f_o' = 0$)

$y^e = 0;\ F^e = LFf_o'/(f_o-f_o'L)$ (fixed exchange rates general case)

The calculations lead to results similar to those in section 2. Actually equations (9.1), (9.2), (10.1) and (10.2) are somewhat more complicated than (BO1), (M01), (B04) and (M04). But the specification is equivalent and the *property that any fluctuation of r' is fully and instantly reflected in r still holds.*

Table 9. the Case of Fixed Exchange Rates

Monetary policy

$$f_2(1-\rho L)(1-\rho_f L)(r-r') = -LC - \rho_f Lf + (B_2(L)(q-q')+(1-\rho_f)B_2'(L)L(S-S^*)) + f_3(B_3(L)+(1-\rho_f)B_y(L))Ly + f_4(\rho_f-\rho')Lq + q_2 b_3^{-1}\rho_p Lv_p \quad (9.1)$$

Budgetary policy

$$(1-\rho_y L)g = (B(L)+(1-\rho_y)B_y(L))Ly - \beta_1'(L)L(q-q') - (1-\rho_y)B_1(L)L(S-S^*) + q_2 b_3^{-1}\rho_p Lv_p + i_2 B_i(L)L(1-L)(r-\rho' Lq' - b_3^{-1}\varphi_\rho Lv_p) \quad (9.2)$$

with

$$v_p = (q-b_1 y-\rho' Lq')(1+b_2 b_3^{-1}L)$$

$$LB_1'(L) = B_1(L) - B_1(0)$$

$$LB_2'(L) = B_2(L) - B_2(0)$$

$$LB_3(L) = B_y(L)(1-L) - B_y(0)$$

$$q_1 = B_1(0) : b_o = B_y(0) : q_2 = B_2(0)$$

$$LB(L) = B_y(L) - B_y(0)$$

$$C = F(1-f_o'/(f_o-f_o'L))$$

Table 10. The Case of Flexible Exchange Rates

Monetary policy

$$f_2(1-\rho L)(1-\rho_f L)(r-r'-\epsilon^e) = (B_2(L)L(q-q'-\epsilon) + (1-\rho_f)B_2'(L)L(S-S^*)$$

$$+ f_3(B_3(L)+(1-\rho_f)B_y(L))Lv + f_4(\rho_f-\rho')Lq + q_2 b_3^{-1}\rho_p Lv_p \quad (10.1)$$

Budgetary policy

$$(1-\rho_y L)g = (B(L)+(1-\rho_y))B_y(L)Ly - B_1'(L)L(q-q'-\epsilon) - (1-\rho_y)B_1(L)L(S-S^*) + q_2 b_3^{-1}\rho_p Lv_p + i_2 B_i(L)L(1-L)(r-\rho' Lq' - b_3^{-1}\rho_p Lv_p) \quad (10.2)$$

4. EMPIRICAL RESULTS

Our empirical results have already been presented in Chauveau (1987). We thus limit ourselves to a few comments

– about the specifications actually selected

– about the French case.

4.1 Specifications

A usual specification states that the actual rate of interest adjusts gradually to the desired one:

$$R - R(-1) = (R^{*}-R(-1)) \qquad (S1)$$

R is the short term domestic interest rate, R(–1) its lagged values, whereas R* designs the desired one. R* is given by equation (3) of section 1 if exchange rates are floating, and by equation (3") in the case of fixed though revisable exchange rates (e.g. when EMS prevail). One may thus write (S1) as

$$R = (1-\mu)R(-1) + [R'+(p^{*}-p'^{*}) - \sum_j a_j FER(-j)/GDP(-j) + \sum_i b_i EXC(-i) + c] \qquad (S2)$$

or

$$R = (1-\mu)R(-1) + \mu[R' + e^{e} - \sum_j a_j FER(-j)/GDP(-j) + \sum_i b_i EXC(-i) + c] \qquad (S'2)$$

The coefficients of R(–1) and R′ sum to one which means that in the long run a one point increase of the foreign interest rate induces a one point raise of the domestic one. This does not hold any more in the short run, the Central Bank reacting slowly. Such a specification may be questioned as empirical observation of Central Bank's behaviour suggests that they react far more quickly to the fluctuations of foreign rates. To take this phenomenon into account, (S2) or (S'2) can be rewritten with the assumption that the adjustment process holds for the gap (DIF = R – R′) between domestic and foreign rates rather than for the domestic rate itself. Hence:

$$DIF = (1-\mu)DIF(-1) + \mu[(p^{*}-p'^{*}) - \sum_j a_j FER(-j)/(GDP(-j) + \sum_i b_i EXC(-i) + c] \qquad (S3)$$

or

$$DIF = (1-\mu)DIF(-1) + \mu'[e^{e} - \sum_j a_j FER(-j)/GDP(-j) + \sum_i b_i EXC(-i) + c] \qquad (S'3)$$

With this new specification any variation of the foreign rate is fully and instantly reflected in the domestic one. This, in turn, seems to be quite excessive and a more general specification, allowing for quick though incomplete adjustment between the two rates can be stated as

$$DIF = (1-\mu)DIF(-1) - d\Delta R' + \mu[(p^*-p'^*) - \sum_j a_j FER(-j)/GDP(-j) + \sum_i b_i EXC(-i) + c] \quad (S4)$$

or

$$DIF = (1-\mu)DIF(-1) - d\Delta R' + \mu[e^e - \sum_j a_j FER(-j)/GDP(-j) + \sum_i b_i EXC(-i) + c] \quad (S'4)$$

The impact of any variation of the foreign rate is immediate if d equals zero. (S4) and (S'4) are equivalent to (S2) and (S'2) respectively when d equals 1. Such a specification permits us to take into account different reaction times of central banks.

Finally, (S4) and (S′4) can be written in the following form:

$$X = R' + (1-\mu)DIF(-1) - d\Delta R' + \mu[(p^*-p'^*) - \sum_j a_j FER(-j)/GDP(-j) + \sum_i b_i EXC(-i) + c] \quad (S5)$$

or $$R = R' + (1-\mu)DIF(-1) - d\Delta R' + \mu[e^e - \sum_j a_j FER(-j)/GDP(-j) + \sum_i b_i EXC(-i) + c] \quad (S'5)$$

which emphasises the 'a priori' restrictions:

– the coefficient of R′ must equal one
– the coefficient of R′ must lie between 0 and –1
– the coefficient of p* and the coefficient of DIF must sum to one
– the coefficient of p′* and the coefficient of p* must sum to zero.

Equations (S5) or (S4) have been used, in econometric applications, for countries whose currency is floating; equations (S'5) or (S'4) for countries belonging the the E.M.S. and whose currency tends to depreciate. As a matter of fact the "foreign" currency has bee assimilated

– for Japan to the US dollar
– for Germany to the US dollar
– for United Kingdom to the DM
– for Italy to the DM
– for France to the DM

For a justification of this simplification see Chauveau (1987).

4.2 The French Case

This study uses quarterly data from 1974:2 to 1978:3 and monthly data from March 1979 to September 1978.

We could have limited this work to the EMS period (from March 1979 to the present) and we could therefore have adopted monthly data. This possibility has been rejected for two reasons: i) it is always better to have an estimation on a long period if behaviours are stable; it is more reliable; ii) it is difficult to include monthly adjustments in existing models which are usually estimated on a quarterly basis. The estimations allow us to suppose that the monetary policy was not really different during the fixed parity system ("snake" and EMS) and in the periods of floating franc. Thus the Banque de France would have managed the Franc/DM parity in a way relatively independent of the official exchange rate system. The Bank would have intervened on the foreign exchange market in order to stabilise the rate of the franc in successive stages.

In this regard, the observation of Figure 2 is significant: through the entire period the actual rate of the franc against the mark has remained close to its theoretical value given by PPP. More precisely, we note that the French franc has experienced long periods of relative stability in–between various points of disruption in the franc's exchange rate curve. The successive stages of stability are dated as follows: 1977:1 to 1981:1, 1982:2 to 1983:1, and 1983:3 to 1986:1.

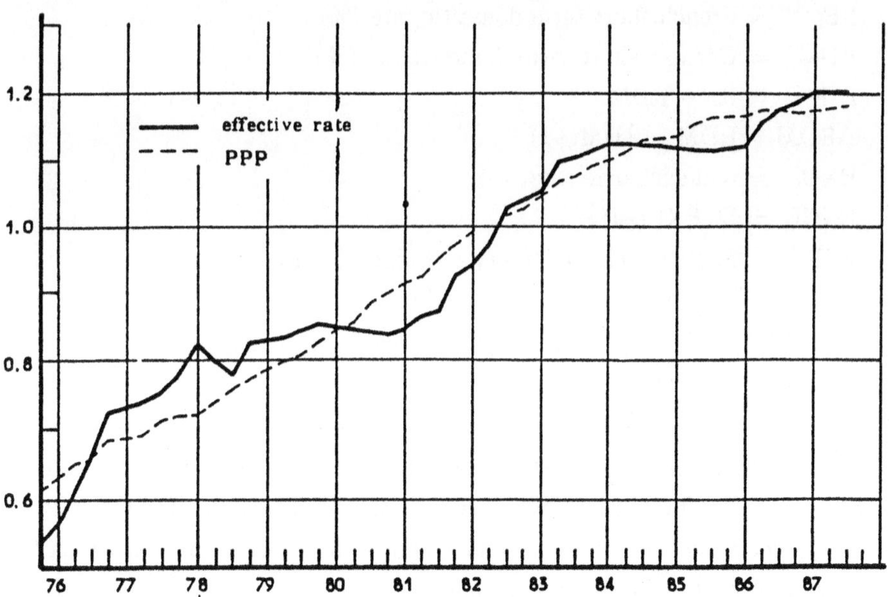

Figure 2

The second subsample (1981:2 to 1983:1) is characterised by successive devaluations and the very beginning period (1975:4 to 1976:4) was the departure from the "snake" which, although it looks more continuous, was very similar to the period of repeated devaluations. The chronology so defined is independent of the existing exchange rate system.

Nevertheless it must be noted that the stabilisation of the franc's rate is more pronounced – stages are more horizontal – when a fixed exchange rate system prevails and that the "break" in 1978 corresponds to a period of intense uncertainty about the franc before the legislative elections and then a return of confidence in the expectations.

Despite some numerous changes that occurred since the first oil crisis, it seems possible to exhibit a stable reaction function which gives fairly good econometric results; those are reported in the following frame and in Table 1, Appendix 2.

Table 11

$$RF = 0.98\ RDM + 0.285\ DIF(-1) - 0.212\ \Delta RDM - 0.025\ FER/GDP$$
$$+\ 5.77\ EXCL + 0.622 + 1.78\ DUM781 + 1.67\ DUM811 + 1.54\ DUM822$$
$$+\ 1.54\ ENTRY$$

with:

RF = French short term domestic rate (%)
RDM = German short term domestic rate(%)
DIF = RF – RDM
ΔRDM = RDM – RDM(–1)
EXC = real exchange rate
EXCL = $\Sigma b_i EXC(-i)$
FER = foreign exchange reserves (million francs)
GDP = French gross domestic product
DUMXXY = dummy variable (XX = year, Y = quarter)
ENTRY = DUM792

Such a specification is well related to our theoretical results. Note that restrictions on coefficients are well verified: the coefficient of RDM equals 0.98; DIF(–1)'s coefficient is between 0 and 1 and RDM's coefficient is between 0 and –1. Nevertheless, two differences are apparent:

- The expected growth rate of the exchange rate does not appear in the estimation: some attempts to introduce expectations of the exchange rate have been made hypothesising that they depend on the gap between the actual rate and the rate corresponding to the PPP.[4] When the DM rate is above its theoretical value given by PPP, the probability of a devaluation of the French franc increases; the lower the foreign exchange reserves the higher the probability. All these attempts lead to negative results. This should not be surprising given that the level of foreign exchange reserves is highly correlated to the expectations. Reserves decrease quickly in the case of speculation against the franc; they also increase quickly when a foreign currency is controverted. The introduction of gold and foreign exchange reserves in the adjustment makes it difficult to isolate the influence of the anticipation.
- A few dummy variables have been introduced to take into account some expectational events: in the first quarter of 1978, the expectations of exchange rates were particularly unfavourable and provoked an unexpected rise the the French rate. In the second quarter of 1982, the devaluation of the French franc, which had been predicted by markets, was delayed causing similar effects. On the other hand, some abnormal fall or the rate occurred in the first quarter of 1981 and in the second quarter of 1979; in the first case, the Eurodeutschmark's rate rose in an exceptional way and this increase had no impact on the French rate. In the second case, the fall followed the setting of the EMS (the corresponding dummy is named ENTRY).

Four more technical points can be noticed:

(i) As RDM's coefficient is not significantly different from one, it is better to impose that it takes this value by using the regression where the dependent variables is the difference between the French and the German rate. The econometric results, shown in Table 2, Appendix 2, are very similar to the former ones.

(ii) The real exchange rate is smoothed in order to have a negative effect, at the beginning, on the interest rate, and then positive. The coefficients used are proportional to –3, 0, 3, 4, and 5. The total effect is positive as is their sum.

(iii) The autoregressivity of the formulation is low, suggesting that the Bank of France reacts relatively quickly to the evolutions of the foreign exchange reserves and to the real exchange rate.

(iv) Our results imply that the Bank of France reflects immediately 80% of the change in the German rate on the French rate and 20% in the following quarter. This, on the contrary, is a quick reaction.

The adjustments made with monthly data are presented in Appendix 2 (Tables 5 and 6). The results are similar to the previous ones except for two arguments:

- Exchange rate's expectations are probably influenced – or at least have been influenced during this specific period – by the ratio effective exchange rate/central par (RAPP). Its introduction in the adjustment with quarterly data was therefore made impossible because the EMS was not in effect throughout the entire period covered by this data.
- The real exchange rate has been eliminated from the monthly adjustment; its coefficient was insignificant because of multicollinearity.

In the monthly adjustment, we could have used the growth rate of a monetary argument as an advanced indicator of the future exchange rate. A rapid increase in the money stock gives rise to expectations of a devaluation. The test completed with M3 gave insignificant results.

Whatever the specifications, two important results must be emphasised:

- a quick repercussion of the fluctuations of the German short term rate of interest on the French one;
- a very strong influence of the level of the foreign exchange reserves on the interest rate differential between France and Germany

Describing monetary policy with a single equation where the domestic rate is determined by the German rate and by simple considerations about the current account may seem naive or pretentious. Nevertheless, such a specification is not excessive, if we remember that the Central Bank has managed the interest rate in terms of the external constraint; this has been confirmed by several specialists on the French monetary policy and, in particular, by Besnard and Redon (1986).

NOTES

1) If the Central Bank acts on the foreign exchange market, foreign exchange reserves should be incorporated in the "rule".
2) We could as well introduce a utility function whose arguments would be the values of the three targets and take explicitly into account the trade–off between those variables. This would lead to useless complications.
3) Equation (2bis) is obviously equivalent to the following one:
$R - p^* = R' - p'^* + bEXCL + d +$ (2ter).
4) cf. Besnard and Redon (1987).

REFERENCES

Aoki, M. (1985), "Monetary Reaction Functions in a Small Open Economy", *Journal of Economic Dynamics and Control*, 9, pp.1–24

Aoki, M. (1987), "Decentralised Monetary Rules in a Three Country Model", communication aux Journées internationales d'économie monétaire et bancaire, Aix en Provence, Juin.

Artus, P, Y. Barroux and J. Pecha (1987), "Objectif quantitatif de croissance de la masse monétaire et fonction de réaction des autorités monétaires", *Cahiers économiques et monétaires*, 27.

Avouyi Dovi et al (1987), "Evaluation des fonctions de réaction en France, RFA, Royaume uni et choix de la base de temps", O.F.C.E., February, mimeo.

Barroux, Y. and T. Chauveau (1985), "La détermination des taux d'intérèt en France", *Cahiers économiques et monétaires*, 21.

Barroux, Y. and N. Dagognet (1987), Analyse des relations causales entremasses monétaire et base monétaire: l'expérience française", Banque de France, February, mimeo.

Besnard and E. Redon (1986), "Vingt ans de politique monétaire francaise", *Problèmes économiques*, No.1991, September.

Broze, L., C. Gourieroux and Z. Szarfar (1985), "Solution of Dynamic Linear Rational Expectations Models", *Economic Theory*, Vol 1, No. 2

Coudert, V. and R. Topol (1987), "Endogénéeisation des taux d'intérèt par des fonctions de réaction", Working Paper No.87–02, C.E.P.I.I.–O.F.C.E., May.

Chauveau, T. (1987), "La politique de taux d'intérèt des grandes banques centrales", *Révue de l'I.P.E.C.O.D.E.*, No.17, November.

Champsaur, P. and J. Melitz (1982), "Une généralisation du choix des instruments de politique monétaire", *Annales de l'I.N.S.E.E.*, No.46, pp.61–80.

Metric (1981), "Une modélisation de l'économie francaise", Paris, I.N.S.E.E. (ouvrage collectif)

Theil, H. (1964), *Optimal Decision Rules for Government and Industry*, North–Holland, Amsterdam.

Turnovsky, S.J. (1977), *Macroeconomic Analysis and Stabilisation Policy*, Cambridge University Press, Cambridge.

Villa, P. (1986), "Règles de gestion du taux d'intérèt", C.E.P.R.E.M.A.P., No.8609, March.

APPENDIX 1

$$d_y = ((c_1 - m_1)u - i_1(1-d))$$

$$d_0 = (c_0 + i_0 + x_0 k - m_0)/(1-d_y)$$

$$d_1 = i_1/(1-d_y)$$

$$d_2 = i_2/(1-d_y)$$

$$d_3 = x_2 k/(1-d_y)$$

$$d_3' = (c_2 + m_2)/(1-d_y)$$

$$d_4 = 1/(1-d_y)$$

$b_1 = p_o/Y$

$b_2 = p_2 = 1 - b_3$

$l_1 = l_1^d u$

$l_2 = l_2^d$

$l_3 = l_3^d$

$f_o = (m_o + m_1 uY^*/S^* + m_2 S^* - (x_2 k))/S^{*2}$

$f_{oo} = m_2/S^*$

$f_1 = m_1 uS^*$

$f_2 = \gtrless k^{-2}$

APPENDIX 2

ABBREVIATIONS

RF	= French short term interest rate
RDM	= German short term interest rate
DIF	= RF – RDM
ΔRDM	= RDM – RDM(–1)
EXCL	= lagged real exchange rate
FER	= foreign exchange reserves
GDP	= gross domestic product
DUMXXY	= dummy variable (DUMXXY = 1 in 19XX Y)
ENTRY	= DUM791

Table 1. Econometric Results, France: quarterly time series

Endogenous variable: RF

Sign	Coefficient	T–Student	Variables
+	.980	(32.6)	RDM
+	.285	(4.4)	DIF(–1)
–	.212	(2.5)	ΔRDM
–	.025	(8.2)	FER/GDP
+	5.772	(4.3)	EXCL
+	.622	(0.5)	1
+	1.783	(3.7)	DUM781
–	1.674	(3.2)	DUM811
+	1.542	(3.1)	DUM822
–	1.535	(3.1)	ENTRY

Period	S.E.E.	R2C	D.W.
1974:2 1987:3	.466	.973	1.400

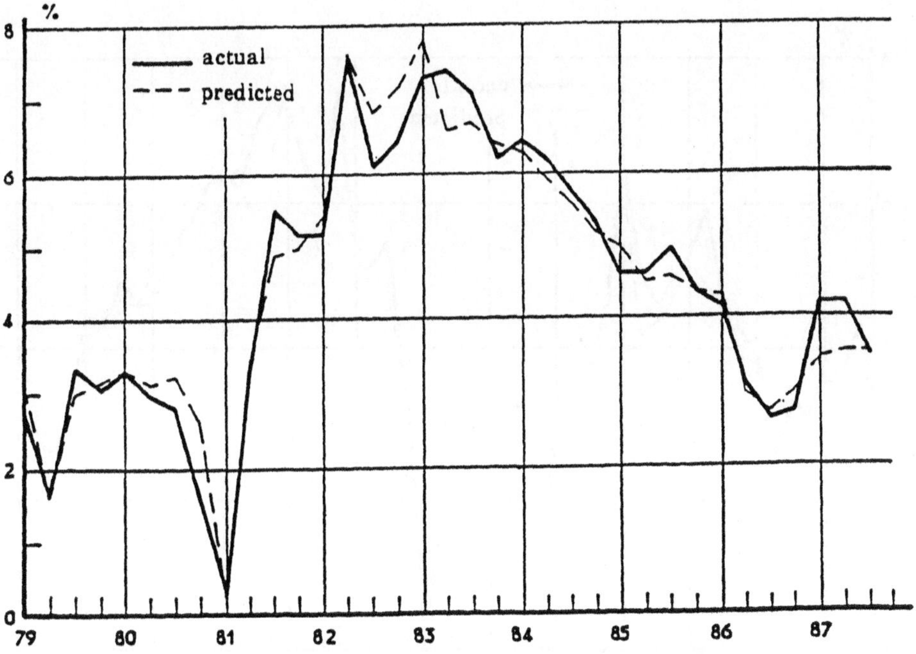

Graph 1

Table 2. Econometric Results, France: quarterly time series

Endogenous variable: DIF = RF – RDM

Sign	Coefficient	T–Student	Variables
+	.303	(5.2)	DIF(–1)
–	.209	(2.5)	ΔRDM
–	.024	(8.6)	FER/GDP
+	5.682	(4.3)	EXCL
+	.424	(0.3)	1
+	1.833	(3.9)	DUM781
–	1.764	(3.5)	DUM811
+	1.510	(3.1)	DUM822
–	1.513	(3.0)	ENTRY

Period	S.E.E	R2C	D.W.
1974:2 1987:3	.463	.914	1.419

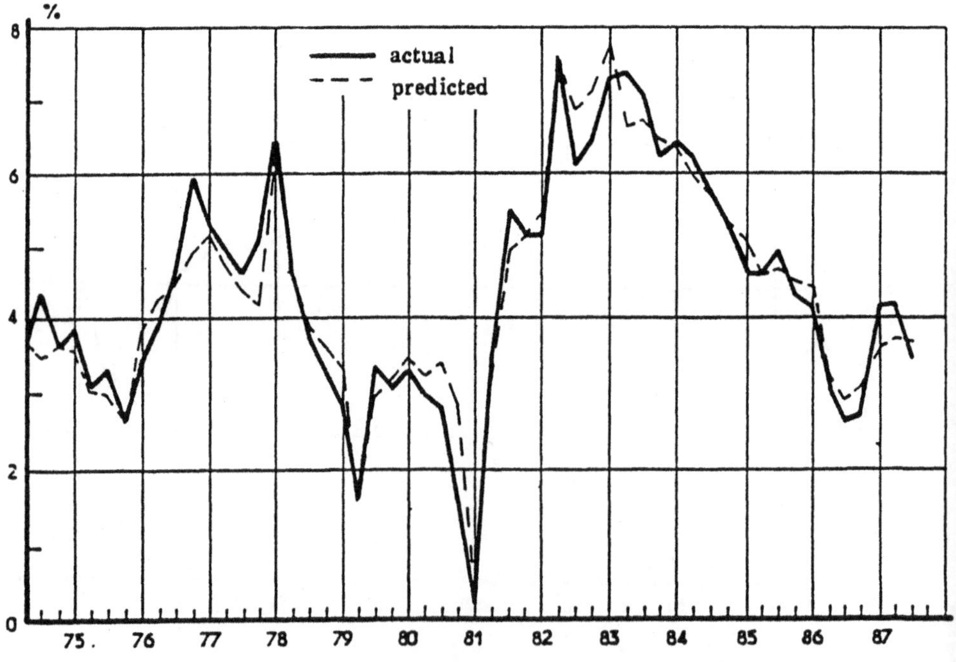

Graph 2

Table 3. Econometric Results, France: quarterly time series

Endogenous variable: DIF = RF – RDM

Sign	Coefficient	T–Student	Variables
+	.384	(4.0)	DIF(–1)
–	.330	(2.8)	ΔRDM
–	.034	(3.2)	FER/GDP
+	6.483	(3.2)	EXCL
+	.657	(0.2)	1
+	1.434	(2.6)	DUM781
–	1.290	(2.3)	ENTRY

Period	S.E.E	R2C	D.W.
1974:2 1980:2	.491	.825	1.490

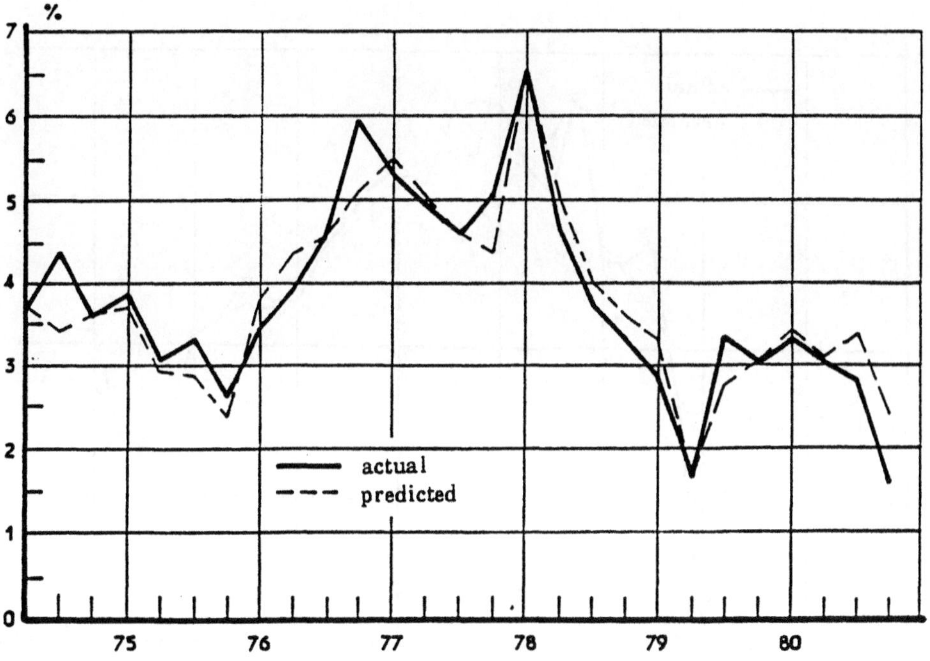

Graph 3

Table 4. Econometric Results, France: quarterly time series

Endogenous variable: DIF = RF – RDM

Sign	Coefficient	T–Student	Variables
+	.264	(3.7)	DIF(–1)
–	.167	(1.2)	ΔRDM
–	.027	(8.5)	FER/GDP
+	6.603	(2.8)	EXCL
+	.057	(0.3)	1
–	1.677	(3.3)	DUM811
+	1.547	(3.1)	DUM822
–	1.473	(2.9)	ENTRY

Period	S.E.E	R2C	D.W.
1979:1 1987:2	.458	.937	1.390

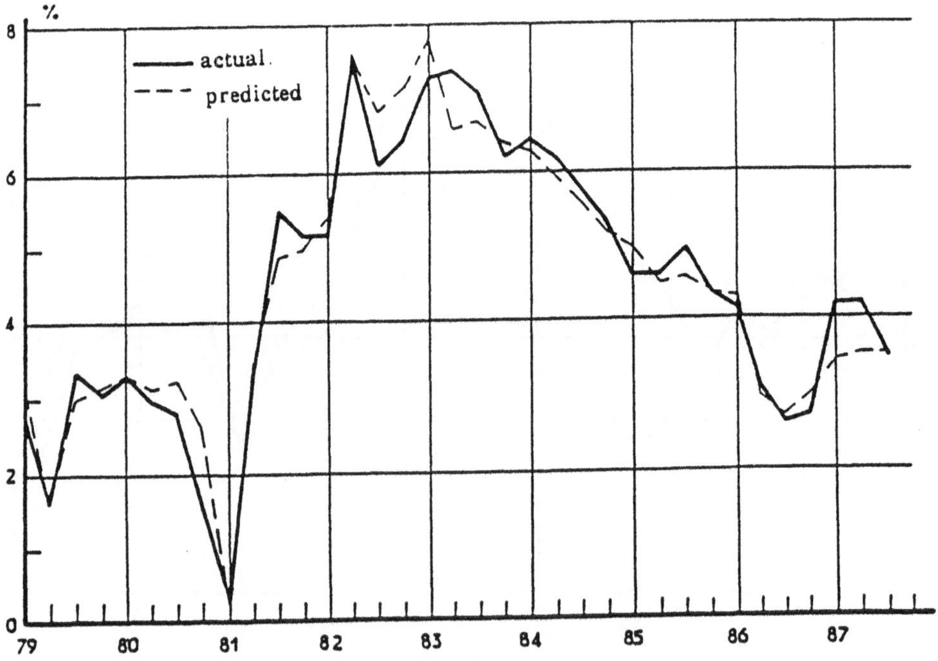

Graph 4

Table 5. Econometric Results, France: monthly series

Endogenous variable: RF

Sign	Coefficient	T–Student	Variables
+	.9691	(60.6)	RDM
+	.6570	(18.9)	DIF(–1)
–	.7126	(7.8)	ΔRDM
–	.0130	(7.6)	FER/GDP
+	13.5951	(3.4)	RAPP
–	10.5829	(2.6)	1
+	3.5429	(8.9)	DUM816
+	1.3194	(4.6)	DUM823+DUM824

Period	S.E.E	R2C	D.W.
1979.3 1987.9	.379	.983	1.786

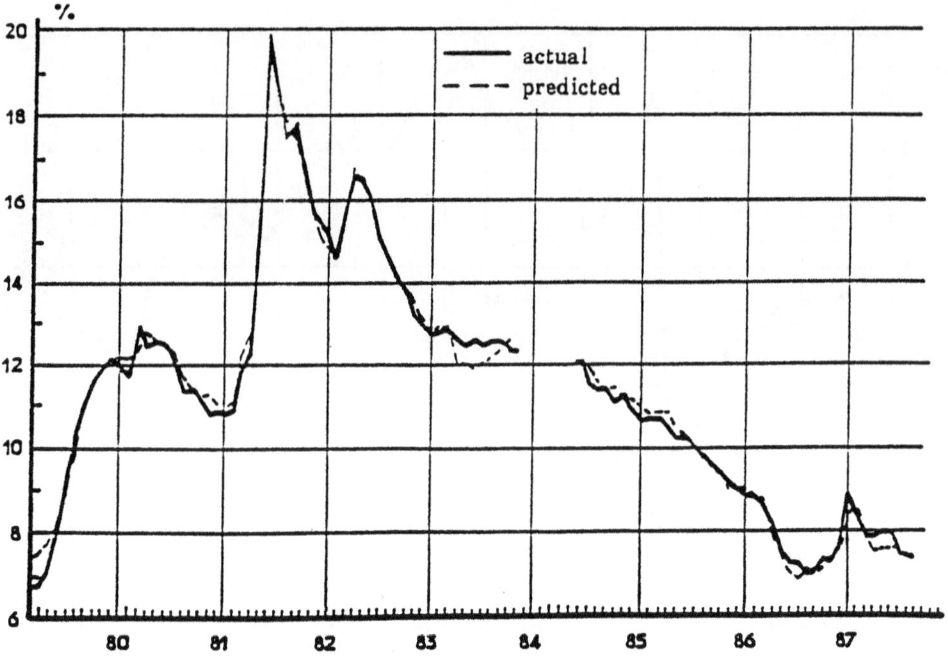

Graph 5

Table 6. Econometric Results, France: monthly series

Endogenous variable: DIF = RF – RDM

Sign	Coefficient	T–Student	Variables
+	.6714	(19.3)	DIF(–1)
–	.7226	(7.8)	ΔRDM
–	.0126	(7.2)	FER/GDP
+	13.5190	(3.3)	RAPP
–	10.8210	(2.6)	l
+	3.3826	(8.5)	DUM816
+	1.2327	(4.2)	DUM823+DUM824

Period	S.E.E	R2C	D.W.
1979.3 1987.9	.379	.983	1.786

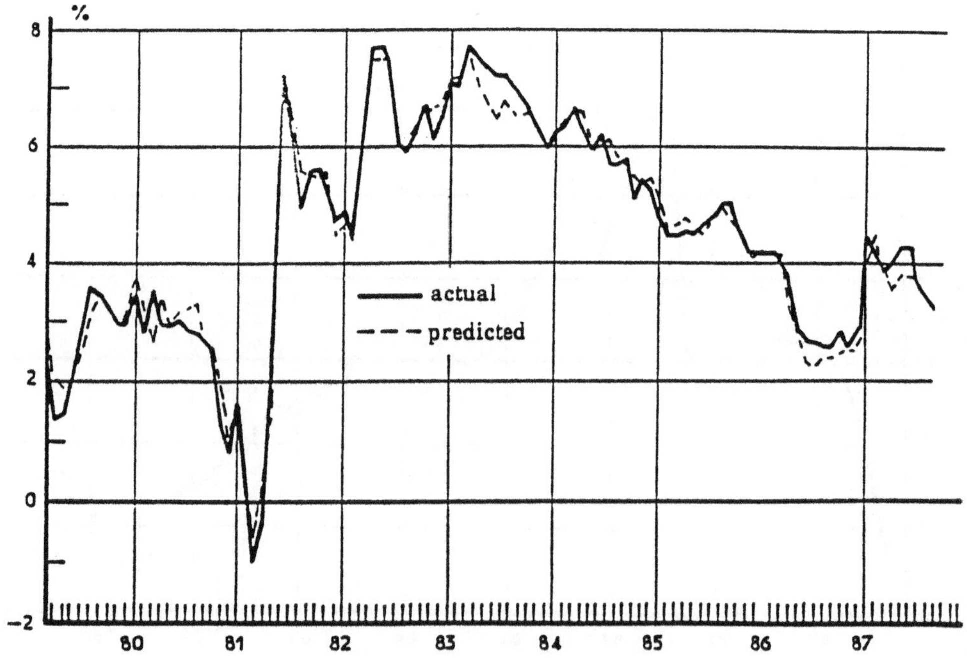

Graph 6

PART II

CREDIBILITY AND REPUTATION

CHAPTER 3

CREDIBILITY, REPUTATION AND THE INDETERMINACY OF MACROECONOMICS

Carlo Carraro, *The University of Venice, Italy and CEPR, London*

1. INTRODUCTION

Suppose the policy problem can be described as a repeated game between two decision makers, and suppose that one of the two players make his strategy conditional on the other player's strategy. This implies that one player decides first, whereas the other player decides only after having observed the first player's strategy. The policy problem is therefore sequential. For example, private agents' behaviour may be constrained by the existence of contracts, so that at each stage, private agents sign contracts first, and the policy maker decides its policy only after having observed the agents' strategy.

This framework has often been used in macroeconomics. Several examples are proposed in the literature on the time–inconsistency problem, and the issue of international co–ordination[1]. The different macroeconomic problems that fit the sequential framework described above have been analysed under alternative rules of the game. There are papers that assume that expectations have a strategic role (e.g. Barro–Gordon, 1983; Backus–Driffill, 1985), and papers that determine the subgame perfect equilibrium of the game by ruling out the asymmetry between the players (see Pohjola's 1986 survey). As pointed out in Carraro (1985b) and Rogoff (1986), most papers solve this game without realising that its outcome is not uniquely determined. Furthermore, the wide literature on the Folk Theorem (see Fudenberg–Maskin, 1986, Abreu, 1988) tells us that indeterminacy cannot be ruled out by changing the time horizon of the game or the assumptions on the information available to players. Indeterminacy is therefore part of macroeconomic analysis, and it affects all descriptive and normative conclusions.

P. Artus and Y. Barroux (eds.), Monetary Policy, 63–78.

In this paper we try to solve the indeterminacy problem by slightly changing the rules of the game as follows. Suppose both players want to achieve their own desired outcome. The player who decides second is assumed to have a greater strategic power; he can thus threaten the first player in order to achieve his desired outcome[2]. Given the asymmetry between the two players, the player who decides second is called the dominant. The questions to be answered are: can the second player announce a strategy such that the first is induced to behave as if he were acting in the second player's interest? How can this strategy be computed? What are the properties of the solution of the game when such a strategy is announced by the dominant (second) player? What are the properties of the dominant player's optimal strategy?

By answering these questions, we want to show that a unique outcome can be achieved, if one player is dominant (i.e. if we allow one player to choose among all feasible outcomes). In such a case, of course, he tries to achieve his most favorable outcome, and he thus needs to coordinate his action with the other player's action. The latter has no incentive to comply with the dominant player's desired outcome, and must therefore be appropriately threatened. Will these threats be effective and credible? The answer will be shown to depend on the dominant player's reputation, thus enabling us to determine plausible conditions for the uniqueness of the outcome of the policy game. However, the normative content of this result will be shown to be limited, because reputation is a subjective parameter, that can hardly be evaluated.

Going back to our example, this paper determines that particular policy maker's strategy that induces private agents to behave as if they were acting in the policy maker's interest. This provides a great advantage to the policy maker. If indeed the monetary authority or the government can announce a strategy that implies the minimisation of their loss function with respect not only to their own decision variables, but also with respect to the private agents' variables, then it is obvious that, in general, a lower loss can be achieved, i.e. it becomes easier for the policy maker to attain his desired outcome (examples are provided in Carraro, 1985a,b; 1988a).

We name the strategy that enables the policy maker to achieve his desired outcome Stackelberg trigger strategy (STS), where the name Stackelberg is used to denote the asymmetry of players' strategies. An effective and credible STS strategy can easily be shown to be the policy maker's best policy.

The structure of the paper is the following: section 2 defines the basic game.

It analyses indeed the constituent policy game and defines effectiveness and credibility of some of the Stackelberg trigger strategy. Section 3 then determines the equilibria of the repeated game, both in the presence of complete and of incomplete information, and introduces the indeterminacy problem. It is also shown under what conditions can the dominant player achieve his desired outcome, i.e. there exists a unique (Stackelberg trigger strategy) equilibrium of the repeated game. Section 4 discusses the theoretical implications of these results and analyses the role of macroeconomics when its determinacy is appropriately taken into account.

2. THE BASIC POLICY GAME

Let us start the analysis by presenting the constituent policy game. Let us assume that there are only two decision–makers: the dominant and the dominated player, that we denote with the letters D and F respectively. Let $V_D(s_D, s_F)$ and $V_F(s_D, s_F)$ be the players' loss functions, where $s_i \epsilon S_i$, i=D,F, denotes player i–ths strategy and S_i is his strategy space. The loss functions v_i, i=D,F, are assumed to be defined, continuous and bounded on $S = S_D \times S_F$ and each V_i is assumed to be convex with respect to s_i.

The "rules of the game" are as follows: the dominant player aims at achieving a given desired outcome (s_D^*, s_F^*). He therefore threatens the other player in order to induce him to choose the strategy s_F^*. If the dominated player indeed chooses s_F^*, then the dominant player chooses s_D^*. In this case the players' losses are V_D^* and V_F^*. If the dominated player does not comply with the dominant player's desired outcome and chooses s_F^o, then the dominant player has two possible choices. First, he can accommodate the other player's strategy and choose $s_D^o = R_D(s_F^o)$, where:

$$R_i(s_j) = \arg\min V_i(s_i, s_j) \qquad i=D,F \qquad (1)$$

are the players' *best reply functions.* The mappings $R_i(s_j)$, i=D,F, define player i's optimal reaction to player–j's strategy and are assumed to be contractions for simplicity[3].

The second possibility is to punish the nominated player who has not chosen s_F^*, by using the punitive strategy s_D^p. In the first case, the players' losses are V_D^o and V_F^o; in the second case, the losses are V_D^p and V_F^p. The strategies s_D^p and s_F^o will later be defined.

The extensive form of this game is described by Figure 1:

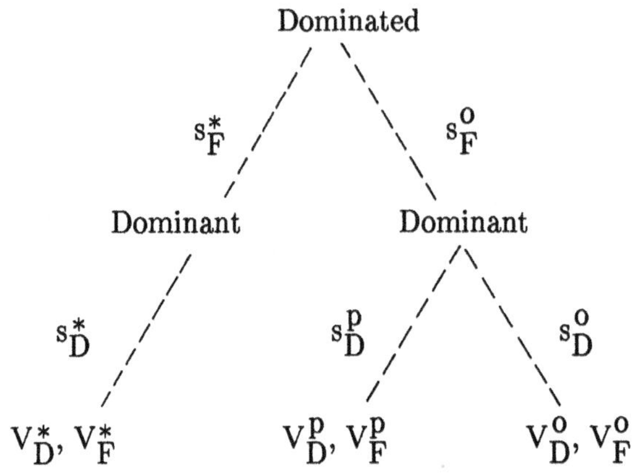

Figure 1. The extensive form of the constituent game

Given the above rules of the game, the dominant player's strategy is defined by the decision function $s_D(s_F)$ which belongs to the set Σ_D. The normal form of the *constituent game* $\tau(N,S,V)$ is defined by the set of players N, the strategy space S and the loss vector $V = (V_D V_F)$.

In order to relate our results to recent findings in the engineering literature, we assume that the dominant player's desired outcome coincides with his best outcome ("Team Solution" in the engineering literature). This assumption is not necessary and the results below hold even when (s_D^*, s_F^*) is not the dominant player's best outcome. We define (s_D^*, s_F^*) as:

$$(s_D^*, s_F^*) = \arg \min_{s_D, s_F} V_D(s_D, s_F) \tag{2}$$

Notice that this implies $s_D^* = R_D(s_F^*)$.

The CLS problem can be described in the following way: find a *Stackelberg trigger strategy* $s_D^{ts}(s_F)$ such that:

$$s_F^* = \arg \min_{s_F} V_F[s_D^{ts}(s_F), s_F] \tag{3a}$$

$$s_D^* = s_D^{ts}(s_F^*) \tag{3b}$$

where backward induction is used to solve the game. In other words, the CLS problem is solved if the dominant player can determine a strategy s_D^{ts}, such that the other player is induced to behave as if he were minimising the dominant player's loss function. The solution of the dominated player's problem, given

$s_D = s^{ts}_D$, must indeed be $s_F = s^*_F$, the dominant player's desired strategy. Moreover, when the dominated player plays s^*_F, the dominant player's best reply must be s^*_D.

For example, let

$$s^{ts}_D = s^*_D + h(s_F, s^*_F) \tag{4}$$

where the function $h(\cdot)$ is defined as

$$h(s_F, s^*_F) = \begin{cases} 0 & \text{if } s_F = s^*_F \\ s^p_D(s_F) & \text{otherwise} \end{cases} \tag{5}$$

and where $s^p_D(s_F)$ must be such that:

$$\arg\min_{s_F} V_F(s^{ts}_D, s_F) = \arg\min_{s_F} V_D(s^*_D, s_F) \tag{6}$$

If (6) is satisfied, we have $s_F = s^*_F$ and (4) and (5) imply $s_D = s^*_D$. The function h(.) is called *threat function* since it defines a set of threats (or incentives) that are used by the dominant player in order to induce the other player to choose the strategy s^*_F.

We name the strategy (4)(5) Stackelberg trigger strategy and we define a *Stackelberg trigger strategy equilibrium* as the equilibrium in which the dominant player achieves his desired outcome.

Two important problems affect the existence of the Stackelberg trigger strategy:

(i) the dominated player may prefer to be penalised by the dominant player rather than adopt his desired strategy if the dominated player's loss is lower under the punitive strategy, i.e. if

$$V_F(s^*_D, s^*_F) > V_F(s^{ts}_D, s_F) \qquad \text{for some } s_F \epsilon S_F \tag{7}$$

(ii) the threat announced by the dominant player and defined by the punitive strategy s^p_D may not be credible if he finds it advantageous to follow a strategy which differs from the announced one when s_F does not coincide with s^*_F, i.e. if the inequality

$$v_D(s^{ts}_D, s_F) > v_D[R_D(s_F), s_F] \qquad \text{for some } s_F \epsilon S_F \tag{8}$$

holds and is perfectly anticipated by the dominated player.

In order to study the first problem, we rule out, for the moment, the credibility problem and we assume that the dominant player commits himself to carrying out the declared strategy.

We define the most punitive strategy $s^p_D(s_F)$ as the dominant player's strategy which maximises the other player's loss function any time he does not comply with the policy selected for him by the dominant player, i.e.

$$s^p_D(s_F) = \arg\max_{s_D} V_F(s_D, s_F) \tag{9}$$

Having assumed that the dominant player is committed to carrying out the announced strategy, the dominated player's optimal strategy is:

$$s_F = \begin{cases} s^*_F & \text{if } V^{st}_F \geq V^*_F \\ s^p_F & \text{otherwise} \end{cases} \tag{10}$$

where

$$s^p_F = \arg\min_{s_F} \max_{s_L} V_F(s_L, s_F) \tag{11}$$

and $V^{st}_F = (V_F(s^{ts}_D(s^p_F))$. Equation (10) implies $s_F = s^*_F$ if $V^*_F \geq V^{st}_F$. In other words, the dominant player can induce the other player to comply with all the outcomes that belong to the following region:

$$IR = \{(s_D, s_F), s_D \epsilon S_D, s_F \epsilon S_F: V_F(s_D, s_F) \leq V^{st}_F\} \tag{12}$$

The set IR is called *inducible region* (Tolwinski,1983). In words, the inducible region defines all points in the strategy space that the dominated player prefers to the conflict with the dominant player, because they imply lower losses than the disagreement loss V^{st}_F.

The previous remarks lead us to define the most powerful dominant player's strategy as:

$$s^{ts}_D(s_F) = \begin{cases} s^*_D & \text{if } s_F = s^*_F \\ s^p_D(s_F) & \text{otherwise} \end{cases} \tag{13}$$

where $s^p_D(s_F)$ is defined by (9).

Summing up: if the desired outcome (s^*_D, s^*_F) is such that $V_F(s^*_D, s^*_F) > V^{st}_F$, then the dominant player cannot induce the other player to choose s^*_F. If (s^*_D, s^*_F) cannot be induced by s^{ts}_D as defined by (13) and (9), it cannot be induced by any other STS strategy. All equilibrium outcomes of the game $\tau(N,S,V)$ belong to IR. The minimum loss that the player can achieve is

$$\bar{V}_D = \min_{s_D, s_F \epsilon IR} V_D(s_D, s_F) \tag{14}$$

These conclusions hold under the assumption that the dominant player commits himself to carrying out his declared threat strategy. Analogous results can be found in Tolwinski (1983).

We now relax the assumption that the dominant player can commit himself to the strategy (13) and we analyse the credibility of the Stackelberg trigger strategy. Suppose the dominated player does not believe s^{ts}_{L}. He thus believes that the dominant player will adopt his single–play best reply function $R_D(s_F)$ for any $s_F \epsilon S_F$. Hence, given the "rules of the game", the dominated player computes his optimal strategy in the following way:

$$s^o_F = \arg \min_{s_F} V_F[R_D(s_F), s_F] \tag{15}$$

The relative loss is $V^o_F \equiv V_F(s^o_D, s^o_F)$, if the dominant player accommodates and chooses s^o_D. The loss is $V^p_F \equiv V_F(s^p_D(s^o_F), s^o_F)$ if the dominant player carries out the the punishment. Since we assumed $s^*_D = R_D(s^*_F)$, we have $V^o_F \leq V^*_F$ by construction. Furthermore, the dominated player can be induced to choose s^*_F only if $V^p_F \geq V^*_F$. The inducible region therefore becomes:

$$IR = \{(s_D, s_F), s_D \epsilon S_D, s_F \epsilon S_F: V_F(s_D, s_F) \leq V^p_F\} \tag{16}$$

The following inequalities thus hold:

$$V^o_F \leq V^*_F \leq V^p_F \tag{17}$$

When the dominated player does not choose s^*_F, the dominant player chooses between his single–play best reply $s^o_D = R_D(s^o_F)$ and the punitive strategy $s^p_D(s^o_F)$. In the one–stage game that we are considering, the definition of best–reply function implies $V^p_D \equiv V_D(s^p_D(s^o_F), s^o_F) \geq V_D(s^o_D, s^o_F) \equiv V^o_D$. Furthermore, the definition of desired outcome implies:

$$V^*_D \leq V^o_D \leq V^p_D \tag{18}$$

It would not make sense indeed to specify a desired outcome providing the dominant player with a loss greater than V^o_D.

Inequalities (17) and (18) make it possible to prove the following proposition:

Proposition 1: *If complete information is assumed and the dominant player is not committed to carrying out his threats, the only subgame perfect equilibrium of the constituent sequential game $\tau(N,S,V)$ is (s^o_D, s^o_F).*

Proof: From Figure 1 and (18), it is easy to conclude that $R_D(s_F)$ is the dominant player's strategy. By anticipating this, the dominated player always chooses s_F^o because of inequalities (16). Hence, $s_D^o = R_D(s_F^o)$ and s_F^o are the equilibrium strategies of the game. This proves the proposition.

3. REPEATED GAMES AND MULTIPLE OUTCOMES

The result derived in Proposition 1 is fairly obvious, and does not tell us anything about the indeterminacy problem. However, it is well–known that multiple outcomes arise even when the constituent game has a unique solution, if that game is repeated and suitable conditions are satisfied. A seminal result was provided by Friedman (1971), who showed that all outcomes that Pareto dominates the subgame perfect equilibrium (s_D^o, s_F^o) can be sustained as equilibrium outcomes if: (i) the game is infinitely repeated; (ii) players adopt trigger strategies; (iii) each player's discount factor is sufficiently close to one. This Folk theorem is extended to finitely repeated games in Friedman (1985), Benoit–Krishna (1985), Fudenberg–Maskin (1986). Extensions to games with incomplete information are provided by Kreps–Wilson (1982) and Milgrom–Roberts (1982). Other related important results are in Abreu (1986, 1988).

These results enable us to conclude that multiple outcomes cannot be ruled out, once the policy game is repeated (see Carraro, 1985a, 1987; Rogoff, 1986). In this paper, however, we argue that there exists a possible solution to the indeterminacy problem, if we allow one player to choose among the feasible outcomes. This solution is based on the asymmetry of the players, and on the strategic role of threats.

Figure 1 makes it clear that each stage of the policy problem that we are analysing is defined by a sequential game, where the dominated player decides first, taking as given the dominant player's Stackelberg trigger strategy. The "rules of the game" previously described are thus analogous to those that characterise the so–called Chain–Store game. The analysis of the repeated game will therefore make use of recent results on such a game (Selten, 1978; Kreps–Wilson, 1982a).

The simplest way of introducing a multi–stage policy problem is to assume that the game between the policy maker and economic agents is repeated a finite (or infinite) number of times. Each stage depends on the previous ones only as far as the players are not memoryless, i.e. the information set at time t, where $1 \leq t \leq T$ and $T \leq \infty$ defines the length of the game, contains the decisions of the players in the previous stages.

A multi–stage framework gives us the possibility of providing new insight into the credibility problem, and to start discussing indeterminacy problem.

In the previous section, we have shown that the ability to raise threats can greatly reduce the dominant player's loss, provided that the other player is convinced that the dominant player is really committed to his threat, if the circumstances arise in which he claims he would use it. However, we have seen that the action following from the execution of threats is generally not optimal with respect to the dominant player's loss function at the time of their realisation. If the game is repeated T times, however, the dominant player may find it advantageous to carry out his threats in the first stages of the game in order to induce the other player to adopt the desired strategy in the following periods.

In other words, the punitive strategy, though irrational in a single play of a game, may well be rational in repeated play. The reason is that a carried–out threat enhances the dominant player's credibility in doing the apparently irrational thing in a single play so that, over the long run, the dominant player may develop a sufficiently fearsome reputation to deter future undesired actions by the dominated player. Thereby, while losing in the short run, the dominant player can gain over time.

This argument, however, can be shown to be correct only under special assumptions.

If the game is repeated, the players' (closed loop) strategies are the sequences $\sigma_i = (v_{i1}...v_{iT})$, i=D,F, where: (i) $v_{Ft}(h_t)$ is the dominated player's function at stage t and $h_t = \{(s_{D1},s_{F1}) \ ... \ (s_{Dt-1},s_{Ft-1})\}$ is the history of the game; (ii) $v_{DT}(h_t,s_{Ft})$ is the dominant player's function. The set of decision functions for player i is $\Sigma_{it} = \{v_{it} \,|\, v_{it}: S_i^t \rightarrow S_{it}\}$, where $S_F^t = S_1 x S_2 x ... x S_{t-1}$, $S_D^t = S_F^t x S_{Ft}$, and $S_t = S_{Dt} x S_{Ft}$, t = 1...T. The single–play strategies $s_{it} = v_{it}(h_{if})$, i = D,F, $h_{Ft} = h_t$, $h_{Dt} = (h_t,s_{Ft})$, belongs to S_{it}. The players' intertemporal losses $V_i(\sigma_D,\sigma_F)$, i=D,F, are assumed to be the average of the single–play losses. We summarise these assumptions by denoting the *repeated game* as Γ(N,S,V,T). Because we are analysing a class of games which should capture the main features of macroeconomic policy problems, we only consider *finitely* repeated games. Infinite time independent games can hardly account for the frequent changes of regime that occur in policy problems.

The dominant player's desired outcome is ($s_{Dt}=s_D^*$, $s_{Ft}=s_F^*$; t=1...T). We thus define a *Stackelberg trigger strategy equilibrium of the repeated game* as the equilibrium in which the dominant player achieves his desired outcome at all stages of the game. If this equilibrium exists, the game has a unique outcome,and the indeterminacy problem is solved.

It is well known that one equilibrium of the repeated game is constituted by the single–play equilibrium (s_D^o, s_F^o) at each stage of the game. Using backward induction, it is also possible to show that this is the unique equilibrium of the finitely repeated game, if complete information is assumed, and the constituent game has a unique solution (Selten, 1978; Friedman, 1985). The proof starts from the last period by showing that at t=T the dominant player has no incentive to punish the other player when s_F differs from s_F^*, since no remaining period exists where the dominant player can get $V_D^o - V_D^*$. Therefore, at $t = N - 1$, the dominant player has no effect on the last stage $(s_D = s_D^o)$. Therefore, at $t = T - 1$, we certainly have $s_{Dt-1} = s_D^o$. This argument can be repeated at each stage, thus proving that $(s_{Dt} = s_D^o, s_{Ft} = s_F^o; t = 1...T)$ is the unique subgame perfect equilibrium of the game.

However, recent papers by Rosenthal (1981), Kreps–Wilson (1982a), Milgrom–Roberts (1982), have shown that other equilibria of the finitely repeated game can be determined when incomplete information is introduced into the model. Let us therefore assume that the dominated player is uncertain whether the punitive action will be carried out at stage t of the game. Since the dominant player finds it profitable to punish the other player only when $V_D^p \leq V_D^o$, an equivalent assumption is that the dominated player does not know with certainty the dominant player's loss function.[4]

Using inequalities (17), we have:

$$1 \geq (V_F^* - V_F^o)/(V_F^p - V_F^o) \equiv b \geq 0 \tag{19}$$

Furthermore, defining $a = (V_D^o - V_D^*)/(V_D^p - V_D^o)$, we can re–write the sequential policy game described in the previous section by using the following normal form, where the players' losses have been re–normalised:

Table 1. The Chain Store Game

		Dominated	
		s_F^*	s_F^o
Dominant	$R_D(s_F)$	a,0	0,b
	$s_D^p(s_F)$	/	–1,b–1

This normal form coincides with the normal form of the Chain Store game analysed by Kreps–Wilson (1982a). We can thus determine the sequential equilibria of the policy game.

The dominated player's uncertainty about the dominant player's loss function implies that, at each stage t, he assesses a probability p_t that the dominant player's loss function is such that $V_D^p \leq V_D^o$, so that the dominant player finds it profitable to carry out his threats. At stage t+1, p_{t+1} will be determined on the basis of the dominant player's decision at time t. The standard *Bayes' rule* is assumed to be used to compute p_{t+1} on the equilibrium path. Probability assessments off the equilibrium path are defined in Kreps–Wilson (1982a).

Let δ be the initial probability that the dominant player finds it profitable to punish the other player whenever s_F differs from s_F^* at t=1 (i.e. $p_o = \delta$), and assume that both players remember the moves of the game, as the game progresses. Therefore, we are dealing with a game with imperfect information and perfect recall (see Kreps–Wilson, 1982a).

An equilibrium concept which is analogous to Selten's subgame perfect equilibrium, but which takes into account the uncertainty introduced into the model is the sequential equilibrium described in Kreps–Wilson (1982b). We thus want to determine the sequential equilibria of the finitely repeated game described by Table 1.

The function p_t is defined by the following four equations

If $s_{Ft} = s_F^*$, at stage t, then $p_{t+1} = p_t$. (20a)

If $s_{Ft} \neq s_F^*$, $p_t > 0$ and the dominant player's reaction is $s_{Dt} = s_D^p$, (20b)

$$\text{then } p_{t+1} = \max (b^{T-t}, p_t).$$

If $s_{Ft} \neq s_F^*$, p_t and either $s_{Dt} = s_D^o$ or $p_t = 0$, then $p_{t+1} = 0$. (20c)

$p_o = \delta$ (20d)

where δ, the prior probability that the dominant player carries out the punishment whenever s_{Ft} differs from s_F^*, can be interpreted as the policy maker's *reputation.*

Furthermore, let us consider the following players' strategies:

Dominant player: If $v_D^p \leq v_D^o$, the dominant player always chooses s_D^p when s_F differs from s_F^*. If $v_D^p > v_D^o$ and t=T, then $s_{Dt} = R_D(s_{Ft})$. If $s_{Ft} \neq s_F^*$, t<T and $p_t \geq b^{T-t}$, then $s_{Dt} = s_D^p$. If $s_{Ft} \neq s_F^*$, t<T and $p_t \geq b^{T-t}$, and then $s_{Dt} = s_D^p$ with probability $((1-b^{T-t})p_t)/((1-p_t)b^{T-t})$ and $s_{Dt} = s_D^o$ with complementary probability. If $s_{Ft}=s_F^*$, then $s_{Dt} = s_D^*$ at all stages of the game.

Dominated player: If $p_t > b^{T-t+1}$, then $s_{Ft} = s_F^*$. If $p_t < b^{T-t+1}$, then $s_{Ft} = s_F^o$. If $p_t = b^{T-t+1}$, then $s_{Ft} = s_F^*$ with probability 1/a.

Suppose (s_D^*, s_F^*) belong to IR. The following proposition can then be proved:

Proposition 2: *The strategies and probability assessments given above constitute a sequential equilibrium of the game* $\Gamma(N,S,V,T)$.

Proof: Kreps–Wilson (1982a, p.259).

In general, this implies that multiple outcomes can be sustained as equilibrium outcomes. We want to show however under what conditions the dominant player can achieve his desired outcome at all stages of the game. This is shown by the following proposition:

Proposition 3: *If* $(s_D^*, s_F^*) \epsilon IR$ *and* $\delta > b$, *the player's strategies and probability assessments given above sustain the sequence* ($s_{Dt} = s_D^*$, $s_{Ft} = s_F^*$; *t=1,...T) as a sequential equilibrium of the finitely repeated game* $\Gamma(N,S,V,T)$.

Proof: from Kreps–Wilson (1982a), Proposition 1, we have that $p_t > b^{T-t+1}$ implies $s_{Ft} = s_F^*$. Being b<1, δ>b is necessary and sufficient for $p_t > b^{T-t+1}$ at any t=1,2,...T. Therefore, $s_{Ft} = s_F^*$ for t=1,2,...,T. The dominant player's consequent rational reaction is $s_{Dt} = s^*_D$ at any t=1,2,...,T, so that the sequence ($s_{Dt}=s^*_D$, $s_{Ft}=s^*_F$; t=1,...,T) can be sustained as a sequential equilibrium of the repeated game.

This proposition shows under what conditions there exists a Stackelberg trigger strategy equilibrium of the game. In other words, the policy maker can successfully choose his most favorable outcome among the feasible outcomes of the sequential game, if his strategy satisfies the (effectiveness and credibility) conditions provided in Proposition 3. Let us examine more carefully the condition $\delta > b$. It can be written as

$$\delta > (V^*_F - V^o_F)/(V^p_F - V^o_F) \tag{21}$$

so that it will be more easily satisfied when $V^*_F - V^o_F$ is small and $V^p_F - V^o_F$ is large, i.e. when:

(i) the dominated player's relative loss accepting the dominant player's desired strategy is small;

(ii) the dominated player's relative loss when the dominant player's threats are actually carried out is large.

(iii) his reputation δ is large.

4. INDETERMINACY AND THE ROLE OF MACROECONOMICS

Let us analyse the implications of the above results. At least from a descriptive viewpoint, the existence of multiple solutions is rather troublesome. Is there any way to reduce the multiplicity of possible outcomes previously emphasised? Rogoff(1986) remarks that multiplicity arises from the introduction of discontinuous state–dependent trigger strategies. If players'strategies must be a continuous function of state variables, then Rogoff (1986) argues that the unique time–consistent (subgame perfect) solution of the sequential policy game is the subgame perfect equilibrium (s^o_D,s^o_F) at all stages of the game (see Stanford, 1986a; Robson, 1986). This conclusion is generally not true. Multiplicity arises even if strategies are continuous if:

- accelerated ϵ–equilibria of the game with discounting are considered (see Kalai–Stanford, 1985);
- average loss functions are assumed (see Stanford, 1986b);
- continuous state dependent threat strategies, which each player's strategy also depends on the other player's decision, are considered (Kalai–Stanford, 1985);

– memory strategies that depend on the moves in all previous stages of the game are allowed for (see Basar–Olsder, 1982; Friedman–Samuelson, 1988).

In this paper we argue that uniqueness can be achieved if one player (the policy maker) can raise effective and credible threats. Hence, if we are analysing a policy game in which the players' strategic power is not symmetric, and the order of actions is sequential, we know that there exists the possibility to uniquely determine the equilibrium outcome. This is often the case in macroeconomics. Macroeconomics policy games can better be understood by assigning a specific institutional power to the policy maker. A clear example can be found in Carraro–Giavazzi (1988), where an international game between monetary authorities and unions in two countries is analysed.

However, the desired outcome to be achieved through a Stackelberg trigger strategy can be any outcome (s_D^o, s_F^o) that satisfies $s_D^* = R_D(s_F^*)$ and the credibility condition, and that belongs to the dominant player's inducible region. Hence multiplicity cannot be completely ruled out, at least ex–ante. Furthermore, (s_D^*, s_F^*) can be achieved only if the reputation parameter δ is large enough. Being δ a subjective parameter that cannot be observed, this result has a limited normative content. It is indeed difficult to argue ex ante that a given policy will be successful if δ is unknown.

The crucial point is that ex–post uniqueness of the equilibrium outcome can be consistent with ex–ante multiple outcomes. In other words, if the parameters s_D^*, s_F^* and δ are unknown, it is difficult to derive predictive and normative propositions from the above policy model. Only ex–post descriptions can be made.

Is there still a role for macroeconomic policy analysis? The answer is probably positive, even if a new approach must be adopted. Macroeconomics makes large use of equilibrium concepts that identify equilibrium points. The lesson from game theory is that equilibrium concepts define instead equilibrium regions, so that normative conclusions must be derived with respect to these regions. Furthermore, comparative statics should determine movements of these regions with respect to changes of policy variables or of parameters of the model. If the model is accurately specified, this can be enough to give macroeconomics an empirical and normative content.

This is not however the only available solution. Research on the concept of rationality that lies behind game–theoretic equilibrium concepts may lead to the definition of different equilibrium concepts that help reducing multiplicity.

Preliminary results in this direction are contained in Abreu–Rubinstein (1986) and Rubinstein (1986). Furthermore, some of the parameters can be estimated. For example, the policy maker's desired outcome can be inferred by observing his past behaviour, if appropriate econometric techniques are used. A first attempt is provided in Carraro (1988b). This can help reducing multiplicity by restricting the uncertainty on the parameters of the model.

NOTES

1) See, for example, Kydland–Prescott (1977), Barro–Gordon (1983), Rogoff (1985). Backus–Driffill (1985), Carraro–Giavazzi (1987, 1988). A discussion of the role of contracts in macroeconomic policy is contained in Fisher (1986).
2) In Barro–Gordon (1983) and Backus–Driffill (1985), the first player threatens the second in order to achieve a Pareto optimum.
3) For the sake of simplicity we assume that the minimum problem (1) has a unique solution.
4) A similar assumption is used by Kreps–Wilson (1982a) in order to provide a solution to the Chain–Store paradox.

REFERENCES

Abreu, D. (1986), "Extremal Equilibria of Oligopolistic Supergames", *Journal of Economic Theory*, 39, pp.191–225.

Abreu, D. (1988), "On the Theory of Infinitely Repeated Games with Discounting", *Econometrics,* 56, pp.383–96.

Abreu, D. and A. Rubenstein (1986),"The Structure of Nash Equilibrium in Repeated Games with Finite Automata", mimeo.

Backus, D. and J. Drifill (1985), "Inflation and Reputation", *American Economic Review*, 75, pp.530–38.

Barro, R.J. and D. Gordon (1983), "Rules, Discretion and Reputation in a Model of Monetary Policy", *Journal of Monetary Economics*, 12, pp.101–21.

Basar, T. and G.C. Oldser (1982), *Dynamic Non–cooperative Game Theory*, Academic Press, New York.

Benoit, J.P. and V. Krishna (1985), "Finitely Repeated Games", *Econometrica*, 53, pp.905–22.

Carrraro, C. (1985a), *New Methods for Macroeconomic Policy Analysis*, ch. 3, Ph.D. Dissertation, Princeton University.

Carraro, C. (1985b), "Stackelberg Trigger Strategy and Monetary Policy", mimeo, University of Venice.

Carraro, C. (1987), "A Folk Theorem of Monetary Policy", forthcoming in Laussel, D., W. Marois, and A. Soubeyran (eds.), *Monetary Theory and Policy*, Springer Verlag, Berlin.

Carraro, C. (1988a), "Strategic Sequential Interaction between Monetary and Fiscal Policy", mimeo, University of Venice.

Carraro, C. (1988b), "The Tastes of European Central Bankers" forthcoming in De Cecco, M. and A. Giovannini (eds), *Monetary Regimes and Monetary Institutions: Issues and Perspectives in Europe*, Cambridge University Press, 1988.

Carraro, C. and F. Giavazzi (1987), "Policy Instruments and Coalitions in

International Games" in Carraro, C. and F. Giavazzi (eds.), *Game Theory and Policy Interdependence* a special issue of Ricerche Economiche.

Carraro, C. and F. Giavazzi (1988), "Is International Policy Cooperation Really Counterproductive?", CEPR working paper.

Chow, G.C. (1981), *Econometric Analysis by Control Methods*, John Wiley & Sons, New York.

Fisher, S. (1986), "Time Consistent Monetary and Fiscal Policies: a Survey", M.I.T., mimeo.

Friedman, J.W. (1971), "A Non–cooperative Equilibrium for Supergames", *Review of Economic Studies*, 38, pp.1–12.

Friedman, J.W. (1985), Cooperative Equilibria in Finite Horizon Noncooperative Supergames", *Journal of Economic Theory*, 35, pp.390–98.

Friedman, J.W. (1986), *Game Theory with Applications to Economics*, Oxford University Press, Oxford.

Friedman, J.W. and L. Samuelson (1988), "Subgame Perfect Equilibrium with Continuous Reaction Functions", mimeo.

Fudenberg, D. and E. Maskin (1986), "The Folk Theorem in Repeated Games with Discounting or Incomplete Information", *Econometrica*, 54, pp.533–54.

Kalai, E. and W. Stanford (1985), "Conjectural Variations Strategies in Accelerated Cournot Games", *International Journal of Industrial Organisation*, 3, pp.133–52.

Kydland, F. and E.C. Prescott (1977), "Rules Rather than Discretion of Optimal Plans", *Journal of Economic Policy*, pp.473–91.

Kreps, D.M. and R. Wilson (1982a), "Reputation and Imperfect Information", *Journal of Economic Theory*, 27, pp.253–79.

Kreps, D.M. and R. Wilson (1982b), "Sequential Equilibria", *Econometrica*, 50, pp.863–94.

Milgrom, P. and T. Roberts (1982), "Predation, Reputation and Entry Deterrence", *Journal of Economic Theory*, 27, pp.280–312.

Robson, A.J. (1986), "The Existence if Nash Equilibria in Reaction Functions for Dynamic Models of Oligopoly", *International Economic Review*, 27, pp.539–44.

Rogoff, K. (1985), "Can International Monetary Coordination Be Counterproductive?", *Journal of International Economics*, 18, pp.188–217.

Rogoff, K. (1986), "Reputational Constraints on Monetary Policy" mimeo, University of Wisconsin.

Rosenthal, R.W. (1981), "Games of Perfect Information, Predatory Pricing and the Chain–Store Paradox", *Journal of Economic Theory*, 25, pp.92–100.

Rubenstein, A. (1986), "The Complexity of Strategies and the Resolution of Conflict: an Introduction", mimeo.

Schotter, A. (1980), *The Economic Theory of Social Institutions*, Cambridge University Press.

Stanford, W. (1986a), "On Continuous Reaction Function Equilibria in Duolopy Supergames with Mean Payoffs", *Journal of Economic Theory*, 39, pp.233–50.

Stanford, W. (1986b), "Subgame Perfect Reaction Function Equilibria in Discounted Duolopy Supergames are Trivial", *Journal of Economic Theory*, 39, pp.226–32)

Tolwinski, B. (1983), "A Stackelberg Solution of Dynamic Games", *IEEE Transactions on Automatic Control*, pp.85–93.

CHAPTER 4

POLICY CREDIBILITY AND THE LUCAS CRITIQUE SOME NEW TESTS WITH AN APPLICATION TO DENMARK*

Michael Christensen, *Aktivbanken, Vejle, Denmark*

1. INTRODUCTION

The policy announcements of regime changes which have characterized a number of western economies, e.g the United States (October 1979) and United Kingdom (May 1979) have given rise to an enormous theoretical dispute concerning the credibility problems facing a government, e.g. Barro and Gordon (1983) and Backus and Driffill (1985). Also empirical investigations have been carried out to test the disinflationary policies pursued in the United States (see Blanchard 1984 and Perry 1983) to see whether these policies have been credible and it is an empirical test of policy credibility which concerns us in the present chapter[1].

So far empirical analyses of policy credibility have made use of the prediction error method in which they considered model predictions of either the inflation rate (the Phillips curve model) or the nominal interest rate (the term structure model) and arguing that a disinflationary policy has been credible if such predictions overestimate actual values of the inflation rate or the nominal interest rate during the relevant regime period, simply because these models were unable to take account of such regime changes.

However, this may be an unsatisfactory test of the credibility hypothesis because such prediction errors might explain almost anything not considered explicitly in the model. Only in the case in which the residuals are due solely to the absent credibility variable the prediction error method will prove useful in testing the credibility hypothesis. What one should do is of course to include the credibility (policy) variable itself in the model, and test its significance which is exactly what we intend to do here.

P. Artus and Y. Barroux (eds.), Monetary Policy, 79–95.

Being concerned about credibility, it is, however, important to distinguish between the immediate effects occurring after an announcement of a change in policy, which we shall call the announcement effect, and the effects occurring after agents have experienced that the announced policy change really has been pursued, which we shall call the result effect.

In Christensen (1987a) we analysed the policy regime change in Denmark (October 1982) finding some evidence in favour of the Danish exchange rate policy gaining credibility gradually (the result effect). However, this was inferred using the prediction error method. Here we intend to sustain the evidence on policy credibility using an alternative method taking explicit account of the credibility (policy) variable.

The Danish regime change was characterized by several policy changes, where the most important concerned a stabilization of the exchange rate. This policy regime change was important because former governments had pursued continuing devaluations of Danish Kroner, whereas the new policy makers claimed that further discrete devaluations would not be pursued. So far the policy makers have not deviated from this policy inducing a strong Danish currency within the EMS margin, and it therefore seems natural to analyse whether this policy has been credible. If it has been credible, the private sector should have believed the policy makers commitment to this policy and consequently expectations must have been revised.

It is well known that devaluations give rise to inflation and obviously a stabilization of the exchange rate (if credible) must have changed expectations towards lower inflation rates and thereby lower nominal interest rates. We shall, therefore, following the analysis in Christensen (1987a) estimate a modified Fisher interest rate model in order to analyse whether this stabilization of the exchange rate has led to lower nominal interest rates. But instead of concentrating on the prediction errors we shall incorporate a credibility variable, which is measured by the variability of the exchange rate between Danish Kroner and German Mark, explicitly into the interest rate model estimated. The reason why we focus on the exchange rate variability as the policy variable is because the exchange rate policy has been the most important policy change during the conservative regime period. If the hypothesis stated above, i.e. a stabilization of the exchange rate induces lower inflationary expectations and thereby lower nominal interest rates, is correct, it turns out that a necessary condition to sustain high credibility is that the variability of the exchange rate becomes positively correlated with the nominal interest rate, which is the crucial test to be made[2]. However, other policy changes have been pursued as well, e.g. the conservative government claimed an intended aim of reducing inflation rates through restrictive incomes policy as well as reducing the governmental budget deficit. It may, however, be difficult to relate any credibility effects to these two latter policy measures, because the Social Democratic government in office before October 1982 tried to lower inflation rates and budget deficits as well, but without success. In this particular case we shall argue that the exchange rate policy is the appropriate policy to focus on, because under the new conservative government the exchange rate policy has been of superior importance to the other policies, pursued by former governments as well, which has been argued by Taylor (1982) to be a necessary condition for high credibility. As we include the exchange rate variability variable (the policy variable) itself in the model we can test directly any credibility effects of this particular policy regime change.

Closely related to the credibility hypothesis is the Lucas critique which states that policy regime changes affect the parameters of reduced form models, i.e. parameters are policy variant. The usual procedure testing the relevance of the Lucas critique has been to compare regression coefficients across different regime periods, but this method also seems unsatisfactory because parameter instability may be due to general misspecification rather than the Lucas critique. It is therefore important that one allows parameters to vary directly with the policy variable, which we shall do here estimating a varying parameter model, although it is still important to check for general misspecification.

The chapter is organized as follows. Section 2 provides the empirical analysis of the credibility hypothesis concerning the Danish exchange rate policy, and in Section 3 we estimate a varying parameter model, where parameters are allowed to vary directly with the policy variable, in order to test the relevance of the Lucas critique. Section 4 provides some concluding remarks.

2. THE CREDIBILITY HYPOTHESIS

In this section we shall analyse whether the Danish exchange rate policy pursued by the conservative government since October 1982 has been credible. It was shown in Christensen (1987a) that the nominal interest rate is the variable which is probably most sensitive to changes in market expectations and as changes in expectations are crucial in order to discriminate credibility effects it seems natural to concentrate on interest rate determination in this case[3]. We shall therefore specify a modified Fisher interest rate model, where the nominal interest rate is assumed to be determined by lagged nominal interest rates, inflationary expectations, and a foreign interest rate. We specify the following relationship

$$R_t = \alpha_0 + \sum_{i=1}^{6} \alpha_{1i} R_{t-i} + \sum_{i=0}^{6} \alpha_{2i} \Delta\tilde{P}_{t-i} + \sum_{i=1}^{6} \alpha_{3i} R^*_{t-i} + u_t \tag{1}$$

where R_t is the domestic (Danish) interest rate, $\Delta\tilde{P}_t$ is inflationary expectations and R^*_t is the foreign (German) interest rate[4]. (Also money supply growth rate was included in equation (1) in some preliminary regressions but this variable turned out to be of no importance for the sample period used here).

Now, to see the difference between the prediction error method and the "direct" method we shall make use of here, consider equation (1). The prediction error method assumes the error term u_t contains the policy (credibility) variable, i.e. $u_t = f(\tau_t, \epsilon_t)$, where τ_t is the policy variable and ϵ_t is some white noise term, without specifying the exact functional form, where we instead propose

$$u_t = \sum_{i=1}^{6} \alpha_{4i} \tau_{t-i} + \epsilon_t \qquad\qquad \epsilon_t \sim N(0, \sigma^2_\epsilon) \tag{2}$$

i.e we include the credibility (policy) variable explicitly in the regression equation (1), which allows us to test the significance of τ_t as well as the hypothesis of ϵ_t being a white noise term. Combining (1) and (2) we assume the nominal interest rate, R_t and inflationary expectations $\Delta\tilde{P}_t$ are the endogenous variables (see below) and the foreign interest rate R^*_t and the policy variable τ_t are exogenous variables. Although the prediction error method may give some indication of credibility, we shall, however, argue that the specification in (2) gives a more promising test of credibility.

As already mentioned above the policy variable τ_t will be measured by the variability of the exchange rate between Danish Kroner and German Mark, because the most important policy target under the Danish conservative regime has been the exchange rate, which the authorities have kept within the EMS margins. We shall specify the policy variable by the standard deviation of the exchange rate, calculated as

$$\tau = \sqrt{(1/(n-1))} \sum_{i=1}^{n} (e_i - \bar{e})^2 \tag{3}$$

where e_i is the daily exchange rate between Danish Kroner and German Mark and n is the number of observations within a month, which varies from 19 to 23, i.e. we use monthly observations and it is seen from equation (1) that the lag length is 6 months[5].

It is important to infer that it is not the exchange rate itself but its variability that we interpret to be the credibility variable. This means that both appreciations as well as depreciations of the exchange rate within the EMS margins are assumed to have equal effect on credibility. Any change in the exchange rate between Danish Kroner and German Mark will indicate a deviation from the policy announcement of a fixed exchange rate and thereby one would expect the policy maker to lose credibility. In other words, as far as credibility is concerned, it does not matter whether the policy maker revalues or devalues the currency. Credibility is likely to be lost whenever the policy maker reneges on the pegged exchange rate policy[6]. It should also be inferred that by specifying the policy variable by the variability of the exchange rate, we implicitly take account of exchange rate uncertainty and thereby exchange rate expectations, i.e. τ_t may alternatively be interpreted as a measure of risk–aversion.

The nominal interest rate used is a long term (maturity in 2007) interest rate and inflation is measured by the change in the consumer price index. However, it is inflationary expectations rather than actual inflation rates, which determine the nominal interest rate in equation (1). As inflationary expectations are considered an endogenous variable, these have been obtained here by use of a vector autoregression using all available information, that is 6 months lags of actual inflation rates, nominal interest rates, foreign interest rates and of course the exchange rate variability variable. In other words, the available information set is assumed to be

$$I_t = (\Delta P_{t-i}, R_{t-i}, R^*_{t-i}, \tau_{t-i} \,|\, i \in [1,6]) \tag{4}$$

and conditional on this information set inflationary expectations have been obtained by

$$\Delta\tilde{P}_t = \delta_0 + \sum_{i=1}^{6} \delta_{1i}\Delta P_{t-i} + \sum_{i=1}^{6} \delta_{2i}R_{t-i} + \sum_{i=1}^{6} \delta_{3i}R^*_{t-i} + \sum_{i=1}^{6} \delta_{4i}\tau_{t-i} \tag{5}$$

It is unnecessary to present the vector autoregression results here, but merely note that these seemed to fulfill the orthogonality requirements exhibiting no serial correlation. The orthogonality hypothesis has been tested by regressing the inflation forecast error on current values of the Danish and German interest rates and the variability of the exchange rate which by assumption we have excluded from the information set. The assumption is justified since an F–test of joint insignificance can be calculated to give 0.11, where the 5% critical significance value is F(3,75) = 2.73 indicating that the null-hypothesis of orthogonality seems not to be rejected. Following McCallum (1976) we shall not, however, use these vector-autoregression (VAR) predictions in estimating (1), but rather actual inflation rates and then instead use the VAR predictions as instruments, which yields consistent estimates. In this particular case parameter estimates are also asymptotically efficient, since the information set includes the exogenous variables specified in (1), i.e. R_{t-i}, R^*_{t-i} and $\tau_{t-i}, i \in [1,6]$, as argued by Wickens (1982), (see also Pagan (1984)). Finally, the foreign interest rate used is a German long-term interest rate.

We can now turn to the empirical results obtained in estimating equation (1), where we make use of the general to specific estimation technique. The sample period is October 1982 to December 1985 since the conservative government took over in October 1982. We could, however, easily extend the sample period to include observations before October 1982, but since we are particularly interested in analysing the importance of τ_t for determination of the nominal interest rate during the new conservative regime period, attention is devoted to the period October 1982 to December 1985. Using the standard error and the sum of squared residuals to measure the best specification we end up with (6), where a GIVE estimation procedure has been used (see above)

$$\begin{aligned} R_t = \underset{(1.37)}{0.39} + \underset{(0.06)}{0.80}\, R_{t-1} - \underset{(0.06)}{0.20}\, R_{t-6} - \underset{(0.27)}{0.70}\, R^*_{t-2} \\ + \underset{(0.25)}{1.09}\, R^*_{t-5} + \underset{(0.17)}{0.78}(\Delta P_t + \Delta P_{t-1} + \Delta P_{t-2} - \Delta P_{t-6}) \\ + \underset{(0.14)}{0.61}(\tau_{t-1} + \tau_{t-3} + \tau_{t-4}) \end{aligned} \tag{6}$$

$$\text{S.E.} = 0.54 \quad \text{SSR} = 11.15 \quad h = \underset{(1.65)}{1.09} \quad \text{LMF}(6) = \underset{(2.48)}{0.76}$$

$$\text{LMARCH}(6) = \underset{(12.59)}{6.46} \quad \text{BP} = \underset{(18.31)}{9.95} \quad \text{GS} = \underset{(2.46)}{0.13} \quad \text{P} = \underset{(4.15)}{18.25}$$

Here we have standard errors in parentheses below parameter estimates and critical 5% significance values in parentheses below test–statistics. S.E. is the standard error of the regression equation, SSR is the sum of squared residuals, h is Durbin's h–test testing for 1st order autocorrelation, LMF(6) is a modified LM test testing for up to 6th order autocorrelation, given by

$(T-k-m)/m(R^2/(1-R^2))$, where T is the number of sample observations, k is the number of explanatory variables, m is the autocorrelation order (in this case 6) and R^2 is obtained by regressing the residuals obtained from (6) on lagged residuals, as well as all explanatory variables including all lagged dependant variables. LMARCH(6) and BP are heteroskedasticity tests, the former testing for a 6th order ARCH process and the latter is a Breusch–Pagan test, testing for general heteroskedasticity. Finally, GS is an F-test testing the specific model in (6) against the most general specification and P is an F-test testing the significance of the policy variables.

Several interesting results can be inferred from (6). First, it is interesting to observe that the policy variables turn out to be very significant at the 5% level. Actually, three lags of the policy variable seem to have quite a significant influence on how the nominal interest rate is determined all yielding a positive coefficient (data seems to accept that these should have equal weight)[7], indicating first of all that determination of the nominal interest rate is influenced by the policy variable, i.e. the variability of the exchange rate, and second of all that lower exchange rate variability is associated with a lower nominal interest rate. It will be recalled from the discussion that this is a necessary condition to sustain credibility. Furthermore, this is justified considering the P-test, which accepts the significance of the policy variables.

Concerning credibility, we mentioned in the Introduction that it is important to distinguish between an announcement effect and a result effect. As three lags of the exchange rate variability variable have a significant influence on nominal interest rate determination, we infer that it seems as if credibility takes time to establish (it takes up to 4 months, cf. (6))[8].This may be interpreted in terms of a learning process, (i.e. this evidence seems to be in favour of the result effect), whereas it is more uncertain whether we can identify an announcement effect. This is in accordance with the results obtained in Christensen (1987a) where we sustained the presence of a result effect but not an announcement effect. In order to test, at least tentatively, whether an announcement effect is present, we have included a dummy variable in (6), which yields the value 1 in 1982.10m and zero for the rest of the period. This becomes, however, insignificant at the 5% level as an F value gives .67, where the critical significance value is 5.32, indicting that the null-hypothesis cannot be rejected. In conclusion these results give us at least some evidence of the presence of a result effect, (i.e. the Danish exchange rate policy has gained credibility gradually) whereas there seems not to be any immediate effects, (i.e. we reject the presence of an announcement effect).

However, this evidence of policy credibility is very much dependent on whether the policy maker has been successful in keeping the exchange rate fixed (against German Mark). We know for instance that no discrete devaluations nor any discrete revaluations have been pursued by the policy maker. Furthermore, considering Figure 1, where we now compare the conservative regime period with the Social Democratic regime period (before October 1982), it is seen that the standard deviation of the exchange rate has indeed been decreasing during the conservative regime period, i.e. after October 1982, although not immediately after the regime change. The mean of τ_t for the period January 1979 to September 1982 is .9386, whereas it is .7949 for the regime period October 1982 to December 1985. Given this the positive correlation between the nominal interest rate and τ_t sustained by equation (6) is also confirmed comparing Figure 1 with Figure 2, where the nominal interest rate is seen to have been decreasing as well.

Although we have only tentatively sustained that the exchange rate policy has been gaining credibility gradually through a learning process, the significance of the different lags of the exchange rate variability variable in (6) certainly indicates that the Danish interest rate has been falling after October 1982 not merely because of the decrease in the German interest rate (the German interest rate started falling around late 1981), but also because of the decrease in the variability of the exchange rate[9]. This is fully consistent with the interpretation of τ_t as a measure of risk-aversion. If the exchange rate policy has been credible, agents have become less risk-averse compared to the Social Democratic regime period before October 1982 inducing lower exchange rate variability and thereby a lower nominal interest rate. Whether one interprets τ_t as a policy variable or as a measure of risk-aversion, the conclusions hold through.

Secondly, notice from (6) that the German interest rate seems to have a significant influence on the Danish interest rate; actually, two lags of this variable have important influence on the short-run determination of the Danish interest rate. Although one of these yields a negative coefficient contrary to what could be expected we still have a significant positive correlation between the domestic interest rate and the foreign interest rate in the long-run, yielding a coefficient close to one.

Finally, notice that four inflation variables turn out to have a significant influence on nominal interest rate determination, all of these being restricted to

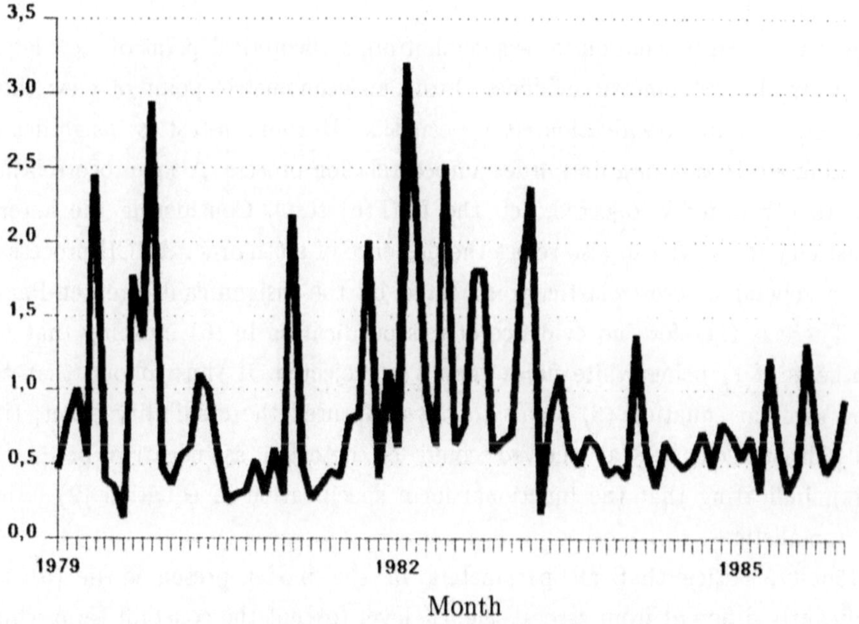

Figure 1. Exchange rate variability

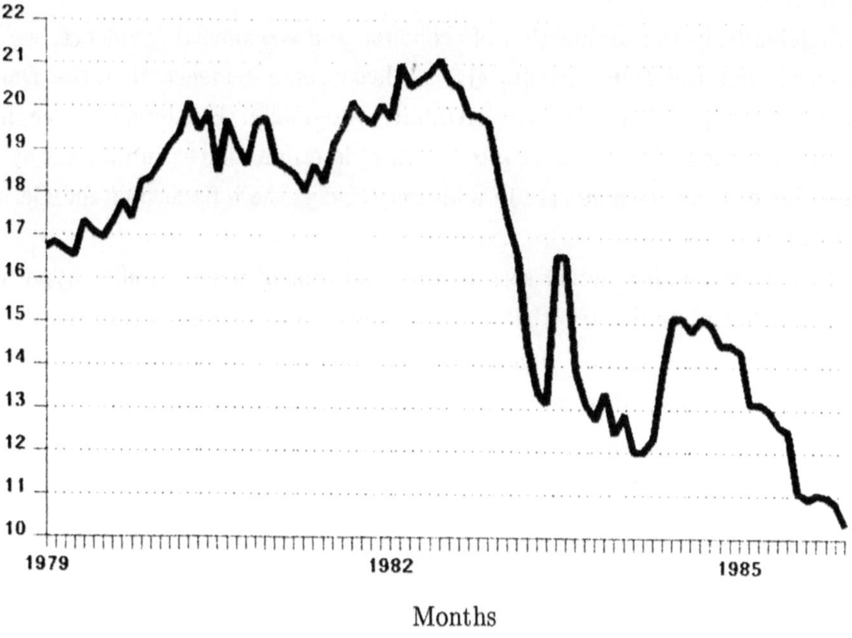

Figure 2. Nominal interest rate

have equal weight.

As these results seem quite reasonable from a theoretical point of view let us now study the econometric evidence. From an econometric point of view there are no signs of misspecification. It is seen that Durbin's h-test is insignificant, indicating a rejection of a first order autocorrelation process. Also autocorrelation of up to 6th order is rejected, (cf. the LMF(6) test). Considering the hetero-skedasticity tests, we can also reject the presence of a 6th order ARCH process as well as general heteroskedasticity indicated by the insignificant Breusch-Pagan test. There is therefore no evidence of misspecification in (6) meaning that the hypothesis of ϵ_t being white noise cannot be rejected. It thus follows that the policy term in equation (6) seems to have captured the credibility effect, (i.e. what Christensen (1987a) showed could be detected as negative prediction errors), indicating that the functional form specification in equation (2) is not that unrealistic.

Finally, notice that all parameters in the model presented in (6) are significantly different from zero at the 5% level (except the constant term which we have included anyway). Also, as indicated by the GS-test, the specific (parsimonious) model in (6) is seen not to be rejected against the general specification.

Judging from the conjunction of economic and econometric evidence, we feel convinced that the above results give at least some evidence that the Danish exchange rate policy has gained credibility gradually. Furthermore, we have provided evidence that nominal interest rate determination is influenced by the variability of the exchange rate in addition to, e.g. the influence of the German interest rate.

This evidence all together seems to be in favour of the credibility hypothesis (high credibility) indicating that stabilization of the exchange rate has led to lower nominal interest rates, since the private sector has indeed responded to the variability of the exchange rate. However, some further analysis is still needed to make precise whether the result effect dominates the announcement effect as the present evidence seems to suggest.

3. THE LUCAS CRITIQUE

Having concluded that the Danish exchange rate policy seems to have been credible the interesting question now is whether this credible regime change has been subject to the Lucas critique, i.e. whether the reduced form parameters estimated in equation (6) are policy variant. Lucas (1976) argued that macro–econometric relations incorporating rational expectations are useless in providing evidence on policy effects. The essence is that reduced form parameters are policy variant, i.e. one cannot base policy evaluations on econometric relationships estimated over periods containing different policy regimes, because estimated parameters change between such regimes. Consider the following structure

$$y_{t+1} = f(y_t, x_t, \theta, \nu_t) \tag{7}$$

where x_t is an arbitrary vector of exogenous variables, θ is a vector of fixed parameters, ν_t is a vector of independent, identically distributed random shocks and y_{t+1} and y_t are vectors of state variables. f is assumed to be known.

The argument is now that a policy regime change does not only affect y_{t+1} through x_t but also through θ, i.e. the parameters are policy variant, indicated as

$$y_{t+1} = g(y_t, x_t, \theta(\varphi), \nu_t) \tag{8}$$

where θ varies systematically with the policy variable φ. Consequently, it is therefore an unrealistic assumption to assume θ to be a vector of fixed parameters. Let us illustrate more clearly the drawbacks from an econometric point of view of neglecting this dependence.

Writing (7) in specific form, we have

$$y_{t+1} = \theta_0 + \theta_1 y_t + \theta_2 x_t + \nu_t \tag{9}$$

where we now for the sake of illustration assume x_t to be an exogenous policy instrument and y_{t+1} to be a policy target. Given the following policy rule

$$x_t = \varphi_1 y_t \tag{10}$$

we find combining (9) and (10)

$$y_{t+1} = \theta_o + (\theta_1 + \theta_2\varphi_1)y_t + \nu_t = \gamma_o + \gamma_1 y_t + \nu_t \tag{11}$$

where $\gamma_o = \theta_o$ and $\gamma_1 = \theta_1 + \theta_2\varphi_1$

The right–hand side of (11) is the equation estimated by the econometrician. It follows now, however, that a policy regime change inducing a change of φ_1 to φ_2, say, affects γ_1 as well, i.e. γ_1 is policy variant and therefore one must take account of changing parameters if different policy regimes are contained in the sample period[10].

The varying parameter model estimated in order to test the relevance of the Lucas critique is described in Maddala (1982), who suggests a simple linear relationship between the model specific parameters and the policy variable.

Recall equations (1) and (2) and assume now that parameters vary linearly with the policy variable as

$$\alpha_{jit} = \beta_{jio} + \beta_{ji1}\tau_{t-1} + e_{jit} \qquad e_{jit} \sim N(0,\sigma^2_{e_{ji}}) \tag{12}$$

where j=1,2,3,4. The model to be estimated now looks as

$$R_t = \beta_o + \sum_{i=1}^{6} \beta_{1io} R_{t-i} + \sum_{i=1}^{6} \beta_{1i1} R_{t-i}\tau_{t-1} + \sum_{i=0}^{6} \beta_{2io} \Delta P_{t-i} \tag{13}$$

$$+ \sum_{i=o}^{6} \beta_{2i1} \Delta P_{t-i}\tau_{t-1} + \sum_{i=1}^{6} \beta_{3io} R^*_{t-i} + \sum_{i=1}^{6} \beta_{3i1} R^*_{t-i}\tau_{t-1}$$

$$+ \sum_{i=1}^{6} \beta_{4io} \tau_{t-i} + \sum_{i=1}^{6} \beta_{4i1} \tau_{t-1} + v_t$$

where it can be shown

$$VAR(v_t) = \sigma^2_\epsilon + \sum_{i=1}^{6} \sigma^2_{e_{1i}} R_{t-i} + \sum_{i=o}^{6} \sigma^2_{e_{2i}} \Delta P_{t-i} \tag{14}$$

$$+ \sum_{i=1}^{6} \sigma^2_{e_{3i}} R^*_{t-i} + \sum_{i=1}^{6} \sigma^2_{e_{4i}} \tau_{t-i}$$

i.e. it is important to test for heteroscedasticity[11]. It follows from (13) that a joint test of all parameters being policy invariant is

$$H_o: \beta_{1i1} = \beta_{2i1} = \beta_{3i1} = \beta_{4i1} = 0 \tag{15}$$

i.e. the coefficients related to all the cross–terms must all equal zero. It should, however, be mentioned that an acceptance of H_o only indicates a rejection of parameters being related linearly to the policy variable and therefore this is not necessarily a definite rejection of the Lucas critique being relevant. On the other hand, a rejection of H_o could, instead of sustaining the Lucas critique, indicate general misspecification meaning that it is important to test for misspecification, especially heteroskedasticity cf. (14).

Estimating equation (13) we shall extend the sample period to include different regimes so that it is possible to test whether parameters change when the policy variable changes. The estimation period is January 1980 to December 1985. Using this sample period equation (16) presents the estimation results, where parameters are allowed to vary linearly with the policy variable, i.e. the exchange rate variability variable, τ_t.

GIVE Estimates of the Varying Parameter Model for Denmark (Equation (16))

$$R_t = \underset{(0.61)}{-1.33} + \underset{(0.07)}{0.79}\,R_{t-1} + \underset{(0.24)}{0.82}\,R_{t-4} - \underset{(0.21)}{0.58}\,R_{t-5} - \underset{(0.33)}{1.21}\,R_{t-4}\tau_{t-1}$$

$$+ \underset{(0.29)}{0.97}\,R_{t-5}\tau_{t-1} + \underset{(0.74)}{0.99}\,\Delta P_{t-6} + \underset{(0.27)}{0.73}\,\Delta P_{t-1}\tau_{t-1}$$

$$- \underset{(0.90)}{1.56}\,\Delta P_{t-6}\tau_{t-1} + \underset{(0.16)}{0.55}\,R^*_{t-3}\tau_{t-1}$$

$$\text{S.E.} = 0.67 \quad \text{SSR} = 32.55 \quad \text{LMF(1)} = \underset{(4.00)}{1.49} \quad \text{LMF(6)} = \underset{(2.27)}{1.04}$$

$$\text{LMARCH(6)} = \underset{(12.59)}{5.29} \quad \text{BP} = \underset{(15.51)}{12.90} \quad \text{GS} = \underset{(1.97)}{0.70} \quad \text{CHOW} = \underset{(2.02)}{1.41}$$

$$\bar{\tau}_{t-1} = 0.8076$$

Standard errors in parentheses below parameter estimates and 5% critical significance values in parentheses below test statistics.

As an illustration, the estimated parameter related to the variable $R_{t-4}\tau_{t-1}$ is -1.21 and given the mean of τ_{t-1} ($\bar{\tau}_{t-1}$, see (16)) we can calculate the mean of the varying parameter related to R_{t-4} to be equal to -0.16 ($0.82 - 1.21 \cdot 0.8076$, cf. (12)).

It follows from equation (16) that only one of the variables have a fixed coefficient namely R_{t-1}. It is also seen from (16) that some of the varying parameters, although related linearly to the policy variable, turn out with an insignificant constant term, i.e. recalling (12) $\beta_{jio} = 0$. For example, this is the case for the variables ΔP_{t-1} and R^*_{t-3}.

Now we can turn to discuss the evidence presented by equation (16). First of all, it is seen that out of 6 variables, 5 turn out with a varying parameter giving strong support to the Lucas argument (actually only R_{t-1} has a fixed coefficient). There is therefore clear evidence that most of the parameters in (16) respond to the policy variable. However, this result is indeed conditional on the model in equation (16) being well specified. Considering the econometric evidence we see that the LMF(1) test rejects a 1st order autocorrelation process and also a 6th order autocorrelation process is rejected, (cf. the LMF(6) test). Concerning heteroskedasticity, we see from (16) that the ARCH statistic rejects the presence of an ARCH process[12], and the Breusch–Pagan test rejects general hetero–

skedasticity, which may seem quite surprising, as the BP test is specified in accordance with (14). Recalling Note 10 and equation (12) above, this rejection of general heteroskedasticity indicates that parameters vary deterministically with the policy variable, i.e. there are no obvious signs of misspecification in (16), and therefore parameter estimates must be considered to be asymptotically efficient. Finally, we have calculated the Chow–test in order to test whether a structural change takes place in October 1982. We see that the null-hypothesis of no structural change cannot be rejected, which gives further support to the evidence (see Note 11) that the varying parameter approach has captured any structural change.

Furthermore, notice that the parsimonious regression equation in (16) is not rejected against the general specification (equation (13)) as indicated by the GS-test accepting the null hypothesis[13]. Finally, we infer that no policy variables appear significantly different from zero in (16), besides from their importance determining the varying parameters.

From this evidence we can conclude that there seems to be an obvious relationship between model specific parameters and the policy variable, in this case the variability of the exchange rate and it follows that it cannot be rejected that the Lucas critique has been relevant in connection with the Danish policy regime change in October 1982.

4. CONCLUDING REMARKS

In the preceding sections we have tried to give some evidence of policy credibility and the relevance of the Lucas critique concerning the Danish policy regime change in October 1982. It has been argued that methods to test for policy credibility and the relevance of policy variant parameters used so far are unsatisfactory and some more promising tests have been proposed. First, it was argued that the prediction error method might give misleading results because such prediction errors may explain almost everything over and above credibility effects, e.g. general misspecification. Instead we suggest that the credibility (policy) variable should be incorporated explicitly into the specific model so that an explicit test of its significance can be made. Measuring this credibility variable by the variability of the exchange rate (the exchange rate between Danish Kroner and German Mark) we have been able to put forward some evidence of the Danish exchange rate policy gradually gaining credibility.

Secondly, we argued that a test of the importance of the Lucas critique only considering parameter instability between different regime periods is unsatisfactory because parameters may differ across the sample period due to general misspecification rather than because of policy changes. Instead we suggest a varying parameter model, where parameters are related linearly to the policy variable, i.e. the standard deviation of the exchange rate. Using this model, we were able to sustain very significant correlations between model specific parameters and the policy variable indicating that the Lucas critique indeed has been important with respect to the Danish policy regime change in October 1982.

Finally, it should be mentioned that these results seem to be quite robust as the results obtained in the present chapter are in line with the results obtained in Christensen (1987a) although the test methods differ considerably. However, it should be mentioned that some problems are still present. For instance, measuring the policy variable by the standard deviation of the exchange rate and thereby restricting credibility to be affected equally by appreciations and depreciations of the Danish currency may turn out to be inappropriate. Further analysis along this line is therefore needed.

NOTES

*) This chapter is part of my Ph.D. thesis submitted to the University of Southampton, December 1987. Comments on previous versions of this chapter from Keith Blackburn, Paul Turner, David Currie, John Driffill, Torben M. Andersen, Per B. Overgaard and an anonymous referee are gratefully acknowledged. Also discussions with Joergen Damgaard, Nils Gottfries, Manfred Holler, Svend Hylleberg, Peter Jensen, and Soeren B. Nielsen have been useful. Best thanks to Henning Bunzel for computational assistance and Privatbanken, Copenhagen from which valuable data was obtained.

1) See Blackburn and Christensen (1989) for a survey of the credibility literature.
2) It could be argued that one really ought to include the policy rule (exchange rate rule) simultaneously into the model rather than just the policy variable. However, it is not at all obvious what the exact rule specification looks like in this case
3) In Christensen (1987b) we consider different Phillips curve relations and argue that prices adjust sluggishly which implies that the Danish disinflationary policy seems to have been lacking credibility.
4) Since the German interest rate is included as an independent variable in equation (1) it seems relevant to measure the dependent variable by the difference between the Danish and the German interest rates. However, such a restriction turned out to produce inferior results compared to the results presented below.
5) The lag length is chosen arbitrarily to be 6 months although a more general dynamic specification might prove more appropriate.
6) Assuming revaluations and devaluations to affect the policy makers credibility equally may be too restrictive an assumption.

7) Such restrictions imposed on parameter estimates provide without loss of information additional degrees of freedom, although no theoretical justification can be given to sustain these.
8) See also Cagan and Fellner (1984), who argue that credibility takes time to establish.
9) The decrease in the variability of the exchange rate may not, however, be due entirely to the pursued fixed exchange rate policy but also the fact that the rate of depreciation of the Danish Kroner has been decreasing after October 1982.
10) Essentially, parameter constancy (invariant parameters) is what Engle et al (1983) call superexogeneity.
11) It is important to infer that the model in (13) per definition exhibits heteroskedasticity, which gives inefficient parameter estimates. However, this rests on the assumption that parameters are related stochastically to the policy variable (see (12)). If instead parameters vary deterministically with the policy variable there is no theoretical reason to expect the presence of heteroskedasticity in model (13).
12) The ARCH-test can be interpreted in terms of misspecification through a structural change, see Engle (1982). As this test seems not to accept any ARCH process, there is some evidence that the varying parameter approach has captured any structural change.
13) It is inferred from (16) that ΔP_{t-6} and $\Delta P_{t-6}\tau_{t-1}$ are not significant at the 5% level, but these have been included anyway, because excluding these (16) turned out being misspecified.

REFERENCES

Backus, D. and J. Driffill (1985), "Inflation and Reputation", *American Economic Review*, 75, pp.530–38.

Barro, R.J. and D.B. Gordon (1983), "Rules, Discretion and Reputation in a Model of Monetary Policy", *Journal of Monetary Economics*, 12, pp.101–22.

Blackburn, K. and M. Christensen (1989), "Monetary Policy and Policy Credibility: Theories and Evidence", *Journal of Economic Literature*, 27, pp.1–45.

Blanchard, O.J. (1984), "The Lucas Critique and the Volcker Deflation", *American Economic Review*, 74, 211–15.

Cagan, P. and W. Fellner (1984), "The Costs of Disinflation, Credibility and the Deceleration of Wages 1982–1983", in W. Fellner (ed.) *Essays in Contemporary Economic Problems – Disinflation*, American Enterprise Institute, Washington.

Christensen, M. (1987a), "On Interest Rate Determination, Testing for Policy Credibility and the Relevance of the Lucas Critique – Some Danish Experiences", *European Journal of Political Economy*", 3, pp.369–88.

Christensen, M. (1987b), "Disinflation, Credibility and Price Inertia – A Danish Exposition", *Applied Economics*, 19, pp.1353–66.

Engle, R.F. (1982), "Autoregressive Conditional Heteroskedasticity with Estimates of the Variance of United Kingdom Inflation", *Econometrica*, 50, pp.987–1007.

Engle, R.F., D.F. Hendry and J.F. Richard (1983), "Exogeneity", *Econometrica*, 51, pp.277–304.

Lucas, R.E. Jr. (1976), "Econometric Policy Evaluation – A Critique", in K. Brunner and A.H. Meltzer (eds.) *Carnegie Rochester Conference Series on Public Policy*", 1, pp.19–46.

Maddala, G.S. (1982), *Econometrics*, McGraw–Hill, 4th Edition, London.

McCallum, B.T. (1976), "Rational Expectations and the Estimation of Econometric Models: An Alternative Procedure", *International Economic Review*, 17, pp.484–90.

Pagan, A. (1984), "Econometric Issues in the Analysis of Regressions with Generated Regressors", *International Economic Review*, 25, pp.221–47.

Perry, G.L. (1983), "What Have We Learned about Disinflation?", *Brookings Papers on Economic Activity*, 2, pp.587–602.

Taylor, J.B. (1982), "Establishing Credibility: A Rational Expectations Viewpoint", *American Economic Review*, 72, pp.81–5.

Wickens, M.R. (1982), "The Efficient Estimation of Econometric Models with Rational Expectations", *Review of Economic Studies*, 49, pp.55–68.

PART III

THE DEMAND FOR MONEY

CHAPTER 5

DYNAMICS OF THE DEMAND FOR MONEY AND UNCERTAINTY : THE US DEMAND FOR MONEY REVISITED*

Erkki Koskela, *University of Helsinki, Finland*
Matti Viren, *Bank of Finland, Helsinki, Finland*

1. INTRODUCTION

It is now commonly agreed that the demand for money function suffers from several problems. In particular, this seems to be the case if it is fitted to US data. At the empirical level these problems boil down to parameter instability of the standard demand for money function (see e.g. Judd and Scadding, 1982 and Roley, 1985 for surveys). In the search to account for parameter instabilities in an empirically satisfactory way one should be able to find a satisfactory solution to many problems like how to measure the relevant concept of money in the light of developments in the financial markets, how to distinguish between exogenous and endogenous variables in the demand for money function and how to specify the functional form and dynamics. While redefining the demand for money concept may to some extent alleviate instability problems, it is hard to argue that the problem lies only in the measurement of money concept. Anyway in what follows we ignore measurement aspects and concentrate on some modelling issues associated with the demand for money. We use US quarterly data over the period 1951:1 – 1983:4.

Typically, the stability of the standard demand for money equation a la Goldfeld has been evaluated by using tests for the stability of the whole regression relationship over time so that the source of instability has not been identified. A way to conduct stability tests, which make it possible to identify particular sources of instabilities is to use the so-called *threshold models,* which have been recently proposed by Tong and Lim (1980). The idea is to scrutinise

P. Artus and Y. Barroux (eds.), Monetary Policy, 99–116.

the parameter constancy by specifying the switching model, where for instance the parameters of the demand for money equation take different values depending on whether the driving "threshold" variables happen to be above or below the (fixed) "threshold" values to be estimated simultaneously with the parameters of the demand for money equation. *The first purpose of the paper* is to apply threshold specifications to the standard demand for money equation.

Given the well-documented instability of the Goldfeld demand for money function it is not surprising that the threshold specifications turn out to outperform the standard one. This raises the question of how it should be respecified to account for the instabilities in such a way that the resulting specifications could be regarded as an approximation to the threshold models. For various reasons an obvious candidate for such a model is the generalised error correction specification (GECM) proposed by Kloek (1984). *The second purpose of the paper* is to compare GECM with the simple error correction mechanism (ECM) and with the partial adjustment mechanism (PAM). Though GECM dominates both ECM and PAM, it still suffers from some problems, particularly from heteroskedasticity of residuals. In the presence of uncertainty and risk aversion, however, inflation and interest rate risk may play an important role. *Finally,* we make an attempt to account for uncertainties associated with variables as additional explanatory variables in the demand for money function. The resulting uncertainty corrected demand for money functions with GECM outperform the other specifications and – unlike them – passes all standard diagnostic tests.

We proceed as follows: section 2 presents the specifications to be estimated, while the estimation results are reported in section 3. Finally, there is a brief conclusion.

2. MODELLING THE DEMAND FOR MONEY

2.1 Partial Adjustment and Threshold Applications

The standard way of modelling the demand for money is to use a simple (transactions) demand for money model as a starting point and write

$$m_t^* = a_o + a_1 y_t^e + a_2 r_t^e + u_t, \quad (1)$$

where m^* denotes the "desired" real money balances, y the real GNP, r the nominal interest rate and the u error term. Because the values of y and r are not necessarily known at (the beginning of) period t, it is preferable to use the "expected" values y and r.

Usually at this point people start thinking about dynamics of (1) and the conventional response is to make use either of a partial adjustment mechanism or an error correction mechanism a la Hendry. Starting with the former if we substitute the actual values of y and r for y^e and r^e respectively and postulate the real partial adjustment mechanism (RPAM) in log terms $m_t = \lambda m_t^* + (1-\lambda)m_{t-1}$, then we end up with

$$m_t = b_o + b_1 y_t + b_2 r_t + b_3 m_{t-1} + u_t, \tag{2}$$

where all variables are expressed in log terms and m refers to the actual real money balances. According to RPAM, economic agents display an instantaneous response to the change in the price level, while a non-instantaneous response to changes in income and interest rate. A more natural assumption is to allow for a non-instantaneous reaction also to the change in the price level; after all economic agents adjust nominal balances. The nominal partial adjustment mechanism (NPAM) is $M_t = \lambda M_t^* + (1-\lambda)M_{t-1}$, where M refers to the log of the actual nominal balances and M* to it's "desired" value, and it can be rewritten as $m_t = \lambda m_t^* + (1-\lambda)m_{t-1} - (1-\lambda)p_t$, where p_t refers to the log of the inflation rate. Substituting y and r for y^e and r^e respectively and using NPAM yields

$$m_t = c_o + c_1 y_t + c_2 r_t + c_3 p_t + c_4 m_{t-1} + u_t, \tag{3}$$

where we have the parameter restrictions $c_4 = -c_3$ if the inflation rate results from NPAM.

Another way of justifying the inflation rate as an explanatory variable in addition to the nominal interest rate in the demand for money function goes as follows: if money function serves as a substitute for real assets and neither the Fisher equation – according to which the nominal interest rate changes one-to-one with respect to the expected inflation rate – nor the "inverted" Fisher equation – according to which the real interest rate changes inversely one-to-one with respect to the expected inflation rate – holds, then both the nominal interest rate and the inflation rate will affect m* so that

$$m_t^* = a_o + a_1 y_t^e + a_2 r_t^e + a_3 p_t^e + u_t. \tag{1'}$$

Assuming the adaptive expectations hypothesis $x_t^e - x_{t-1}^e = \theta(x_t - x_{t-1}^e)$ for the expected variables and the same expectations coefficient $0 < \theta < 1$ gives with $m_t^* = m_t$ the specification which is equivalent to (3) with the two exceptions: given (1′) the error term is now $v_t = u_t - (1-\theta)u_{t-1}$ and the interpretation of the coefficients c_i is different.

In all the specifications presented thus far parameters have been assumed to be stable. For various reasons this may not be the case, however. *First,* in the partial adjustment case it can be shown that if the actual cash balance is not directly a choice variable under stochastic cash flows, but economic agents revise their cash monitoring practices in response to exogenous variables, we can wind up with the nominal adjustment specification, where the parameters of the demand for money function do depend on exogenous variables (see Milbourne and Buckholtz and Wasan (1983), and Smith (1986) for details)[1].

Second, in the case of the adaptive expectations interpretation of (3) there is no compelling reason to suppose a constant adaptations coefficient θ. In fact, by allowing for certain (realistic) elements of uncertainty one can derive an adaptive model with a time-varying adaptations coefficient from a situation, where economic agents form their predictions by using a Bayesian sampling procedure. Under the circumstances where the observations about the variable to be forecasted are composed of two, separately unidentifiable parts, the 'permanent' and 'transient' components, the adaptation coefficient depends on the relative precision of the degree of belief and the interpretation of observation; with a high degree of belief and very "transient" observations θ is close to one (for details, see Turnovsky (1969) and particularly, Lawson (1980))[2].

In the face of various potential explanations for parameter instability one should obviously carry out stability tests. Standard stability tests are not necessarily very helpful, however, because they are based on the assumption that instability is somehow related to time so that they do not allow for the identification of the sources of instability. From the point of view of the identification of the sources of instability the so-called *threshold models* are an obvious candidate. They are based on the assumption that the parameters of the explanatory variables change according to some threshold variable, which can be just time, or explanatory variables themselves. For instance in the case of specification (3) using a threshold specification means fitting the following type non-linear equation into the data

$$m_t = c_o + c_1 y_t + c_2 r_t + c_3 p_t + c_4 m_{t-1} + u_t \quad \text{for all t with } q_t \leq \bar{q} \qquad (4a)$$

$$m_t = c_o^* + c_1^* y_t + c_2^* r_t + c_3^* p_t + c_4^* m_{t-1} + u_t^* \quad \text{for all t with } q_t > \bar{q}, \qquad (4b)$$

where u_t and u_t^* are error terms and where q is a threshold variable and $\bar{q}$ is its corresponding (fixed) threshold value. If the error variances are equal, then one can write out a modified threshold model of the form

$$m_t = c_o + c_1 y_t + c_2 r_t + c_3 p_t + c_4 m_{t-1} + c_o' d \tag{5}$$

$$+ c_1' y_t' + c_2' r_t' + c_3' p_t' + c_4' m_{t-1}' + u_t',$$

where u_t' is an error term and d=1 for all t with $q_t \le \bar{q}$ and 0 otherwise, $y_t' = y_t$ for all t with $q_t \le \bar{q}$ and 0 otherwise and similarly for r_t', p_t' and m_{t-1}'. The advantage of (5) over (4) is that it allows for testing the equality of parameters in the two regimes by means of testing the significance of the additional variables d, y_t', r_t', p_t' and m_{t-1}' (for further details of the methodology of threshold models, see the seminal paper by Tong and Lim (1980)).

Except that threshold models provide a way of testing for stability of the specifications, they can be justified on two other grounds. First, they provide a rough approximation to more general linear structures in the lack of knowledge of precise parameterization; in particular, they provide an approximation to varying-parameter specifications, which may result from the earlier presented reasons. Second, threshold models are a natural way to evaluate the so-called "*multi-geared adaptive expectations hypothesis*" presented by Flemming (1976). This is a sort of synthesis between rational expectations and adaptive expectations to avoid the strong assumptions of the former and (in some cases) systematic errors of the latter; for instance if the price-level variable has exhibited no trend in recent years, then this is the variable to which economic agents will apply the adaptive expectations hypothesis. However, if the price-level variable has a trend, while its rate of change variable, the inflation rate, has not, then the adaptive schema will be used to predict the inflation rate variable.[3] And analogously for other expected variables.

2.2 Generalized Error Correction Specification

If the threshold models of type (4) or (5) outperform standard linear specifications like (2) and (3), then either the non-linear threshold specification gets support and/or the outperformance can be interpreted as showing parameter instability of standard linear models. In the latter case the question of how the linear specifications should be modified in order to account for instabilities has to be faced.

An obvious way to proceed is to make use of the generalized error correction mechanism (GECM) proposed and discussed by Kloek (1984). In this connection it may be specified as follows

$$\Delta m_t = b_o + b_1(m-y)_{t-1} + b_2(m-y)_{t-2} + b_3\Delta y_t + b_4\Delta y_{t-1} \qquad (6)$$

$$+ b_5\Delta r_t + b_6\Delta r_{t-1} + b_7\Delta p_t + b_8\Delta p_{t-1} + u_t,$$

where Δ refers to the first differences of the variables and where $(m-y)_{t-1}$ and $(m-y)_{t-2}$ are the so-called error correction terms. According to (6) the change in the real money balances depends on the change in the current and lagged values of the explanatory variables and on the lagged discrepancies between the real money balances and the real income, the so-called error correction terms.[4]

The specification (6) have several attractive features. First, by dropping the error correction term $(m-y)_{t-2}$ and the lagged differences of the explanatory variables we wind up with the simplest example of the error correction mechanism (ECM)

$$\Delta m_t = b_o + b_1(m-y)_{t-1} + b_2\Delta y_t + b_3\Delta r_t + b_4\Delta p_t + u_t \qquad (7)$$

Second, the specification (6) represents an approximation to threshold models presented earlier in the sense that excluding the error correction terms the right-hand side variables can be written in terms of first and second differences (a "gear shift") and threshold models provide a way to evaluate "gear shifts" in the explanatory variables.[5] Third, the specification allows for varying velocity of money in the long run (for an analysis of the circumstances in which the specifications of type (6) or (7) represents optimal responses of economic agents in a dynamic environment, see Nickell (1985)).

Specifications of the demand for money presented earlier, while differing in detail, have one common characteristic: they have the certainty equivalence property in the sense that even though we have referred to uncertainties as a reason for varying parameter models, the expectation variables have been formulated by means of the expected values only. It is obvious, however, that changes in the degree of uncertainty may play an important role as a factor affecting the pattern of money holdings by risk-averse economic agents.

First, for well-known portfolio theoretic reasons uncertainty about nominal rates of return, inflation and covariance between nominal rates of return and inflation may affect money holdings as additional explanatory variables (for various ways of justifying this, see Buiter and Armstrong (1978), Fischer (1975) and Boonekamp (1978)).

Second, as suggested earlier, one can derive a time-varying and uncertainty sensitive specification from a situation, where economic agents form their predictions under uncertainty by using a Bayesian sampling procedure (see

Turnovsky (1969), and particularly Lawson (1980)). Moreover, Walsh (1984) has recently suggested how the parameters of the demand for money function – derived from portfolio theoretic framework in the presence of nominal interest rate and inflation uncertainty – can themselves depend on stochastic properties of interest rate and inflation.[6] For both of these reasons, changes in uncertainty may affect via parameters of the explanatory variables.

In practice it is very difficult, if not impossible, to distinguish between the two channels of influence of uncertainty variables. In this paper we do not try to tackle this issue, but introduce uncertainty variables additively as additional explanatory variables into the GECM specification (6).

More specifically, we introduce the nominal rate of return uncertainty variable – measured by the variance of the interest rate v_r – the inflation rate uncertainty variable – measured by the variance of the inflation rate v_p – and the hedging variable – measured by the covariance between the nominal rate of return and the inflation rate, cov – as augmented variables. Denoting the expected values by superscript e we end up with the following uncertainty-corrected GECM specification:

$$\begin{aligned}\Delta m_t = {} & b_o + b_1(m-y)_{t-1} + b_2(m-y)_{t-2} + b_3\Delta y_t + b_4\Delta y_{t-1} \\ & + b_5\Delta r_t^e + b_6\Delta r_{t-1}^e + b_7\Delta p_t^e + b_8\Delta p_{t-1}^e + b_9\Delta v_{rt} \\ & + b_{10}\Delta v_{rt-1} + b_{11}\Delta v_{pt} + b_{12}\Delta v_{pt-1} + b_{13}\Delta cov_t \\ & + b_{14}\Delta cov_{t-1} + u_t\end{aligned} \tag{8}$$

The purpose of the empirical part of the paper is to estimate and compare the relative performance of the specifications (2) – (8) by using the US quarterly data over the sample period 1951:1 – 1983:4

3. EMPIRICAL RESULTS

The US data over the period 1951:1 – 1983:4 to be used are quarterly, seasonally adjusted – with the exception of nominal interest rates, which are seasonally unadjusted – and derived mainly from Business Conditions Digest. The money stock is the conventional M1, GNP is used as a proxy for y and the respective price deflator as the relevant price series. As the proxy for the opportunity cost of holding money we used the three-month Treasury bill rate (RTB).[7]

3.1 The Goldfeld Specification and Threshold Models of the Demand for Money

It is well-known that the real partial adjustment demand for money function (2) has shown a rather poor performance, particularly, when the data from the 1970s and 1980s has been used in the estimations (Judd and Scadding (1982), see also Koskela and Virén (1986)). The estimation results of (2) and (3) indicate clearly that the inflation rate serves as an important explanatory variable in the demand for money function.

Using quarterly US data over the period 1951:1 – 1983:4 yields a standard error .00824 for specification (2) and .00686 for the specification (3) with the t-value of the inflation rate being 7.59. Moreover, we cannot reject the NPAM $c_4 = -c_3$ ($F(1,128) = .56$) over the whole estimation period. If we go a bit further and estimate the following unrestricted model in terms of the inflation rate

$$m_t = c_o + c_1 y_t + c_2 r_t + c_3 P_t + c_4 P_{t-1} + c_5 m_{t-1} + u_t \qquad (3')$$

where P_t indicates the log of the price level, then the hypothesis that $c_3 = -c_4$ cannot be rejected either ($F(1,127) = 2.26$) in conformity with NPAM. But using the fact $M = m + P$ (3′) can be rewritten as $M_t - c_5 M_{t-1} = c_o + c_1 y_t + c_2 r_t + (1+c_3)P_t + (c_4 - c_5)P_{t-1} + u_t$ and assuming $c_3 = -1$ and $c_4 = c_5 = 1$ yields $M_t - M_{t-1} = c_o + c_1 y_t + c_2 r_t + u_t$. Unfortunately, we cannot reject the coefficient restrictions leading to this specification either so that over the whole estimation period the change in the nominal money balances seems to depend on the real GNP and the nominal interest rate; this is clearly a finding that is not consistent with any standard theoretical analysis of the demand for money.[8] This last result is a kind of artifact, which does not hold over subsamples. For instance in the case of subsamples 1951:1 – 1967:2 and 1967:3 – 1983:4 the parameter restrictions $c_3 = -1$ and $c_4 = c_5$ can clearly be rejected (the chi square statistic is 6.6 in both cases).

In light of the above mentioned weaknesses of specifications (2) and (3) it is appropriate to seek for a better alternative. Next we turn to consider threshold models of the demand for money (4) and (5), which were presented in section 2.

The test procedure consists of fitting the linear model (3), the threshold model (4) and the modified threshold model (5), where the inflation rate was decomposed into price level components, into the data sample by using p_t, r_t, rate growth of y_t, time and inflation variance v_p alternatively as threshold variables. The estimation results with the inflation rate p as the threshold variable are presented in Table 1 both over the whole estimation period and across two sub-periods. The values of the threshold were determined by using the

Table 1. Estimation Results with Threshold Specifications

Constant	m_{-1}	y	r	P	P_{-1}	SEE	$\bar{p}$	SBIC
1951.2 – 1983.4								
–.283 (2.50)	1.010 (40.15)	.057 (3.43)	.500 (4.84)	–.695 (3.87)	.664 (3.68)	.0046	p<3.86 n=66	–686.6
.134 (0.70)	.942 (19.07)	.030 (1.44)	–.089 (1.84)	–1.298 (6.74)	1.296 (6.80)	.0074	p>3.86 n=65	–613.3
			SBIC = –1286.25		z = 19.96			
1951.2 – 1967.2								
.633 (1.64)	.855 (11.87)	.149 (3.49)	–.326 (2.68)	–.699 (3.48)	.502 (2.36)	.0042	p<2.54 n=46	–478.7
1.174 (5.99)	.669 (16.89)	.218 (8.54)	–1.115 (5.89)	–.212 (1.39)	.020 (0.12)	.0019	p>2.54 n=18	–207.9
			SBIC = –679.7		z = 16.82			
1967.3 – 1983.4								
.078 (0.34)	1.055 (20.42)	–.082 (1.65)	–.271 (3.90)	–.572 (1.87)	.623 (2.12)	.0056	p<6.88 n=42	–412.7
2.403 (2.42)	.266 (1.00)	.392 (2.89)	.148 (1.34)	–1.402 (3.42)	1.153 (2.54)	.0072	p>6.88 n=23	–208.2
			SBIC = –616.5		z = 18.69			

m = log(M/P), y = log(GNPQ), r = RTB/100, $\bar{p}$ indicates the value of the inflation threshold, SBIC the value of the Schwartz information criterion for a linear model, and finally z an chi square test statistic (with 6 degrees of freedom) for the hypothesis that the coefficients above and below the threshold are equal. This statistic is computed assuming that error variances for the both model structures (above and below the threshold) are equal.

Schwartz Bayesian information criterion (SBIC).[9] The threshold models were estimated by non-linear LS using the program by Luukkonen (1983).

Both on the basis of the Schwartz Bayesian information criterion and of the value of the LR-statistic (calculated for the modified threshold model) the linear specification (3) is outperformed by threshold specifications. Moreover, the particular choice of the threshold variable did not seem to matter; e.g. for the whole sample period almost the same data points were chosen by the threshold variables p, rate of change y, time and inflation variance[10]. All in all, threshold models clearly outperform linear specification (3). An unattractive feature of threshold estimation is that the time works out roughly as well as other threshold variables. Therefore, we turn to consider specifications which would account for these instabilities.

3.2. Error Correction Specifications for the Demand for Money without and with Uncertainty Variables

In this section we first compare the error correction specifications (6) and (7) with the NPAM specification (3). The OLS estimation results are reported in Table 2 together with a number of test statistics. The following features of results merit attention.

First, the "generalized" ECM seems to outperform both the nominal partial adjustment version (3) and the simple ECM (7) in almost all respects. The better performance of (6) is displayed by the standard error of equations, Godfrey's LM autocorrelation statistics, Jarque-Bera test for normality of residuals, and various types of CUSUM tests. Second even though (6) outperforms (3) and (7) in terms of most diagnostics, it suffers from heteroskedasticity of residuals. This is indicated by the CUSUMQ test statistic, which for (6) – as well as for (3) and (7) – exceed the standard levels of significance. A more direct evidence is provided by Engle's Autoregressive Conditional Heteroskedasticity (ARCH) test statistic, which in all cases exceeds the standard levels of significance (for details of ARCH-methodology, see Engle (1982)).

A way to try to interpret the finding that residuals of the demand for money equations suffer from heteroskedasticity is to pay attention to the possibility that changes in uncertainty over time have played an important role as a factor affecting the pattern of money holdings by risk-averse economic agents. Let us now return to estimation results obtained by using the GECM augmented with various uncertainty variables, i.e. the specification (8).[11]

In order to check roughly whether the augmented variables play any role in alleviating the heteroskedasticity problems of (6) we preceded as follows: First we constructed time-series proxies for the expected inflation and the interest rate by using simple univariate AR(4) models. Then the one-period ahead predictions were used for expected values, the squared prediction errors for the variance terms and the covariance terms were derived by using the corresponding cross-products of the prediction errors. The AR(4) models were estimated recursively so that the expected values were conditional only to the information which was

Table 2. OLS Estimation Results for Equations (3), (6) and (7)

A Coefficient Estimates

$$\hat{m}_t = -\underset{\substack{(0.55)\\(0.53)}}{0.051} + \underset{\substack{(47.15)\\(45.93)}}{0.979}m_{t-1} + \underset{\substack{(5.28)\\(5.29)}}{0.026}y_t - \underset{\substack{(2.81)\\(2.60)}}{0.113}r_t - \underset{\substack{(7.59)\\(5.95)}}{0.931}p_t \qquad (3)$$

$$\Delta\hat{m}_t = -\underset{\substack{(0.76)\\(0.72)}}{0.003} - \underset{\substack{(0.40)\\(0.34)}}{0.001}(m-y)_{t-1} + \underset{\substack{(4.49)\\(4.42)}}{0.323}\Delta y_t + \underset{\substack{(0.29)\\(0.22)}}{0.025}\Delta r_t - \underset{\substack{(3.87)\\(3.21)}}{0.496}\Delta p_t \qquad (7)$$

$$\Delta\hat{m}_t = -\underset{\substack{(1.03)\\(1.10)}}{0.003} + \underset{\substack{(6.37)\\(5.55)}}{0.442}(m-y)_{t-1} - \underset{\substack{(6.40)\\(5.58)}}{0.443}(m-y)_{t-2} + \underset{\substack{(3.77)\\(3.64)}}{0.217}\Delta y_t \qquad (6)$$

$$+ \underset{\substack{(6.13)\\(5.36)}}{0.492}\Delta y_{t-1} - \underset{\substack{(0.12)\\(0.08)}}{0.008}\Delta r_t - \underset{\substack{(8.37)\\(5.44)}}{0.540}\Delta r_{t-1} - \underset{\substack{(6.21)\\(6.72)}}{0.680}\Delta p_t - \underset{\substack{(0.97)\\(1.15)}}{0.100}\Delta p_{t-1}$$

B Test Statistics

Equation	(3)	(7)	(6)	5% critical value
R^2	0.983	0.228	0.613	..
100*SEE	0.686	0.805	0.579	..
D–W	1.484	1.296	2.205	1.57/1.78
LM1	3.008	4.327	1.704	1.645
LM2	0.606	1.118	0.266	1.645
LM3	0.846	1.759	0.170	1.645
LM4	0.956	0.778	0.350	1.645
J–B	19.257	17.594	5.389	5.991
ARCH4	18.3	17.28	24.96	9.49
Chow 67:4	4.467	1.748	1.540	1.96
F–H	5.853	1.558	2.266	1.96
Homogeneity	2.108	1.314	0.962	1.57
Cusum(b)	0.710	1.141	0.702	0.948
Cusum(f)	0.862	0.636	0.208	0.948
Cusumsq(b)	0.267	0.276	0.228	0.145
Cusumsq(f)	0.403	0.335	0.362	0.145

$m = \log(M/P)$, $y = \log(GNPQ)$, $r = RTB/100$, $p = \log(P_t/P_{t-1})$, Δ indicates first differences, numbers in parentheses immediately below the coefficient estimates are standard t-ratios; below them are White's heteroskedasticity adjusted t-ratios. LMi's denote Godfrey's LM autocorrelation statistics, J-B is the Jarque-Bera test for normality of residuals, ARCH4 is Engle's autocor–relation conditional heteroskedasticity statistic with 4 lags, Chow 67:4 is the Chow stability test statistics for the period 1967:4, F-H is the Farley-Hinich (F) test for the hypothesis that parameters follow a linear trend, Homogeneity is a F test for parameter stability w.r.t. 6 nonoverlapping periods (with 20 observations in each of them), and finally Cusum and Cusumsq are the stability statistics which are computed both backwards (b) and forward (f). The critical values are based on the number of degrees of freedom of equation (6).

available at the moment the predictions have been made. Finally, the constructed variance and covariance terms were introduced into the specification (6) taking into account its "generalized" ECM type. The corresponding OLS estimation results are presented in Table 3, where the variance and covariance terms are denoted by v_r, v_p and cov respectively.

On the basis of estimation results presented in Table 3 one can readily conclude that introducing the additional variance and covariance terms into the specification (6) and using the predicted values for r and p instead of their actual values clearly helps to improve the performance of the underlying demand for money function; comparing the estimation results with those in equation (6) of Table 2 indicates that both the standard error of the estimate is now considerably smaller and the specifications now pass all standard diagnostic checks including ARCH test statistic.[12] Moreover, according to F-test statistics the hypothesis that the variance and covariance terms are equal to zero can be rejected at standard significance levels.

Turning to economics of the money demand specification presented in Table 3 we should point out first, that the so-called error correction terms will cancel each other out; this means that in the long run the model does not reduce to a constant level of velocity or to a constant growth level of velocity which would be independent of nominal interest rate, inflation rate and real income.[13] Second, the income elasticity of the demand for money lies on the range .71 – .74, which sounds very plausible.[14] Finally, as far as the signs of the other explanatory variables are concerned, the nominal interest rate and inflation rate are of the expected sign, though in the specification (10) the inflation terms will offset each other. On the basis of portfolio theoretic considerations it is reasonable to expect that the variance of nominal interest rate, v_r, affects positively, while the covariance between the prediction errors of the nominal interest rate and inflation, cov, negatively. The latter seems to be the case, while the sign of v_r is "wrong". Thus the estimation results do not completely obey this portfolio theoretic conjecture. But we should keep in mind that these uncertainty terms may also (or solely) affect "multiplicatively" via the coefficients of the demand for money functions from which we have abstracted in our empirical implementation.

Table 3. Estimation Results with Uncertainty Corrected Demand for Money Specifications

$$\Delta m_t = -\underset{\substack{(1.19)\\(1.29)}}{0.003} + \underset{\substack{(5.55)\\(5.30)}}{0.439}(m-y)_{t-1} - \underset{\substack{(5.58)\\(5.34)}}{0.440}(m-y)_{t-2} + \underset{\substack{(3.40)\\(3.77)}}{0.189}\Delta y_t \tag{9}$$

$$+ \underset{\substack{(6.78)\\(6.99)}}{0.550}\Delta y_{t-1} - \underset{\substack{(9.43)\\(7.12)}}{0.433}\Delta r^*_t - \underset{\substack{(2.89)\\(2.56)}}{0.148}\Delta r^*_{t-1} - \underset{\substack{(4.87)\\(5.41)}}{0.611}\Delta p_t + \underset{\substack{(1.22)\\(1.33)}}{0.148}\Delta p_{t-1}$$

$$- \underset{\substack{(3.30)\\(2.70)}}{0.188}\Delta v_{rt} - \underset{\substack{(1.65)\\(1.60)}}{0.091}\Delta v_{rt-1} - \underset{\substack{(2.06)\\(1.87)}}{0.241}\Delta cov_t - \underset{\substack{(0.28)\\(0.23)}}{0.031}\Delta cov_{t-1}$$

$R^2 = .688$, 100*SEE = .530, D–W = 2.075, LM1 = .639,
LM2 = .450, LM3 = .114, LM4 = .678, J–B = .466,
ARCH = 1.77, Chow = .616, F(4) = 4.158

$$\Delta m_t = \underset{\substack{(1.36)\\(1.41)}}{0.004} + \underset{\substack{(4.58)\\(4.87)}}{0.394}(m-y)_{t-1} - \underset{\substack{(4.60)\\(4.91)}}{0.396}(m-y)_{t-2} + \underset{\substack{(3.20)\\(3.23)}}{0.193}\Delta y_t \tag{19}$$

$$+ \underset{\substack{(5.76)\\(6.31)}}{0.517}\Delta y_{t-1} - \underset{\substack{(10.27)\\(\ 8.14)}}{0.500}\Delta r^*_t - \underset{\substack{(2.64)\\(2.59)}}{0.147}\Delta r^*_{t-1} - \underset{\substack{(1.15)\\(0.99)}}{0.373}\Delta p^*_t + \underset{\substack{(1.17)\\(1.05)}}{0.379}\Delta p^*_{t-1}$$

$$- \underset{\substack{(2.09)\\(2.11)}}{0.377}\Delta v_{pt} - \underset{\substack{(1.57)\\(1.55)}}{0.272}\Delta v_{pt-1} - \underset{\substack{(3.51)\\(3.13)}}{0.214}\Delta v_{rt} - \underset{\substack{(1.77)\\(1.74)}}{0.105}\Delta v_{rt-1}$$

$$- \underset{\substack{(2.63)\\(2.74)}}{0.327}\Delta cov_t - \underset{\substack{(0.22)\\(0.19)}}{0.027}\Delta cov_{t-1}$$

$R^2 = .646$, 100*SEE = .570, D–W = 2.119, LM1 = 1.144,
LM2 = 0.24, LM3 = .732, LM4 = .828, J–B = 1.377,
ARCH4 = 4.96, Chow = .540, F(6) = 3.888

r* (p*) denotes the predicted value of r (p) given by an AR(4) model which is estimated recursively from the beginning of the sample period. v_p, v_r and cov are corresponding variance and covariance terms (which are constructed by using the (squared) prediction errors of the respective variables). The coefficient of v_r is multiplied by 100, and the coefficient of v_p, in turn is divided by 100. F(4) and F(6) denote F-test statistics for the hypothesis that the variance and covariance terms are equal to zero. Otherwise notation is the same as in Table 2. For computer capacity reasons we could calculate the Cusumsq-test for neither specification (9) nor for specification (10). But keeping the parameters of the error correction terms fixed produced results which passed in terms of the Cusumsq-statistic.

4. CONCLUDING REMARKS

In this paper we have revisited the demand for money specifications by using US quarterly data over the sample period 1951:1 – 1983:4. The reasons why we have used US data are first that standard specifications are particularly problematic in this case and second that the demand for money has been so extensively studied with this data that it therefore provides a convenient benchmark case for presenting and testing specifications.

Given the well-known weaknesses of the standard partial adjustment specifications we first estimated the nonlinear threshold models of the demand for money. They are based on the assumption that parameters of the demand for money change according to some threshold variable, which can be just time or explanatory variables themselves. An attractive feature of threshold models is therefore that they provide a way to test for non-linearities in terms of explanatory variables thus making it possible to identify sources of instability in linear models.

The threshold models outperformed linear specification in all cases including the case where time was used as the threshold variable. Therefore we turned to consider more general specifications which could account for instabilities. This led us to the so-called error correction type models; they displayed a better performance than partial adjustment specifications, but suffered from hetero–skedasticity of residuals. Finally, we extended the error correction models by introducing uncertainty variables – variance of nominal interest rate, variance of inflation rate and covariance between the nominal interest rate and the inflation rate – as augmented variables into the demand for money functions. The resulting uncertainty-corrected generalized error correction specifications passed all standard diagnostic checks including heteroskedasticity test statistics and showed mostly reasonable properties in terms of the size of elasticities and signs of explanatory variables. Though the results are preliminary we feel that modelling uncertainties in the connection of more general dynamics than partial adjustment is a promising area and provides a number of agendas for further theoretical and empirical research.

NOTES

*) We are indebted to Juoni Kokko for research assistance. Financial support from the Yrjö Jahnsson Foundation and the Nordic Economic Research Council is gratefully acknowledged. An earlier version of this paper was presented at the 1987 European Meeting of the Econometric Society, in Copenhagen, August 24–28, 1987.

1) Under slightly different assumptions Santomero and Seater (1981) have presented a model with variable adjustment, where the partial adjustment parameter changes over time in response to exogenous shocks. By presenting a theory of how assets are searched out and how excess balances are worked off, they emphasize money's role as a "shock absorber" during periods of disequilibrium.
2) Lawson (1980) has also presented how this Bayesian procedure could be operationalised in practice.
3) Thus according to this "gear-shift hypothesis" expectations are formed adaptively on the lowest-order difference of the process of variable to have shown no trend in recent years. See Vanderkamp (1972) for an early attempt to implement this idea in the case of the specification of the wage equation.
4) Generally, and here as well, co-integration of the error correction part is assumed. Recent work on methods for testing the unit root can be used to test for co-integration (see Granger and Engle (1987) for details).
5) The dynamics featuring in (6) can also be justified in terms of expectations. Thus, assuming for instance adaptive expectations in terms of p_t^e (only) in equation (1′) the following model can be derived:

$$m_t = a_o\theta + a_1y_t - a_1(1-\theta)y_{t-1} + a_2r_t \tag{9}$$
$$- a_2(1-\theta)r_{t-1} + a_3\theta p_t + (1-\theta)m_{t-1} + u_t - (1-\theta)u_{t-1},$$

where θ is the adaptive expectations coefficient specified earlier. By differencing and rearranging terms one obtains the following specification:

$$\Delta m_t = a_1\Delta y_t + (1-\theta)(1-a_1)\Delta y_{t-1} + a_2\Delta r_t \tag{10}$$
$$- a_2(1-\theta)\Delta r_{t-1} + a_3\theta\Delta p_t + (1-\theta)(m-y)_{t-1}$$
$$- (1-\theta)(m-y)_{t-2} + u_t - (2-\theta)u_{t-1} + (1-\theta)u_{t-2}.$$

Clearly, this specification is close to the GECM specification (6). It is only that (9) imposes certain parameter restrictions which are not present in (6). However, the estimation results which will be presented in Table 2 correspond fairly closely to this specification.
6) More specifically, *after some approximations* Walsh presents the following demand for money function

$$m_t = h_o + h_1(y_t - \bar{y}_t) + h_2(r_t^e - r_t) + u_t, \tag{1}$$

where the demand for money depends positively on the income "innovation" ($\bar{y}_t$ = the trend value of y_t) and negatively on the expected nominal rate of return on bonds, where r_t and r_t^e refer to actual and expected bond prices. It is important to stress that the parameters h_i ($i = 0, 1, 2$) can be interpreted in terms of the variance of the bond price, the covariance between inflation and the price of bonds and the coefficient of relative risk aversion. The parameters will change, when those variables are subject to changes for instance as a result of changes in monetary policy rules. Thus we have here an example of the Lucas critique extended to account for uncertainties. (See Walsh (1984) for details).

7) A detailed description of the data is available from the authors upon request.

8) By using the US quarterly data over the period 1951:1 – 1983:4 the OLS estimation of the specification (3) gave the following results

$$m_t = \underset{(1.00)}{-0.94} + \underset{(40.45)}{1.005} m_{t-1} + \underset{(1.43)}{0.013} y_t - \underset{(3.24)}{0.135} r_t - \underset{(7.81)}{0.952} P_t + \underset{(7.85)}{0.963} P_{t-1}$$

100*SEE = 0.679, D-W = 1.557, where t-values are in parentheses. Clearly, on the basis of coefficient estimates we can reject neither the hypothesis that the sum of the coefficients of P_t and P_{t-1} is zero, nor the (joint) hypothesis that the coefficient of P_t is –1 *and* that the coefficient of P_{t-1} is equal to the coefficient of m_{t-1} (in this joint hypothesis case the chi square statistic with 2 degrees of freedom is 4.). Moreover, if one tests the joint hypothesis in the context of the specification (3′) that $c_5 = c_4 = -c_3$, then the same chi square test statistic with 3 degrees of freedom is now 4.8, which fails to exceed levels of significance. Thus we wind up with an equation of the type

$$M_t - M_{t-1} = c_o + c_1 y_t + c_2 r_t + u_t.$$

9) In their seminal paper Tong and Lim (1980) suggested the use of the Akaike information criterion (AIC) as the main specification criterion of threshold models. In contrast with SBIC it has, however, a tendency to overestimate the dimension of the model particularly in large samples. In the context of threshold models this tendency to overestimate the dimension means selecting a threshold model with a positive probability even asymptotically though the true model is linear (see e.g. Geweke and Meese (1981) and Teräsvirta and Luukkonen (1985)).

10) A complete set of results is available from the authors upon request.

11) The uncertainty variables have been used with some success as augmented variables in the conventional demand for money function in Koskela & Virén (1987), in which it is shown using US quarterly data over the sample period 1952:2 – 1982:4 that the nominal rate of return uncertainty variable tends to have a significantly positive effect and the inflation hedging variable a significantly negative effect on the demand for money.

12) As for the interest rate, we also experimented with the yield on long-term Treasury bonds. The results were qualitatively similar to those presented in the paper. Hence, they have not been reported. A full set of results is available from the authors upon request.

13) Alternatively, one can refer to the adaptive expectations specification (9) presented in fn. 5. Notice, that this specification implies very reasonable parameter values, particularly in terms of the adjustment coefficient θ.

14) Recently, Rose (1985) has also estimated an error correction type specification using M1 money concept for US data, which outperforms the standard partial adjustment specifications when estimated from early 1950s up till 1973. He reports the steady–state income elasticity .57. Unfortunately, however, the extension of the sample until the end of 1981 has the effect of rejecting the stability of his ECM type demand for money model. Taylor (1986) has also estimated ECM type demand for money models for three European countries, West Germany, the Nether–lands and France, using M2 money concept. The income elasticity turns

out to be 1 for West Germany and the Netherlands, but surprisingly high 1.64 for France. Neither Rose (1985) nor Taylor 1986) use uncertainty variables in their specifications.

REFERENCES

Boonekamp, C.F.–J. (1978), "Inflation, Hedging and the Demand for Money", *American Economic Review*, pp.821–33.

Buiter, W.H. and C.A. Armstrong (1978), "A Didactic Note on the Transactions Demand for Money and Behavior Towards Risk", *Journal of Money, Credit, and Banking*, pp.529–38.

Engle, R.F. (1982), "Autoregressive Conditional Heteroskedasticity with Estimates of the Variance of U.K. Inflation", *Econometrica*, pp 987–1008.

Engle, R.F. and C.W.J. Granger (1987), "Co–Integration and Error Correction: Representation, Estimation, and Testing", *Econometrica*, pp.251–76.

Fischer, S. (1975), "The demand for Index Bonds", *Journal of Political Economy*, pp.509–34.

Flemming, J. (1976), *Inflation*, Oxford University Press, Oxford.

Geweke, J. and R. Meese (1981), "Estimating Regression Models of Finite but Unknown Order", *International Economic Review*, pp.55–70.

Judd, J.P. and J.L. Scadding (1982), "The Search for a Stable Money Demand Function: A Survey of the Post–1973 Literature", *Journal of Economic Literature*, pp.993–1023.

Kloek, T. (1984), "Dynamic Adjustment When the Target is Non–Stationary", *International Economic Review*, pp.315–26.

Koskela, E. and M. Virén (1986), "Endogenous Policy, Structural Shift and the Demand for Money", *Weltwirtschaftliches Archiv*, pp.647–56.

Koskela, E. and M. Virén (1987), "Inflation, Hedging and the Demand for Money: Some Empirical Evidence", *Economic Inquiry*", pp.251–65.

Lawson, T. (1980), "Adaptive Expectations and Uncertainty", *Review of Economic Studies*, pp.305–20.

Luukkonen, R. (1983), "SURVO 76: Programs for Time Series Analysis, Department of Statistics", *University of Helsinki, Research Report No. 40.*

Milbourne, R.D., P. Buckholtz and M.T. Wasan (1983), "A Theoretical Derivation of the Functional Forms of Short Run Money Holdings", *Review of Economic Studies*, pp.531–41.

Nickell, S. (1985), "Error Correction, Partial Adjustment and All That: An Expository Note", *Oxford Bulletin of Economic and Statistics*, pp.119–29.

Roley, V.V. (1985), "Money Demand Predictability", *Journal of Money, Credit, and Banking*, pp.611–41.

Rose, A.K. (1985), "An Alternative Approach to the American Demand for Money", *Journal of Money, Credit, and Banking*, pp.439–55.

Santomero, A.M. and J.J. Seater (1981), "Partial Adjustment in the Demand for Money: Theory and Empirics", *American Economic Review*, pp.566–78.

Smith, G.W. (1986), "A Dynamic Baumol–Tobin Model of Money Demand", *Review of Economic Studies*, pp.465–69.

Taylor, M.P. (1986), "From the General to the Specific: The Demand for M2 in Three European Countries", *Empirical Economics*, pp.243–61.

Teräsvirta, T. and R. Luukkonen (1985), "Choosing between Linear and Threshold Autoregressive Models", in O.D. Anderson (ed.), *Time Series Analysis: Theory and Practice*, North–Holland, Amsterdam, pp.129–37.

Tong, H. and K.S. Lim (1980), "Threshold Autoregression: Limit Cycles and Cyclical Data", *Journal of the Royal Statistical Society*, pp.245–92.

Turnovsky, S.J. (1969), "A Bayesian Approach to the Theory of Expectations", *Journal of Economic Theory*, pp.220–27.

Vanderkamp, J. (1972), "Wage Adjustment, Productivity and Price Change Expectations", *Review of Economic Studies*, pp.61–72.
Walsh, C.E. (1984), "Interest Rate Volatility and Monetary Policy", *Journal of Money, Credit and Banking*, pp.133–50.

CHAPTER 6

ANALYSIS OF THE RELATIONSHIP BETWEEN MONEY STOCK AND MONETARY BASE: THE FRENCH EXPERIENCE DURING THE PERIOD OF QUANTITATIVE CONTROLS ON CREDIT (1973–1985)

Y. Barroux and N. Dagognet, *Banque de France, Paris, France*

1. INTRODUCTION

For the past fifteen years, the French money stock has been regulated by means of quantitative controls on credit. Under this method, and given the usual habits of the French banks, the monetary base has moved in relation to changes in the money stock in keeping with a familiar theoretical model known as the "credit divisor", which is chiefly governed by public behaviour towards notes. The purpose of the present paper is to analyse changes in this ratio (B/M) over the past fifteen years and uncover their main explanatory factors. The method used consists of pairing a classic money demand function with a divisor–type relation, and of inferring from this a monetary base (or divisor) determination equation which is specified as a directly estimated error–correction model.

We shall present in turn the institutional framework of the analysis, the statistical series used, the specifications applied, the econometric results obtained and their interpretation.

2. THE ANALYTICAL FRAMEWORK

Quantitative credit controls were the prime method of monetary regulation in France from December 1972 onwards, and they were only effectively discarded at the beginning of 1987. So for fourteen years, control of the money stock depended on control over the money stock counterparts, e.g., external monetary creation, limitations on Treasury recourse to monetary financing, controls on bank lending to the economy. The main reasons why the monetary authorities opted for this

P. Artus and Y. Barroux (eds.), Monetary Policy, 117–129.

mode of regulation have been explained on many occasions. They include a reluctance to vary interest rates too suddenly or too widely, for fear of weakening the exchange rate (cf. external constraints) and imperiling some of our financial institutions (cf. the heterogeneous nature of the banking system). In this context, the now traditional analysis of money supply based on control of the monetary base by the Central Bank and relying on the stability of the credit multiplier is no longer tenable, and the description of the method of monetary regulation refers to what is known as the "credit divisor" approach.

Whereas the credit multiplier model assumes that an increase in the monetary base precedes any increase in the money stock, the credit divisor approach acknowledges that, for a monetary system in which monetary base supply is not restricted and therefore in which banks can be certain of obtaining the Central Bank money that they need at a rate of interest close to the previous rate, growth in the money stock – or rather the decisions that lead to this growth – may precede an increase in the monetary base. In that case, the traditional relation of cause and effect is reversed, and the monetary base – or the increase in it – results from the money stock (or from the change in it). In actual fact, if we look at things in terms of the behaviour of the commercial banks, it is the supply of credit which gives rise to the need for Central Bank money, because of leakages triggered by the creation of money thus initiated (e.g. the increase in notes in the hands of the public and in compulsory bank reserves). In fact, in the absence of any change in the other counterparts, changes in credit and money are identical.

Although this mechanism is less important in a period when the control of the money stock relies on the imposition of credit ceilings, it is worth taking a look at the stability of the relationship that grew up, in the course of the past fourteen years, between the monetary base and the money stock, at a time when money market intervention techniques and control over bank liquidity are enjoying renewed favour as methods of monetary regulation. In view of the foregoing, needless to say, the approach used has been the demand approach, for both monetary base and money stock. This is not to say that at any given moment agents have held the stock of notes, reserves or currency that they wished to hold. On the contrary, we took the view that the relation whose stability needed to be tested concerned the desired levels of aggregates, whereas demand patterns tended, by means of simple processes of adjustment over time, to draw closer to the levels of stocks effectively desired.

Before presenting the statistical series used, one last point deserves to be touched upon: it concerns the different definitions of the monetary base and money stock aggregates that might be used. In this respect, we have adopted a broad definition of the money stock (M3R), which allows us to circumvent institutional problems (e.g. the distinction between banks and savings institutions) and comes down to considering all financial institutions managing demand and short term deposits as able, and liable, to create money. Further, whereas other authors (Guillaumont–Jeanneney, 1978) have suggested including in the monetary base deposits with the Treasury and savings institutions, we have preferred a narrow definition of this last aggregate, restricting it, roughly speaking, to the liabilities of the Banque de France, namely notes in circulation and reserves held by banking financial institutions with the Central Bank. This definition would appear to be compatible with the one adopted for the money stock and corresponds to an operational concept of the monetary base from the Central Bank's point of view.

3. THE STATISTICAL SERIES STUDIED

"Central Bank money" comes under three headings of unequal importance (figures are for end–April 1986):

- notes issued by the Banque de France (excluding the Central Bank for the "départements d'Outre–Mer"): 202.7 billion;
- the Treasury's current account (credit) with the Central Bank: 54.9 billion;
- the accounts of commercial banks obliged to meet the required level of compulsory reserves (consequently including "free reserves"): 30.2 billion.

It is immediately apparent that the "Treasury account" and "required reserves" components are far more variable than "notes in circulation".

- In the case of the Treasury current account, whose amount and variations are governed primarily by factors of an institutional nature (e.g. changes in the system of Banque de France advances to the Central Government), it seems logical, for the purpose of this analysis, not to take it into account when calculating the "monetary base" aggregate. This is tantamount to deducting it from the "Treasury liabilities" counterpart, in other words, regarding this counterpart as net of the Treasury credit account.
- With respect to the reserves maintained by commercial banks, which are also liable to sharp short term swings, we have opted for the principle of eliminating the "mechanical" effects produced on this item by changes in the

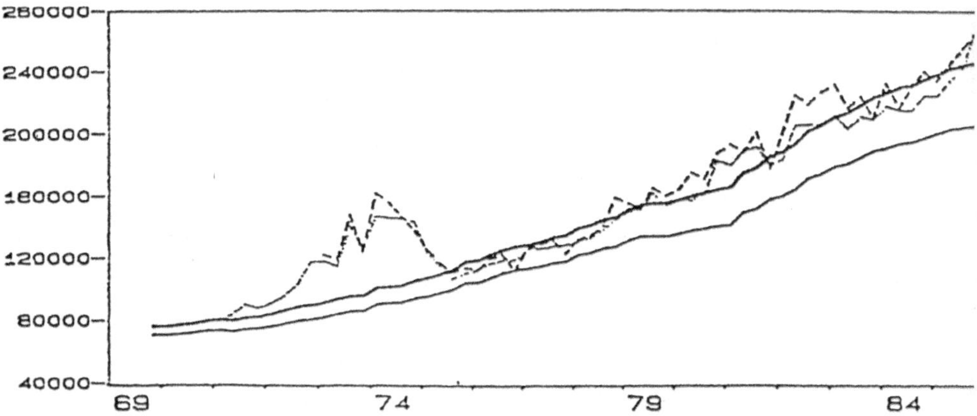

millions of francs

————————	Notes issued
···········	Adjusted base
—+—+—+—+	Notes + compulsory reserves
– – – – – – –	Notes + compulsory reserves + Treasury account

Figure 1. Different definitions of Central Bank money

level of the reserve requirement ratios. We have applied the following procedure for the purpose of theoretical correction:

If $B_1(t)$ ... $(B_n(t)$ are the statutory bases for calculating reserves at the respective rates of $\tau_1(t)$, $\tau_2(t)$, ..., $\tau_n(t)$, (for instance, at present $\tau_1 = 5\%$ for B_1 = demand deposits; $\tau_2 = 1\%$ for B_2 = term deposits, etc.), and if L(t) is the amount of excess reserves maintained by the banks, the level of reserves as shown in the Central Bank's liabilities will be:

$$R(t) = \sum_{i=1}^{n} \tau_t(t) B_i(t) + L(t)$$

We may therefore calculate reserves at theoretical constant rates $\bar{\tau}_1$, $\bar{\tau}_2$, ..., $\bar{\tau}_n$, by means of the equation:

$$\bar{R}(t) = \sum_{i=1}^{m} \bar{\tau}_i B_i(t) + L(t)$$

where $\bar{\tau}_1$ represents the constant rate chosen at an arbitrary date, applied to the base $B_1(t)$ at each period t, so that

$$R(t) = \underbrace{\sum_{i=1}^{n} \tau_i(t)B_i(t) + L(t)}_{\text{observed reserves}} = \underbrace{\sum_{i=1}^{m} (\tau_i(t)-\bar{\tau}_i)B_i(t)}_{\text{effect of rate changes}} + \underbrace{\sum_{i=1}^{m} \bar{\tau}_i B_i(t) + L(t)}_{\bar{R}\text{, reserves calculated at constant rate}}$$

In the same manner, albeit with a few approximations dictated by statistical considerations, we may define a series (R) of required reserves at constant rates. The rates used were 5% for demand deposits, 1% for term deposits, and 0% for bank credits. M3R is fully included in the reserves base.

The "adjusted monetary base" aggregate thus subjected to econometric analysis consists of:

– notes issued by the Banque de France,
– required (theoretical) reserves at constant rates.

These two (quarterly) series were corrected for seasonal variations. The definition of this "adjusted monetary base" aggregate is close to that of the "quantity of Central Bank money" currently used in the Federal Republic of Germany.

Once the impact of changes in required reserve rates has been eliminated, and taking into account the low level of these rates during the period under investigation, variations in the "adjusted base" aggregate turn out to be governed almost entirely by those in the "notes" component. So it is not surprising to find that, when related to GDP or to other money aggregates, the adjusted base displays a familiar downwards trend.

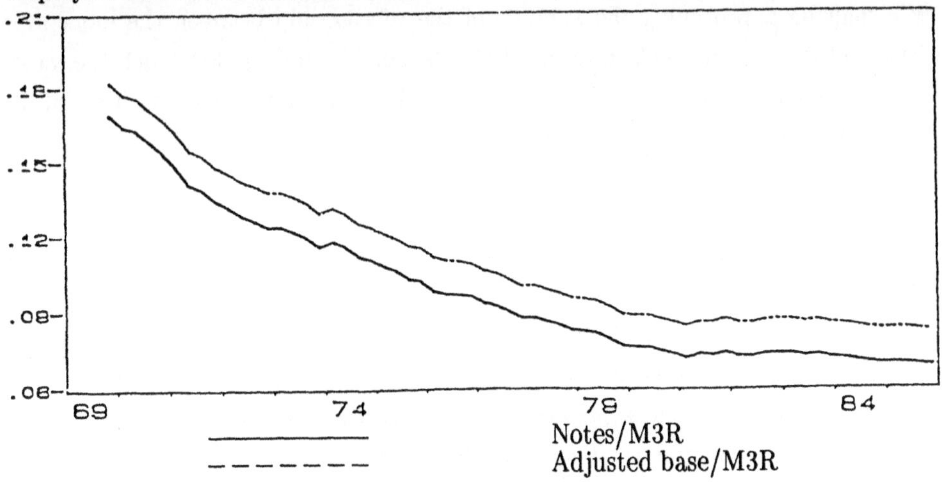

Figure 2. Adjusted base as a proportion of M3R

Analysed in terms of growth rate, the aggregate is subject to wide quarterly swings. This instability diminishes when one considers growth over 2 or, better, 4 quarters.

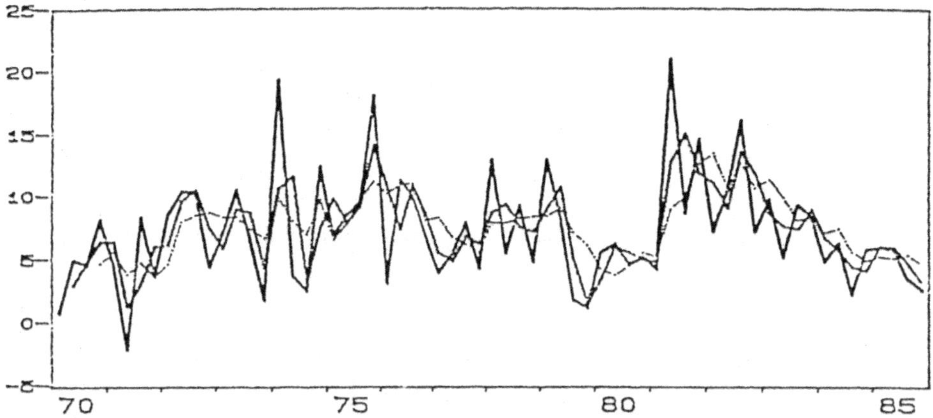

per cent ------ over 1 quarter
——— over 2 quarters
+++++++ over 4 quarters

Figure 3. Twelve–month change in adjusted base

These findings are in line with those of Frochen and Maarek (1979), with the proviso that switching to an adjusted aggregate will attenuate its swings.

4. SPECIFYING THE ECONOMETRIC RELATIONSHIP

We shall be approaching the analysis of the relationship between the monetary base and the money stock in terms of the demand for money, for which the most commonly used specification is the following: for a broad aggregate such as M3R, the level that economic agents deem to be optimal is M* such that

$$\frac{M^*}{p} = g(Q^*)^{\delta_1}(i_1)^{\gamma_1} \tag{1}$$

M^*/p = "real" desired holdings

Q^* = exponential smoothing of GDP volume, which is a rough indicator of the level of wealth accumulated by economic agents

i_1 = a rate of interest paid on assets substitutable for M

δ_1, γ_1 = corresponding coefficients of elasticity

g = constant

or, in logarithms

$$\text{Log}\left[\frac{M_t^*}{p_t}\right] = \delta_1 \text{ Log}(Q_t^*) + \gamma_1 \text{ Log}(i_{1,t}) + c_1 \qquad (2)$$

and the specification tested describes a simple process of adjustment of the actually observed aggregate M/p around its equilibrium level M*/p:

$$\text{Log}\left[\frac{M_t}{p_t}\right] = (1-\mu) \text{ Log}\left[\frac{M_{t-1}}{p_{t-1}}\right] + \mu \text{ Log}\left[\frac{M_t^*}{p_t}\right] \qquad (3)$$

where $\mu \epsilon]0,1[$ is a characteristic parameter of the speed of adjustment. From equations (2) and (3) one can easily derive a self–regressive equation capable of being subjected to econometric analysis:

$$\text{Log}\left[\frac{M_t}{p_t}\right] = (1-\mu) \text{ Log}\left[\frac{M_{t-1}}{p_{t-1}}\right] + \delta_1' \text{ Log}(Q_t^*) + \gamma_1' \text{ Log}(i_{1,t}) + c_1' \qquad (4)$$

One can apply the same type of analysis to the narrow "monetary base" aggregate. Indeed, it is not unreasonable to assume that its components (and more particularly notes in circulation) are subject to demand on the part of non–financial agents in order to conduct transactions or just to hold them (as a financial asset): these are the underlying theoretical determinants of the foregoing econometric specification.

This brings us to a monetary base demand equation whose specification is identical to the money demand function (4):

$$\text{Log}\left[\frac{B_t}{p_t}\right] = (1-\lambda) \text{ Log}\left[\frac{B_{t-1}}{p_{t-1}}\right] + \delta_2 \text{ Log}(Q_t^*) + \gamma_2 \text{ Log}(i_{2,t}) + c_2 \qquad (5)$$

where logically i_2, the interest rate on short term assets capable of being substituted for unremunerated reserves, is the money market rate.

Indeed, one can point to another theoretical foundation of a "monetary base demand". The existence of a credit divisor or – which is practically the same thing – of an equilibrium relation for B/M may be expressed in the form:

$$\frac{B}{M} = f(i_1, i_2, ...) \qquad (6)$$

By means of a simple adjustment procedure, one plausible specification would be:

$$\text{Log}(B^*) = \text{Log}(M^*) + k \qquad (7a)$$

$$k = k(i_1, i_2, ...) \qquad (7b)$$

$$\text{Log } (B) = (1-\theta)\text{Log}(B-1) + \text{Log}(B^*) \qquad (7c)$$

This last equation could also be written as:

$$\text{Log}\left[\frac{B}{p}\right] = (1-\theta)\ \text{Log}\left[\frac{B}{p}\right]_{-1} + \theta\ \text{Log}\left[\frac{B^*}{p}\right] - (1-\theta)\ \text{Log}\left[\frac{p}{p_{-1}}\right] \tag{8}$$

hence

$$\text{Log}\left[\frac{B}{p}\right] = (1-\theta)\ \text{Log}\left[\frac{B}{p}\right]_{-1} + \theta\ \text{Log}\left[\frac{M^*}{p}\right] + \theta k - (1-\theta)\ \text{Log}\left[\frac{p}{p_{-1}}\right] \tag{9}$$

and, if (M^*/p) is given by the long term money demand relation (2), it becomes

$$\text{Log}\left[\frac{B}{p}\right] = (1-\theta)\ \text{Log}\left[\frac{B}{p}\right]_{-1} + \theta\delta_1\ \text{Log}(Q^*) + \theta\gamma_1\ \text{Log}(i_1)$$
$$- (1-\theta)\ \text{Log}\left[\frac{p}{p_{-1}}\right] + c_3 \tag{10}$$

This last relationship offers a clear justification of the adoption of the same theoretical specification for B as for M, with two provisos:

- equation (10) depends on i_1, the rate of alternative holdings to M, but i_2, the rate of interest applying to interest–earning monetary assets that are substitutable for B, enters the equation in so far as the divisor k itself depends on it.
- equation (10) includes the inflation rate, $\text{Log}(p/p_{-1})$, as an explanatory variable.

The econometric adjustments made on the basis of equations (4), (5) and (10) appear to be acceptable for the money stock M (estimate period 1973.1 – 1985.4). On the contrary, they appear to be poor for the monetary base: the values of the Student statistic for certain coefficients in the equations are less than 2 in absolute terms; furthermore, the long term elasticity of B relative to the money market rate is more or less nil. On the other hand, values for the speed of adjustment are plausible in both cases, and the elasticity of B relative to Q^* has the expected sign, which merely reflects the long term decline in the proportion of notes in financial assets as a whole. Tests have shown that incorporating additional explanatory variables into the demand function is not entirely satisfactory. We have therefore sought a different approach, by transforming the above equations so as to be able to analyse the ratio B/M directly.

To do this we have retreated the equations (7c) deflated and (3):

$$\begin{cases} \text{Log}\left[\frac{B}{p}\right] = (1-\lambda)\left[\frac{B}{p}\right]_{-1} + \lambda\ \text{Log}\left[\frac{B^*}{p}\right] \\ \\ \text{Log}\left[\frac{M}{p}\right] = (1-\mu)\text{Log}\left[\frac{M}{p}\right]_{-1} + \mu\ \text{Log}\left[\frac{M^*}{p}\right] \end{cases}$$

These two equations can be rewritten in the following form:

$$\text{Log}\left[\frac{B}{B_{-1}}\right] = -\lambda\ \text{Log}(B_{-1}) + (1-\lambda)\text{Log}\left[\frac{p}{p_{-1}}\right] + \lambda\ \text{Log}\ B^* \tag{11a}$$

$$\text{Log}\left[\frac{M}{M_{-1}}\right] = -\mu\ \text{Log}\left[M_{-1}\right] + (1-\mu)\text{Log}\left[\frac{p}{p_{-1}}\right] + \mu\ \text{Log}(M^*) \tag{11b}$$

By multiplying the former by μ, the latter by $(-\lambda)$ and by adding them, one obtains

$$\mu\ \text{Log}\left[\frac{B}{B_{-1}}\right] - \lambda\ \text{Log}\left[\frac{M}{M_{-1}}\right] = \lambda\mu\ \text{Log}\left[\frac{M}{B}\right]_{-1} - (\lambda-\mu)\text{Log}\left[\frac{p}{p_{-1}}\right] + \lambda\mu\ \text{Log}\left[\frac{B^*}{M^*}\right] \tag{12}$$

or

$$\text{Log}\left[\frac{B}{B_{-1}}\right] = \frac{\lambda}{\mu}\ \text{Log}\left[\frac{M}{M_{-1}}\right] - \lambda\ \text{Log}\left[\frac{B}{M}\right]_{-1} + \frac{\mu-\lambda}{\mu}\ \text{Log}\left[\frac{p}{p_{-1}}\right] + \lambda\ \text{Log}\left[\frac{B^*}{M^*}\right] \tag{13}$$

We can recognise equation (13) as the specification of an error correction model, with two complementary explanatory variables, namely:

- the inflation rate, $\text{Log}\left[\frac{p}{p_{-1}}\right] \simeq \frac{p - p_{-1}}{p_{-1}}$
- the desired level of the ratio B/M, namely B^*/M^* which is a function of permanent income Q^* and of certain interest rates.

It is this "error correction" type model which serves as a basis for the econometric estimates that follow. It can also be written in terms of the levels of the variables (rather than in terms of their growth rates) by means of a trivial algebraic transformation:

$$\text{Log}\left[\frac{B}{M}\right] = \frac{\lambda-\mu}{\mu}\ \text{Log}\left[\frac{M}{M_{-1}}\right] + (1-\lambda)\text{Log}\left[\frac{B}{M}\right]_{-1} + \frac{\mu-\lambda}{\lambda}\ \text{Log}\left[\frac{p}{p_{-1}}\right] + \lambda\ \text{Log}\left[\frac{B^*}{M^*}\right] \tag{14}$$

5. ECONOMETRIC FINDINGS

The econometric test deals almost precisely with the preceding theoretical specification, provided three modifications are made:

- the introduction of a dummy variable "POST81" with a value of 0 prior to 1981 and 1 after that date, so as to be able to chart the divergence of the Base/M3R ratio trend which occurred in the first quarter of 1981, this movement being ascribable in its entirety to the sudden spurt in the amount of notes withdrawn from the banks by the public;

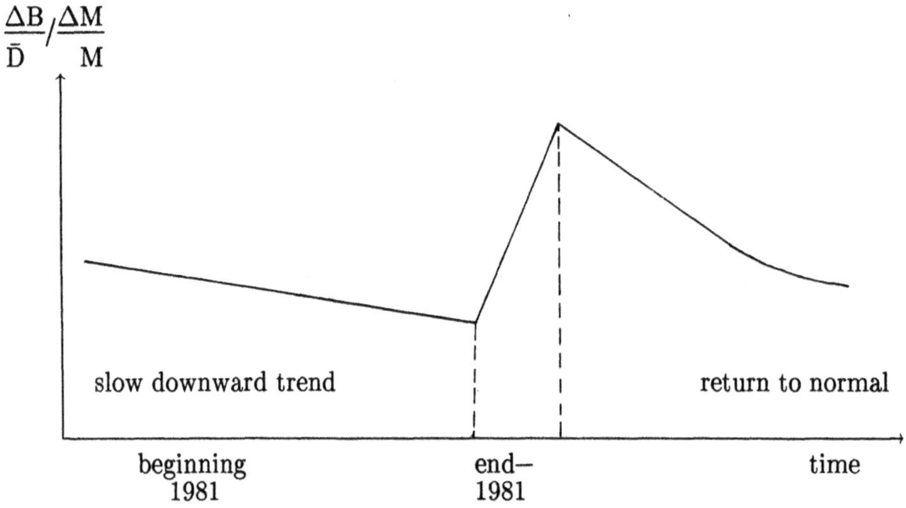

Figure 4

- the presence of another dummy variable in 1974.1 to take account of disturbances due to a bank strike in that period;
- the absence of the "inflation rate" variable, which does not appear to be econometrically significant.

The following adjustment is obtained:

$$\frac{\Delta B}{B} = \underset{(3.0)}{0.43}\,\frac{\Delta M}{M} - \underset{(-5.7)}{0.30}\,\mathrm{Log}\left[\frac{B}{M}\right]_{-1} - \underset{(-5.8)}{0.52}\,\mathrm{Log}(Q^*)$$

$$- \underset{(-2.0)}{0.015}[\mathrm{LogTMM} - \mathrm{LogTOB}] + \underset{(6.2)}{0.027}\,\mathrm{POST81}$$

$$+ \underset{(4.0)}{0.031}\,\mathrm{DUM74.1} + \underset{(5.8)}{5.7}$$

Standard deviation of error: 0.00726; time frame: 1973.1 – 1985.4

$F = 12.5$; $R^2 = 0.624$; $DW = 2.50$

The corresponding adjustment obtained in using the levels of the variables yields consistent results:

$$\mathrm{Log}\left[\frac{B}{M}\right] = - \underset{(-3.9)}{0.55}\left[\frac{\Delta M}{M}\right] + \underset{(13.9)}{0.71}\,\mathrm{Log}\left[\frac{B}{M}\right]_{-1} - \underset{(-5.8)}{0.51}\,\mathrm{Log}\,Q^*$$

$$- \underset{(-2.0)}{0.015}[\mathrm{Log(MMR)(BR)}] + \underset{(6.2)}{0.027}\mathrm{POST81} + \underset{(4.0)}{0.03}\,\mathrm{DUM74.1} + \underset{(5.8)}{5.6}$$

Standard deviation of error: 0.0071; $F = 447.1$; $R^2 = 0.998$; $DW = 2.50$

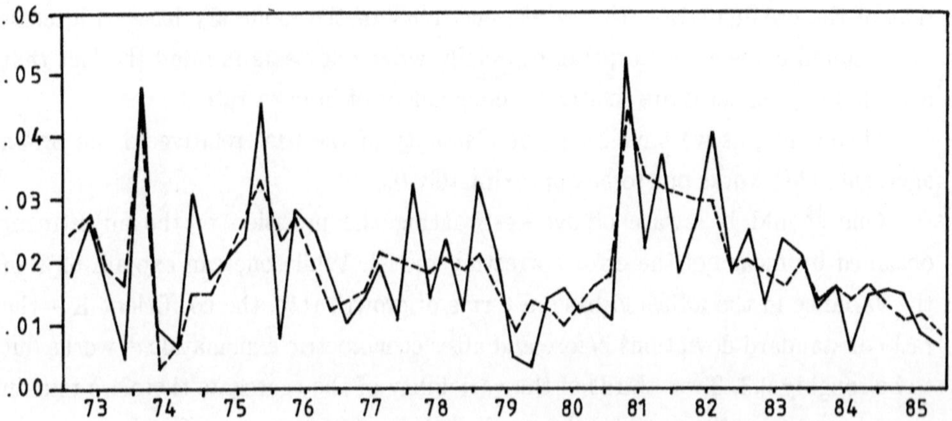

Figure 5. Quarterly rate of change in the (adjusted) base

6. INTERPRETING ECONOMETRIC RESULTS

On the basis of the level–specified error correction model, we can calculate directly the elasticities of the ratio B/M relative to the money market rate and the bond rate respectively.

$$\text{Log}\,\frac{B}{M} = \theta\,\text{Log}\left[\frac{B}{M}\right]_{-1} + \epsilon\,\text{Log(i)} + \text{other variables} \Longrightarrow \frac{d\left[\frac{B}{M}\right] / \left[\frac{B}{M}\right]}{d\,i/i}$$

is worth $\frac{\epsilon}{1-\theta}$ in the long run.

Given that we have forced equality upon the two elasticities in the adjustment (by choosing Log(TMM)[1] – Log(TOB)[2] as an explanatory variable), their common value is –0.015/(1–0.71), which is to say:

Long term elasticity of ratio (B/M) relative to TMM ≃ –0.05

Long term elasticity of ratio (B/M) relative to TOB ≃ +0.05

This is a very weak value. This suggests that, over the period covered by the estimate, the linkages between monetary base and money stock were not all that dependent on changes in the difference between long and short term rates. This result can be accounted for entirely by the weak sensitivity of the monetary base to interest rates earned on alternative assets. In direct estimates of demand functions, this sensitivity appears to be 3 to 5 times lower than for the broad aggregate. If the logic governing the workings of the monetary system is indeed that of the credit divisor, this weak sensitivity of the monetary base to interest rates should come as no surprise, especially when one bears in mind the fact that note–holding patterns are relatively independent of interest rates.

Meanwhile, as we have seen, the elasticity of the base relative to the broad aggregate (M) works out to be approximately 0.5.

One should be aware of over–estimating the precision of the adjustment obtained by means of the error correction model. While one can explain 62% of the variance in the adjusted base in terms of growth rate, the coefficient R – the ratio of standard deviations before and after econometric explanation – works out to be roughly 0.3. Two–thirds of the variability of the aggregate therefore remain unexplained; in other words, the statistical series appear to suffer from strong residual interference.

7. CONCLUSION

There is a certain statistical regularity in the movements of the ratio monetary base/money stock during the period 1973 to 1985. Its profile is influenced by certain variables (permanent income, interest rates), as predicted in the laws of economic theory. However, it looks as if the ratio B/M fluctuates fairly widely around its trendline, and econometric analysis is able to chart fluctuations only imperfectly.

These findings are neither all that surprising nor disappointing. Throughout the whole of the period under review, the form of regulation applied by the monetary authorities – which depend on quasi–direct control of the quantity of money – made the monetary base rather less important than it often is in the creation of money, and tended to diminish the sensitivity of short term variations in the base to interest rate swings. Now that this method of regulation is being replaced by a system based on intervention in the money market, i.e. on interest rate management, we can expect the "bank reserves" component to start obeying a different set of behavioural rules from those in operation until now, and the monetary base to appear far more sensitive to interest rates.

NOTE

1) TMM: money market rate
2) TOB: long term bonds yield

REFERENCES

Bruneel, D. and J.P. Patat (1985), "Dix ans de régulation monétaire (les incidences de l'encadrement du crédit)", *Cahiers Economiques et Monétaires*, no. 18.

Burger, A.E. and R.H. Rasch (1977), "Revision of Monetary Base", Federal Reserve Bank of Saint Louis (July).

Debonneuil, X. and Y. Barroux (1985), "Liens entre les instruments et les objectifs intermédiaires de la politique monétaire: quelques éléments de réflexion", Banque de France, Note.

Frochen, P. and G. Maarek (1979), "Réfléxion sur le concept de base monétaire en France", *Cahiers Economiques et Monétaires*, no. 11.

Frost, P.A. (1977), "Short Run Fluctuations in Money Multipliers and Monetary Control", *Journal of Money, Credit and Banking* (February).

Guillaumont–Jeanneney, S. (1978), "L'instabilité du multiplicateur de crédit en France compromet–elle l'efficacité de la politique d'open–market?", *Economie et Sociétés*, série MO, no. 1.

Le Bourra, J. (1962), "Création de la monnaie et multiplicateur de crédit", *Revue Economique*, 13.

PART IV

CAUSALITY ANALYSIS AND THE EFFECTS OF MONETARY POLICY

CHAPTER 7

CAUSAL RELATIONSHIPS BETWEEN MONEY AND INCOME IN THE SPANISH ECONOMY

A.Aznar and F.J. Trivez, *University of Zaragoza, Spain*

1. INTRODUCTION

An important issue in empirical macroeconomics is to determine whether or not changes in the money supply affect the real sector variables. Different models have been proposed, based on alternative sets of assumptions, and in which the absence or presence of money illusion plays an important role in determining the type of relationships between nominal and real variables.

We find a first class model in which, assuming perfect information and market clearing assumptions, there is no sign of money illusion, and in which the variations in some nominal variables only affect other nominal variables but have no effect on real variables.

A second class of model assumes market clearing and rationally formed expectations. An important implication in these models is that only unanticipated movements in the money supply affect the level of economic activity. Predicted movements in the money supply will produce no movement in real output, since they do not affect the typical supplier's view of his relative price. The unanticipated changes in money supply, by their very nature, are random and therefore the authorities cannot use monetary policy to reduce the fluctuations in output. There is a non–controllable money illusion and no monetary policy can have any systematic impact upon the level of real output.

Finally, there is a third class of model in which an assumption of sticky prices is incorporated with rational or other types of expectation schemes and in which money illusion appears. In these models both anticipated, as well as unanticipated, money changes affect real output and a monetary policy can be

P. Artus and Y. Barroux (eds.), Monetary Policy, 133–161.

drawn in order to control the fluctuations in output.

What is more relevant from our point of view is that all these alternatives formulate different empirical relationships between real and nominal variables, in particular between real National Income and Money Supply.

In a series of papers, Barro (1977, 1978), Barro and Rush (1980), Leiderman (1980) and Rush (1986) presented empirical evidence supporting the hypothesis that derivations of output from its natural rate are affected only by unanticipated monetary changes, these being defined as the residuals of the relation which account for the money supply behaviour.

Following an alternative procedure, Mishkin (1982a, 1982b) and Gordon (1982), find support for the alternative proposition that there is some short term influence of anticipated money growth on output.

In this paper, following an alternative approach outlined in McGee and Stasiak (1985), we consider a bivariate vector autoregressive model for real output and money supply. Then, using some concepts from what we might call the "causality literature", we design a new test procedure and we apply it to quarterly data from the Spanish economy.

The paper is organised as follows: in Section 2 we present the model and the definition and tests of causality, making reference to some works in which the relation between income and money supply is analysed using causality concepts. Section 3 summarises the econometric model selection process used. Section 4 presents the empirical results for the Spanish economy. The last section highlights some of the results and conclusions and also presents some suggestions for future research.

2. MODEL AND DEFINITION OF CAUSALITY

Granger (1969) has proposed a definition of "causality" in econometric systems which has frequently been applied in empirical work. Briefly, a time series $\{x_t\}$ is said to "cause" another time series $\{y_t\}$ if past values of x are useful for predicting y_t when the past values of y have been taken into account. The definition is symmetric for y causing x, and feedback is said to exist if causality is present in both directions. In what follows, we shall assume that the domain of relevant information is restricted to past values of x and y, x and y are jointly covariance stationary time series with autoregressive representation, and the set of predictors is constrained to be linear in past x and y.

Consider the following bivariate vector autoregressive model:

$$\begin{bmatrix} A(L) & B(L) \\ C(L) & D(L) \end{bmatrix} \begin{bmatrix} y_t \\ x_t \end{bmatrix} = \begin{bmatrix} u_{1t} \\ u_{2t} \end{bmatrix} \tag{1}$$

where A(L), B(L), C(L) and D(L) are polynomials in the lag operator, that under the normalisation rule adopted can be written as:

$A(L) = 1 - a_1 L - a_2 L^2 - \dots ;$ $C(L) = -c_o - c_1 L - c_2 L^2 - \dots$

$B(L) = -b_o - b_1 L - b_2 L^2 - \dots ;$ $D(L) = 1 - d_1 L - d_2 L^2 - \dots$

L being the lag operator, so that $L^n Z_t = Z_{t-n}$

u_{1t} and u_{2t} are random variables, with:

$$E\left[\begin{bmatrix} u_{1t} \\ u_{2t} \end{bmatrix} (u_{1s} u_{2s})\right] = \begin{cases} \Sigma & \text{if } t=s \\ 0 & \text{if } t \neq s \end{cases} \tag{2}$$

where

$$\Sigma = \begin{bmatrix} \sigma_{11} & \sigma_{12} \\ \sigma_{21} & \sigma_{22} \end{bmatrix} \tag{3}$$

As Granger (1982) says: "the concept of causality ... is essentially a reduced–form causality, because the time lag between cause and effect is central, and vital, for the definition".

According to this, the appropriate definition of causality must be established from the reduced form of (1), which can be written as:

$$\begin{bmatrix} y_t \\ x_t \end{bmatrix} = \begin{bmatrix} \bar{\pi}_{11}(L) & \bar{\pi}_{12}(L) \\ \bar{\pi}_{21}(L) & \bar{\pi}_{22}(L) \end{bmatrix} \begin{bmatrix} y_t \\ x_t \end{bmatrix} + \begin{bmatrix} v_{1t} \\ v_{2t} \end{bmatrix} \tag{4}$$

where

$$\begin{bmatrix} \bar{\pi}_{11}(L) & \bar{\pi}_{12}(L) \\ \bar{\pi}_{21}(L) & \bar{\pi}_{22}(L) \end{bmatrix} = \frac{1}{1-b_o c_o} \begin{bmatrix} \bar{A}(L) + b_o \bar{C}(L) & \bar{B}(L) + b_o \bar{D}(L) \\ \bar{C}(L) + c_o \bar{A}(L) & \bar{D}(L) + c_o \bar{B}(L) \end{bmatrix} \tag{5}$$

$$\begin{bmatrix} v_{1t} \\ v_{2t} \end{bmatrix} = \frac{1}{1-b_o c_o} \begin{bmatrix} u_{1t} + b_o u_{2t} \\ u_{2t} + c_o u_{1t} \end{bmatrix} \tag{6}$$

$$E\left[\begin{bmatrix} v_{1t} \\ v_{2t} \end{bmatrix} (v_{1s} \quad v_{2s})\right] = \begin{cases} \Omega & \text{if } t=s \\ 0 & \text{if } t \neq s \end{cases} \tag{7}$$

with

$$\Omega = \begin{bmatrix} w_{11} & w_{12} \\ w_{21} & w_{22} \end{bmatrix} = \begin{bmatrix} 1 & -b_o \\ -c_o & 1 \end{bmatrix}^{-1} \Sigma \begin{bmatrix} 1 & -b_o \\ -c_o & 1 \end{bmatrix}^{\prime -1} \tag{8}$$

being

$$\begin{bmatrix} \bar{A}(L) & \bar{B}(L) \\ \bar{C}(L) & \bar{D}(L) \end{bmatrix} = \begin{bmatrix} A(L) & B(L) \\ C(L) & D(L) \end{bmatrix} - \begin{bmatrix} 1 & -b_0 \\ -c_0 & 1 \end{bmatrix} \tag{9}$$

From this reduced form, Granger's definition of causality can be established, namely that y does not cause x if:

$$\bar{\pi}_{21}(L) = 0 \tag{10}$$

Alternatively, x does not cause y if:

$$\bar{\pi}_{12}(L) = 0 \tag{11}$$

Consequently, x and y are independent if neither causes the other. That is:

$$\bar{\pi}_{21}(L) = 0 \quad \text{and} \quad \bar{\pi}_{12}(L) = 0 \tag{12}$$

Alternative procedures have been proposed in the literature as practical tests for the presence and direction of causality, namely: a cross–correlation technique, suggested by Pierce and Haugh (1977), which is essentially a test of independence rather than a test for causal direction; a one–sided distributed lag approach implied by Granger (1969) and formalised by Sargent (1967); a two–sided distributed lag method advanced by Sims (1972); and a modified version of the Sims' test developed by Geweke (see Harvey, 1981 and Geweke et al, 1983). A detailed discussion of these procedures can be found in Trivez (1986) and Aznar and Trivez (1986).

Since the publication of Sims' (1972) pathfinding paper on the relationship between money and income, we have witnessed an outpouring of empirical studies that utilise one or more of the foregoing procedures to test the relationship between these economic magnitudes. A sample of this extensive literature can be found in Table 1. The first column comprises the name of the authors and the dates of publication of their work; the second column specifies the procedures used to test for causality (Granger's, Sims', Pierce–Haugh's and Hsiao's); in the third column, we determine the variables used for the procedures; in the fourth, the period considered and country of reference are recorded; in the fifth, the type of data employed (yearly or quarterly, seasonally adjusted or not, as well as, if they are used in logarithms, the first differences or levels); and finally, in the sixth column, we set out the main results obtained with regard to the direction of causality.

A major problem associated with the use of these tests, however, is the arbitrary determination of the order of the autoregressive process. In recent years, some alternative procedures have been proposed based on Akaike's

Table 1(a)

AUTHORS	METHOD	VARIABLES	PERIOD COUNTRY	DATA FILTER	RESULTS
SIMS (1972)	SIMS	M = (MB, M1) NGNP	1947-1969 U.S.A.	Q.D. (S.A.) $(1-0.75L)^2$ (ln)	$M1 \rightarrow NGNP$ $MB \rightarrow NGNP$
BARTH and BENNETT (1974)	SIMS	M = (M1, M2) GNP	1957-1972 CANADA	Q.D. (S.A.) $(1-0.75L)^2$ (ln)	$M1 \overset{d}{\underset{d}{\leftrightarrows}} GNP$ $M2 \perp GNP$
ELLIOT (1975)	SIMS	ΔM $\bar{\Delta} NGNP$	1953-1969 U.S.A.	Q.D. (S.A.) $(1-0.75L)^2$ (ln)	$\Delta M \rightarrow \Delta NGNP$
SHARPE and MILLER (1975)	SIMS	M1 GNP	1957-1974 CANADA	Q.D. (S.A.) $(1-0.75L)^2$	$M1 \rightarrow GNP$
WILLIAMS, GOODHART and GOWLAND (1976)	SIMS	M = (M1, M3) GDP = (RGDP, PGDP)	1958-1971 U.K.	Q.D. $(1-a_1L-a_2L)(1-L)$	$GDP \rightarrow M1$ $M1 \rightarrow PGDP$
AUERBACH and RUTNER (1978)	SIMS	M1 GNP	1953-1973 CANADA	Q.D. (S.A.) AR and MA filters (ln)	$M1 \overset{d}{\rightarrow} GNP$
MEHRA (1978a)	SIMS	$m = \frac{M}{PGNP}$ y = RGNP	1952-1972 U.S.A.	Q.D. (S.A.) $(1-KL)^2; 0<K<1$	$y \not\rightarrow m$

Table 1(b)

AUTHORS	METHOD	VARIABLES	PERIOD COUNTRY	DATA FILTER	RESULTS
MEHRA (1978b)	SIMS	ΔMB ΔGNP = (ΔRGNP, ΔNGNP, ΔPGNP)	1952-1972 U.S.A.	Q.D. (S.A.) $(1-K1)^2$; $0<K<1$	ΔMB $\rightarrow$ ΔRGNP ΔMB $\rightarrow$ ΔNGNP ΔMB $\rightleftarrows$ ΔPGNP
BRILLEMBOURG and KHAN (1979)	PIERCE-HAUGH and SIMS	M NNP = (RNNP, NNPN, PNNP)	1870-1975 U.S.A.	A.D. ARIMA filter	M $\rightarrow$ NNNP
FEIGE and PEARCE (1979)	I) PIERCE-HAUGH II) GRANGER III) SIMS	M = (M1, MB) NGNP	1947-1969 U.S.A.	Q.D. (S.A. and S.U.) METHOD I: ARIMA filter METHOD II: Δln METHOD III: $(1-0.75L)^2$ (1-L) and ARIMA filter	METHOD I: Independence METHOD II: Independence METHOD III: M1 $\rightarrow$ GNP M2 $\rightarrow$ GNP
HSIAO (1979a)	HSIAO (Akaike's FPE)	M = (M1, M2) NGNP	1955-1977 CANADA	Q.D. (S.A.) (Δ^2ln)	M1 $\rightleftarrows$ NGNP NGNP $\rightarrow$ M2
HSIAO (1979b)	HSIAO (Akaike's FPE)	M = (M1, M2) NGNP	1947-1977 U.S.A.	Q.D. (S.A.) $(1-L)(1-0.75L)^2$ (ln)	M1 $\rightleftarrows$ NGNP M2 $\rightarrow$ NGNP
MEHRA and SPENCER (1979)	I) SIMS II) GRANGER	ΔMB ΔNGNP	1952-1974 U.S.A.	Q.D. (S.A.) $(1-KL)^2$; $0<k<1$	ΔMB $\rightarrow$ ΔNGNP
MIXON, PRATT and WALLACE (1979)	GRANGER	(U.S.) M1 (U.K.) NGNP	1962-1977 U.S.A.-U.K.	Q.D. (S.A.) (ln)	(USA) M1 $\not\rightarrow$ (UK) NGNP during the PFER (1962-1970) (USA) M1 $\rightarrow$ (UK) NGNP during the PFLER (1974-1977)

Table 1(c)

AUTHORS	METHOD	VARIABLES	PERIOD COUNTRY	DATA FILTER	RESULTS
PAUTLER and RIVARD (1979)	SIMS	M=(M1,M2,M3,M4,M5,M6,MB) NGNP	1947-1976 U.S.A.	Q.D. (S.A.) $(1-0,75L)^2$ (ln)	M → NGNP except: M6 ⇄ NGMP MB ⊥ NGNP
SARLO (1979)	SIMS	M=(M1,M2,M3) GNP	1952-1961 (PFLER) and 1962-1970 (PFER) CANADA	Q.D. (S.A.) AR and MA filters (ln)	M1 → GMP during the PFLER M1 ⊥ GNP during the PFER
HUFFMAN and LOTHIAN (1980)	GRANGER	M* NGNP	a) 1837-1870 b) 1870-1914 c) 1914-1968 d) 1837-1968 U.K.	A.D. (ln and Δln)	a) M → NGNP b) M ⊥ NGNP c) M ⇄ NGNP d) M ⇄ NGNP
CUDDINGTON (1981)	GRANGER	M NGNP	1958-1971 U.K.	Q.D.	NGNP → M
HSIAO (1981)	HSIAO (Akaike's FPE)	M = (M1,M2) NGNP	1947-1977 U.S.A.	Q.D. (S.A.) $(\Delta^2 ln)$	M1 ⇄ NGNP M2 → NGNP
HSIAO (1982)	HSIAO- Multivariate (Akaike's FPE)	M2 NGNP BR	1955-1977 CANADA	Q.D. (S.A.) $(\Delta^2 ln)$	NGNP ⇄ BR BR → M2
KOMURA (1982)	SIMS	M2 GNP=(NGNP,RGNP,PGNP)	a) 1955-1964 b) 1955-1971 c) 1971-1980 JAPAN	Q.D. (S.U.) $(1-KL)^2$; $0<K<1$	a) M2 ⇄ NGNP; M2 ⇄ RGNP; M2 ⇄ PGNP b) M2 ⇄ NGNP; RGNP → M2; PGNP → M2 c) NGNF → M2; RGNP ⊥ M2 → PGNP

Table 1(d)

AUTHORS	METHOD	VARIABLES	PERIOD COUNTRY	DATA FILTER	RESULTS
RAMACHANDRA (1983)	SIMS	M NNP = (RNNP, NNNP)	1951-1971 INDIA	A.D. (Δln)	Independence
KOMURA (1984)	SIMS	M1 GNP = (NGNP, RGNP, PGNP)	a) 1955-1964 (PFER) b) 1955-1971 (PFER) c) 1971-1980 (PFLER) JAPAN	Q.D. $(1-KL)^2; 0<K<1$	a) M1 $\overset{\rightarrow}{\underset{d}{\leftarrow}}$ NGNP; M1 $\overset{\rightarrow}{\underset{d}{\leftarrow}}$ RGNP; M1 ⇆ PGNP b) M1 → NGNP; M1 → RGNP; M1 ⇆ PGNP c) Independence
RAM (1984)	GRANGER	M = (M1, M2) GNP = (NGNP, RGNP, PGNP)	a) 1955-1964 b) 1955-1971 c) 1971-1980 JAPAN	Q.D. (U.S.) Δln	a) M1 → NGNP; M2 → NGNP; M1 → PGNP b) M1 ⇆ NGNP; M1 ⇆ PGNP M2 ⇆ NGNP; M2 → PGNP RGNP → M1; RGNP → M2 c) Independence (or weak causal ordering)

VARIABLES:
M = Money Stock
GNP = Gross National Product
NGNP = Nominal Gross National Product
RGNP = Real Gross National Product
PGNP = GNP deflator
GDP = Gross Domestic Product
RGDP = Real Gross Domestic Product
PGDP = GDP deflator
MB = Monetary Base
RNNP = Real Net National Product
NNNP = Nominal Net National Product
PNNP = NNP deflator
M* = 'High-Powered Money'
BR = Bank Rate (interest rate)
NNP = Net National Product

PERIOD:
PFER = Period of Fixed Exchange Rates
PFLER = Period of Flexible Exchange Rates

DATA:
QD = Quaterly Data
AD = Annual Data
SA = Seasonally Adjusted data
SU = Seasonally Unadjusted data

RESULTS:
A → B = A causes B
$A \underset{d}{\rightarrow} B$ = A weakly causes B
A ↛ B = A does not cause B
⊥ = Independence

information criteria, which fix empirically the order of lags of each variable in the system.

Hsiao (1979a, 1979b, 1981) suggests a procedure based on Akaike's (1969, 1970) final prediction error (FPE) criterion as a practical means of identifying the order of lags of each variable. As Hsiao (1981) says: "the method is appealing because it balances the risk due to the bias when a lower order is selected, and the risk due to the increase of variance when a higher order is selected". Other papers which test causality using Akaike's approach are Tjostheim (1981) and Caines et al (1981).

All these last studies suppose, in fact, alternative strategies for empirical model building, that is, for specifying dynamic models.

Following this line, we propose in the next section an alternative information criterion – the AVE criterion – which can be used to test Granger's causality.

3. ECONOMETRIC MODEL SELECTION PROCESS

In this section we are going to present a brief summary of the process followed in the next section when testing alternative econometric models. For more details, see Aznar (1986).

The process consists of three stages: (1) determination of spherical models; (2) determination of the informative models; and (3) determination of the corroborated models.

3.1 Determination of Spherical Models

By a spherical model we mean a model in which the random part is a white noise process. For models like those commented upon in Section 2, in which lagged dependent variables appear as explanatory variables, the Durbin–Watson test seems to be asymptotically defective vis–à–vis other tests proposed in the literature (see, for example, Nerlove and Wallis, 1966).

The most widely used alternative tests, with better asymptotic properties than those of the Durbin–Watson test, are: the h–test, Durbin (1970); the Box–Pierce test, Box and Pierce (1970); the Ljung–Box test, Ljung and Box (1978), and a series of tests derived around the application of the Lagrange multiplier test to dynamic models (see, for example, Breusch and Pagan, 1980 and Godfrey, 1978).

Although there are many simulation studies in which the properties of some of these tests have been compared, we feel that no clear conclusion has emerged on the relative performance of one of them vis–à–vis the others.

In this paper, we will pay special attention to a recent simulation study by Kiviet (1986). One of the major conclusions of this study is that: "Our Monte–Carlo results corroborate theoretical findings that the Durbin–Watson, Box–Pierce, and Ljung–Box tests for serial correlation should not be applied in regression models with lagged dependent variables". He then finds that the Lagrange multiplier type F–test, (he calls it LMF) appears to have the better properties. Suppose we are testing the null hypothesis of white noise disturbance against the alternative hypothesis of an AR(n) process. The LMF can be written:

$$LMF = \frac{T-k-n}{n} \frac{(RSS_{[x]} - RSS_{[x:\hat{V}_n]})}{RSS_{[x:\hat{V}_n]}} \tag{13}$$

where $RSS_{[x]}$ is the sum of squared residuals from the first equation of (4), which we can write as:

$$y = X\pi + v \tag{14}$$

where:

$$y = \begin{bmatrix} y_1 \\ y_2 \\ \vdots \\ y_T \end{bmatrix}; \quad X = \begin{bmatrix} y_o & y_{-1} & \cdots & y_{-M+1} & x_o & x_{-1} & \cdots & x_{-N+1} \\ y_1 & y_o & \cdots & y_{-M+2} & x_1 & x_o & \cdots & x_{-N+2} \\ \vdots & \vdots & & & \vdots & & & \vdots \\ y_{T-1} & y_{T-2} & \cdots & y_{T-M} & x_{T-1} & x_{T-2} & \cdots & x_{T-N} \end{bmatrix}$$

$$v = \begin{bmatrix} v_{11} \\ v_{12} \\ \vdots \\ v_{1T} \end{bmatrix}; \quad \pi' = \begin{bmatrix} \bar{\pi}^1_{11} \cdots \bar{\pi}^M_{11} & \bar{\pi}^1_{12} \cdots \bar{\pi}^N_{12} \end{bmatrix}$$

having supposed that M and N are the orders of $\bar{\pi}_{11}(L)$ and $\bar{\pi}_{12}(L)$. And $RSS_{[x:\hat{V}_n]}$ is the sum of squared residuals from the regression:

$$\hat{v} = X\gamma_1 + \hat{V}_n\gamma_2 + u \tag{15}$$

where γ_1 and γ_2 are M+N and n–element column vectors of parameters and $\hat{V}_n$ is $T \cdot n$ matrix:

$$\hat{V}_n = (\hat{v}_{-1}, \hat{v}_{-2}, \ldots, \hat{v}_{-n}) \tag{16}$$

being:

$$\hat{v}'_{-i} = (0,\ldots,0,\hat{v}_1,\ldots,\hat{v}_{T-i}) \quad (i=1,2,\ldots,n) \tag{17}$$

As Kiviet (1986) indicates: "... it seems reasonable to ignore the fact that LMF does not have an exact F distribution in dynamic models, and to use critical values from the F distribution with n and T–k–n degrees of freedom".

In this paper we will use this LMF test and other tests based on the Lagrange multiplier test, which can be written as:

$$LM = T \frac{(RSS_{[x]} - RSS_{[x:\hat{V}_n]})}{RSS_{[x]}} \qquad (18)$$

which is distributed, under the null hypothesis, as x_n^2.

3.2 Determination of the Informative Models

Here we restrict our attention to those models which, using the LM and LMF tests, are spherical.

Let y be a dependent variable, and $x_1, x_2, ..., x_k$ a set of variables. Let the j–th model be defined as:

$$M(j): y = X_j\pi_j + v_j \qquad j = 1, 2, ..., m;\ m = M + N \qquad (19)$$

where:

- y : vector of T observations of the dependent variable
- X_j : $T \cdot k_j$ matrix of observations of the k_j variables which occur in the j–th model
- π_j : vector of k_j parameters
- v_j : vector or T error terms of the j–th model.

Suppose that, for a period out of the sample, an observation for the k explanatory variables is available; let x_p be the vector of these k values and let y_p be the unknown value of the dependent variable for that period. The question is how to use the available information in order to determine which model to use from amongst the m model defined in (19) in order to predict that unknown value.

From each model in (19) define the corresponding OLS predictor as:

$$\hat{y}_p(j) = x_{pj}\hat{\pi}_j \qquad (20)$$

where

x_{pj} : the k_j subvector of observations of the variables present in the j–th model

$$\hat{\pi}_j = (X_j'X_j)^{-1}X_j'y$$

If we assume that each model in turn is true[1], we have

$$E_j[\hat{y}_p(j)] = x_{pj}\pi_j \tag{21}$$

$$\mathrm{var}[\hat{y}_p(j)] = \sigma_j^2 x_{pj}(X_j'X_j)^{-1}x_{pj}' \tag{22}$$

Since σ_j^2 is unknown, we define:

$$AVE(j) = \hat{\sigma}_j^2 x_{pj}(X_j'X_j)^{-1}x_{pj}' \tag{23}$$

where

$$\hat{\sigma}^2 = \frac{\hat{v}_j'\hat{v}_j}{T-k_j} \tag{24}$$

and:

$$\hat{v}_j = y - X_j\hat{\pi}_j \tag{25}$$

then we select that model for which the value of AVE is minimum.

Between two models, M_1 and M_2, we say that M_1 is more informative than M_2 if:

$$AVE(1) < AVE(2)$$

Is there any limit in order to determine whether a model is or is not informative? Assume a concrete probabilistic distribution for $y_p(j)$; then consider a particular significance level, ϵ_o, for which two values, d(1) and d(2), can be found, such that:

$$\mathrm{Prob}\ \{|\hat{y}_p(1) - E_1y_p| > d(1)\} = \epsilon_o$$

$$\mathrm{Prob}\ \{|\hat{y}_p(2) - E_2y_p| > d(2)\} = \epsilon_o$$

we can then say that a model is informative if $d(j) < d_o$, where d_o is fixed in such a way that it reflects our desired standards on prediction performance, given ϵ_o.

Alternatively, let us take a particular value of d, d_o, for which two values of ϵ, $\epsilon(1)$ and $\epsilon(2)$, can be found such that:

$$\mathrm{Prob}\ \{|\hat{y}_p(1) - E_1y_p| > d_o\} = \epsilon_{AVE}(1)$$

$$\mathrm{Prob}\ \{|\hat{y}_p(2) - E_2y_p| > d_o\} = \epsilon_{AVE}(2)$$

then we can say that a model is informative if $\epsilon_{AVE}(j) < \epsilon_o$, when ϵ_o is fixed in such a way that it reflects our desired standard of prediction performance, given d_o. Note that to each $\epsilon_{AVE}(j)$ there corresponds a $t_{AVE}(j)$ defined as:

$d_o = t_{AVE}(j) \cdot [AVE(j)]^{\frac{1}{2}}$

In sampling theory we can determine the sample size in such a way that the desired levels of both d and ϵ are satisfied. This is not usually the case in econometrics, where the sample size is given and where we can determine the level of either d or ϵ but not both.

3.3 Determination of the Corroborated Models

We have seen that, in order to be informative, a model has to account for some prediction performance standards. Suppose now that the value of the dependent variable for the non–sample period is available. Let y_p^* be this value. Given this new evidence, can we say that the informative content established previously for each model, in terms of the values taken by d and ϵ, are corroborated by y_p^*?

Define the following statistic:

$$t_{CB}(j) = \frac{y_p - \hat{y}_p(j)}{[var(\hat{y}_p(j))]^{\frac{1}{2}}} \tag{26}$$

then we have:

$\text{Prob}\,\{|t_{CB}(j)| \geq |t_{\epsilon/2}|\} = \epsilon$

For a particular sample, the statistic defined in (26) adopts a particular value, $t^*_{CB}(j)$. If we make $t^*_{CB}(j) = t_{\epsilon/2}$, the corresponding value of ϵ, which we call $\epsilon_{CB}(j)$, is the corroboration significance level of the j–th model. The null hypothesis, H_o: $y_p^* = E_j y$, is rejected for a level of significance equal or greater than $\epsilon_{CB}(j)$.

Assume a particular value of d, d_o. We have seen in the second stage that, given d_o, to each model there corresponds a value of ϵ, $\epsilon_{AVE}(j)$, then we say that the j–th model is corroborated when:

$\epsilon_{CB}(j) > \epsilon_{AVE}(j)$

or, equivalently, when:

$t^*_{CB}(j) < t_{AVE}(j)$

We can go further and order the corroborated models according to the value taken by the statistic:

$$t^*_{CB}(j)^2 + \log \hat{var}[\hat{y}_p(j)] \tag{27}$$

The smaller this statistic is, the higher the degree of corroboration of the corresponding model.

4. EMPIRICAL RESULTS

The data consists of annual growth rates of real GDP, calculated each quarter with respect to the same quarter of the previous year, and the M3 money supply corresponding to the Spanish economy for the period 1965 to 1984. These data are listed in Table A1 in the Appendix.

The values of the autocorrelation function of these two series can be seen in Tables A2(a) and A2(b) in the Appendix. They clearly show that GDP series are individually non–stationary. Since the validity of some statistics used in the process outlined in Section 3 rests on the stationarity of the model, some filtering process must be applied to the data. When studying more than one variable, the relevant question is whether the series are jointly stationary and not whether they are individually stationary. But although our starting point is a bivariate model, we estimate and test each relationship separately, so that univariate models may appear as alternative specifications which are worth considering.

For these reasons we were worried about the stationarity of each individual series. The first step was to take first and second differences, but still some nonstationarity remained. As an alternative we detrended both series, taking the residuals of the regression of each series on time. The values of the autocorrelation function of these two detrended series are presented in Tables A.2(c) and A.2(d) in the Appendix. They show that both series are clearly stationary, and we therefore decided to use them as raw material in our analysis, even though this solution has not been particularly favoured in the recent literature; see, for example, Nelson and Plosser (1982).

To these two detrended series we then applied the procedures outlined in the previous section. First, we eliminated the last two observations and estimated the models corresponding to all combinations of the lags of the two variables, considering up to 8 lags for each. We determined the spherical models, calculating the LM and LMF tests for n=1,2,4 and 8 lags, considering that a model is spherical if the null hypothesis of non–autocorrelation cannot be rejected at the 1% significance level. For all these spherical models, we calculated the values of the AVE and corroboration statistics, using the penultimate observation. Then the same analysis was repeated using the last observation. The final chosen model for each variable is obtained by paying attention to the values of the two statistics in both analyses.

The relevant information for the money supply variable is presented in Tables 2(a) and 2(b), and for real GDP in Tables 3(a) and 3(b). In each table we

Table 2(a). Non-Dominated Models

Independent Variables	AVE	Corroboration	$\sqrt{AVE}$	Prediction Error	$\lvert t_{AVE}\rvert$	$\lvert t_{CB}\rvert$	Conclusion	IMF-1 (IM-1)	IMF-2 (IM-2)	IMF-4 (IM-4)	IMF-8 (IM-8)
M(5)	0.0539	11.0806	0.2331	0.87	4.16	3.74	Yes	4.79 (4.94)	2.42 (5.07)	2.73 (10.81)	1.31 (11.04)
M(5),GDP(2)	0.0977	4.9204	0.3125	0.84	3.10	2.69	Yes	3.02 (3.29)	1.56 (3.44)	2.29 (9.55)	1.53 (12.91)
M(5),GDP(4)	0.1017	4.2265	0.3189	0.81	3.04	2.55	Yes	3.91 (4.33)	1.96 (4.40)	2.48 (10.52)	1.42 (12.51)
M(5),GDP(1)	0.1021	4.4889	0.3195	0.77	3.04	2.40	Yes	5.33 (5.53)	2.63 (5.54)	2.73 (10.93)	1.37 (11.61)
M(5),GDP(5)	0.1379	2.2392	0.3713	0.76	2.61	2.05	Yes	4.65 (5.17)	2.32 (5.24)	2.59 (11.09)	1.43 (12.83)
M(5),GDP(6)	0.1394	1.6628	0.3733	0.71	2.60	1.90	Yes	5.68 (6.32)	2.91 (6.57)	1.89 (8.56)	1.14 (10.79)

Dependent Variable: M; Omitted Observations: Two Last; Distance (d) = 0.97 (25%)

Table 2(b). Non-Dominated Models

Independent Variables	AVE	Corroboration	$\sqrt{AVE}$	Prediction Error	$\lvert t_{AVE} \rvert$	$\lvert t_{CB} \rvert$	Conclusion	IMF-1 (IM-1)	IMF-2 (IM-2)	IMF-4 (IM-4)	IMF-8 (IM-8)
M(6)	0.0591	14.5413	0.2431	1.01	4.24	4.16	Yes	0.17 (0.19)	0.37 (0.85)	0.77 (3.48)	0.48 (4.58)
M(5)	0.0644	13.0006	0.2538	1.00	4.06	3.96	Yes	3.92 (4.09)	2.01 (4.25)	2.57 (10.27)	1.25 (10.57)
M(7)	0.0993	6.2710	0.3151	0.92	3.27	2.92	Yes	0.77 (0.87)	0.42 (0.97)	0.86 (3.90)	0.54 (5.16)
M(5),GDP(6)	0.1528	6.2478	0.3909	1.11	2.63	2.83	No	4.33 (4.92)	2.17 (5.00)	1.81 (8.25)	1.03 (9.86)
M(5),GDP(7)	0.1606	6.0660	0.4007	1.12	2.57	2.80	No	4.54 (5.22)	2.39 (5.57)	2.55 (11.27)	1.38 (12.85)
M(5),GDP(8)	0.1656	5.7018	0.4069	1.11	2.53	2.74	No	4.97 (5.79)	2.90 (6.77)	2.43 (11.00)	1.27 (12.22)
M(7),GDP(2)	0.1846	1.8446	0.4297	0.80	2.40	1.87	Yes	0.18 (0.21)	0.09 (0.21)	0.98 (4.56)	0.90 (8.47)
M(7),GDP(3)	0.2087	1.6914	0.4568	0.82	2.25	1.80	Yes	2.58 (3.27)	2.03 (4.64)	1.22 (5.69)	1.10 (10.28)
M(7),GDP(5)	0.2116	1.6348	0.4600	0.82	2.24	1.78	Yes	2.06 (2.47)	1.06 (2.59)	0.98 (4.79)	0.87 (8.64)
M(8),GDP(2)	0.2127	0.7770	0.4612	0.70	2.23	1.52	Yes	0.33 (0.40)	0.65 (1.57)	0.48 (2.38)	0.83 (8.03)

M(8),GDP(4)	0.2397	0.5910	0.4896	0.70	2.10	1.42	Yes	0.35 (0.43)	0.19 (0.48)	0.22 (1.17)	0.66 (6.81)
M(8),GDP(3)	0.2410	0.4970	0.4909	0.68	2.10	1.38	Yes	1.44 (1.72)	1.29 (3.08)	0.62 (3.09)	0.84 (8.29)
M(8),GDP(5)	0.2493	0.3220	0.4993	0.65	2.06	1.30	Yes	1.38 (1.71)	0.74 (1.86)	0.50 (2.58)	0.63 (6.60)
M(8),GDP(8)	0.2792	-0.0268	0.5284	0.59	1.95	1.11	-	0.03 (0.04)	0.04 (0.10)	0.09 (0.54)	0.70 (7.69)

Dependent Variable: M; Omitted Observations: Last; Distance (d) = 1.03 (25%)

Table 3(a). Non-Dominated Models

Independent Variables	AVE	Corroboration	$\sqrt{AVE}$	Prediction Error	$\lvert t_{AVE}\rvert$	$\lvert t_{CB}\rvert$	Conclusion	LMF-1 (LM-1)	LMF-2 (LM-2)	LMF-4 (LM-4)	LMF-8 (LM-8)
GDP(2)	0.0087	52.8453	0.0933	0.71	5.47	7.59	No	0.07 (0.07)	0.05 (0.10)	2.09 (8.22)	1.86 (14.16)
GDP(3)	0.0093	47.8096	0.0964	0.70	5.29	7.24	No	0.81 (0.86)	0.41 (0.88)	2.23 (8.80)	1.81 (14.00)
GDP(4)	0.0095	46.0514	0.0975	0.69	5.23	7.12	No	1.13 (1.21)	1.03 (2.20)	1.99 (8.08)	1.55 (12.52)
GDP(5)	0.0186	8.1154	0.1364	0.47	3.74	3.48	Yes	3.17 (3.35)	1.56 (3.35)	1.29 (5.54)	1.17 (10.04)
GDP(6)	0.0187	6.4286	0.1367	0.44	3.73	3.22	Yes	0.03 (0.03)	0.79 (1.77)	0.91 (4.04)	1.77 (14.30)
GDP(7)	0.0218	5.8981	0.1476	0.46	3.46	3.12	Yes	0.02 (0.02)	0.14 (0.32)	1.58 (6.86)	1.56 (13.14)
GDP(8)	0.0231	4.3686	0.1520	0.43	3.36	2.85	Yes	0.25 (0.30)	0.26 (0.62)	2.68 (11.07)	1.99 (16.22)
GDP(6),M(2)	0.0663	4.0190	0.2575	0.67	1.98	2.59	No	0.48 (0.55)	0.24 (0.56)	0.65 (3.06)	1.15 (10.32)
GDP(5),M(3)	0.0676	3.7666	0.2600	0.66	1.96	2.54	No	0.95 (1.09)	0.60 (1.39)	2.42 (10.14)	2.15 (17.16)
GDP(5),M(2)	0.0680	3.2035	0.2608	0.63	1.96	2.43	No	1.46 (1.63)	0.72 (1.63)	1.30 (5.74)	1.00 (9.00)

GDP(6),M(4)	0.0724	2.7398	0.2691	0.62	1.90	2.31	No	0.10 (0.12)	0.05 (0.13)	2.50 (10.75)	1.96 (16.45)
GDP(5),M(4)	0.0728	1.7439	0.2698	0.56	1.89	2.09	No	1.65 (1.89)	1.10 (2.54)	3.02 (12.42)	2.16 (17.48)

Dependent Variable: GDP; Omitted Observations: Last Two; Distance (d) = 0.51 (25%)

Table 3(b). Non-Dominated Models

Independent Variables	AVE	Corroboration	$\sqrt{AVE}$	Prediction Error	$\lvert t_{AVE} \rvert$	$\lvert t_{CB} \rvert$	Conclusion	IMF-1 (IM-1)	IMF-2 (IM-2)	IMF-4 (IM-4)	IMF-8 (IM-8)
GDP(2)	0.0124	1.5679	0.1114	0.27	4.13	2.44	Yes	0.09 ((0.10)	0.06 (0.12)	2.30 (8.94)	2.02 (15.17)
GDP(5)	0.0157	1.0000	0.1253	0.28	3.67	2.27	Yes	3.29 (3.46)	1.62 (3.46)	1.33 (5.69)	1.25 (10.56)
GDP(6)	0.0215	-2.8379	0.1466	0.15	3.14	1.00	Yes	0.01 (0.01)	0.81 (1.82)	0.99 (4.41)	1.86 (14.91)
GDP(8)	0.0252	-3.3385	0.1587	0.09	2.90	0.58	Yes	0.28 (0.32)	0.36 (0.85)	2.69 (11.10)	1.08 (16.75)

Dependent Variable: GDP; Omitted Observations: Last; Distance (d) = 0.46 (25%)

list the spherical models which are not dominated. A model is not dominated when there is no other spherical model for which the values of both AVE and corroboration, as defined in (23) and (27) respectively, are smaller than those corresponding to the first model.

These models are ordered according to the value taken by the AVE statistic, which appears in the second column. The corroboration statistic, as defined in (27), is written in the third column. In the fifth column the absolute value of the prediction error is shown. In the sixth, we calculate the implied t_{AVE}–value corresponding to a distance equal to 25% of the true value of the dependent variable; the value of this distance is given in the upper part of each table. The seventh column shows the values of the t_{CB}–statistic as defined in (26). The eight column shows whether or not a model is corroborated by the real value observed (in our case, the omitted value in the previous analysis). We can say that a model is corroborated when the value which corresponds to this model in the seventh column is smaller than the corresponding value in the sixth column or, equivalently, when the absolute value of the prediction error is smaller than the value of the distance assumed. When the value of the t_{AVE}–statistic for a model in the sixth column is smaller than two, a row appears in the eighth column, indicating that this model guarantees that the error of prediction would be smaller than the assumed value less than 95% of times. The values of the LMF and LM statistics used to test the white noise character of the error term are shown in the last four columns.

The process followed in choosing a model, when starting from these tables, is as follows: for each variable we take the models which appear to us to be corroborated models in the two analyses, with two and one omitted observations respectively. From these models we select the one which has the smaller value of the AVE criterion. Following this process, the model finally chosen can be seen in Table 4. For each variable, the best model is the one in which five lags of the dependent variable appear as explanatory variables. Thus, according to Granger's definition of causality established in (10), (11) and (12), we can conclude by saying that money supply (M3) and real GDP were independent in the Spanish economy during the period 1965–1984.

Table 4. Estimates of the Final Chosen Relationships

Independent Variables	Dependent Variables GDP	M
GDP (1)	1.541352 (13.18)	
GDP (2)	–0.776018 (-3.65)	
GDP (3)	0.290379 (1.28)	
GDP (4)	–0.448168 (-2.13)	
GDP (5)	0.276098 (2.42)	
M (1)		1.321266 (11.86)
M (2)		–0.181081 (–0.97)
M (3)		–0.143987 (–0.78)
M (4)		–0.445880 (–2.47)
M (5)		0.393299 (3.56)
$\hat{\sigma}$	0.6371	0.8817

5. CONCLUSIONS

In this paper we have presented an alternative methodology for testing the causality relationships between money and real GDP. We emphasise the use of two Lagrange–type statistics to determine the white noise character of the random term. We then distinguish two moments according to whether or not the real value to be predicted was available. We define statistics to give account of the useful information to be derived in both moments, with the accent on the joint consideration of the values of those statistics.

The results of the causality tests show that both series are independent. Each variable is better predicted by using the past of the own variable than by adding to these past values the past value of the other variable.

We think that this study could be extended along several lines. A first would be to omit more than two observations and then to repeat the analysis presented in this paper, in order to confirm the stability of the above mentioned conclusions. A second line would consist of changing the adopted framework and considering more than two variables. If we take into account more than two variables, then alternative specifications to those considered in this paper may be favoured by the evidence contained in data, and the conclusions about the relationships between nominal and real variables may differ. Further lines of investigation can be followed by interpreting the finally chosen model in the light of concepts such as anticipated and unanticipated monetary changes. Last but not least, some aspects of the methodological alternative presented in this paper might be improved and reformulated; for example, the achievement of the equilibrium between the information and corroboration contents of an econometric model is an open question.

NOTES

* Thanks are due to Luis Carrascón and Jesus Mur for the execution of computations and to a referee for helpful comments and corrections. The research has been supported in part by the "Comisión Asesora de Investigación Científica y Técnica" (CAYCIT), project no. PB85–0339.

1) See Akaike (1969, 1970, 1973) and Amemiya (1980).

REFERENCES

Akaike, H. (1969), "Fitting Autoregressive Models for Prediction", *Annals of the Institute of Statistical Mathematics*, 21, pp.243–47.

Akaike, H. (1970), "Statistical Predictor Identification", *Annals of the Institute of Statistical Mathematics*, 22, pp.203–17.

Akaike, H. (1973), "Information Theory and an Extension of the Maximum Likelihood Principle" in B.N. Petrov and F. Csaki (eds.), *2nd International Symposium of Information Theory*, Akademiai Kiado, Budapest.

Amemiya, T. (1980), "Selection of Regressors", *International Economic Review* 21, pp.331–54.

Auerbach, R.D. and J.L. Rutner (1978), "Causality Test of Canadian Money and Income: A Comment on Barth and Bennett", *Canadian Journal of Economics*, 11, pp.583–94.

Aznar, A. (1986), *Econometric Model Selection: A New Approach*, Kluwer Publishers, Dordrecht, forthcoming.

Aznar, A. and F.J. Trivez (1986), "Propuesta para el contraste de causalidad", *III Encuentros de Econometria y Economia Cuantitativa*, San Lorenzo del Escorial, Madrid, 30 June – 1 July, 1986.

Barro, R.J. (1977), "Unanticipated Money Growth and Unemployment in the

United States", *American Economic Review*, 67, pp.101–15.

Barro, R.J. (1978), "Unanticipated Money, Output, and the Price Level in the United States", *Journal of Political Economy*, 86, pp.549–80.

Barro, R.J. and M. Rush (1980), "Unanticipated Money and Economic Activity" in S. Fischer (ed.), *Rational Expectations and Economic Policy*, The University of Chicago Press.

Barth, J.R. and J.T. Bennett (1974), "The Role of Money in the Canadian Economy: An Empirical Test", *Canadian Journal of Economics*, 7, pp.306–11.

Box, G.E.P. and D.A. Pierce (1970), "Distribution of Residual Autocorrelations in Autoregressive–Integrated Moving Average Time Series Models", *Journal of the American Statistical Association*, 65, pp.1509–26.

Breusch, T.S. and A.R. Pagan (1980), "The Lagrange Multiplier Test and Its Applications to Model Specification in Econometrics", *Review of Economic Studies*, 47, pp.239–53.

Brillembourg, A. and M.S. Khan (1979), "The Relationship Between Money, Income and Prices: Has Money Mattered Historically?", *Journal of Money, Credit and Banking*, 11, pp.358–65.

Caines, P.E., C.W. Keng and S.P. Sethi (1981), "Causality Analysis and Multivariate Autoregressive Modelling with an Application to Supermarket Sales Analysis", *Journal of Economic Dynamics and Control*, 3, pp.267–98.

Cuddington, J.T. (1981), "Money, Income and Causality in the United Kingdom. An Empirical Reexamination", *Journal of Money, Credit and Banking*, 13, pp.343–51.

Durbin, J. (1970), "Testing for Serial Correlation in Least Squares Regression when some of the Regressors are lagged Dependent Variables", *Econometrica*, 38, 410–21.

Elliot, J.W. (1975), "The Influence of Monetary and Fiscal Actions on Total Spending", *Journal of Money, Credit and Banking*, 7, pp.181–92.

Feige, E.L. and D.K. Pearce (1979), "The Casual Causal Relationship Between Money and Income: Some Caveats for Time Series Analysis", *Review of Economics and Statistics*, 61, pp.521–33.

Geweke, J., R. Meese and W. Dent (1983), "Comparing Alternative Tests of Causality in Temporal Systems", *Journal of Econometrics*, 21, pp.161–94.

Godfrey, L.G. (1978), "Testing Against General Autoregressive and Moving Average Error Models when the Regressors Include Lagged Dependent Variables", *Econometrica*, 46, pp. 1293–1301.

Gordon, R.J. (1982), "Price Inertia and Policy Ineffectiveness in the United States, 1890–1980", *Journal of Political Economy*, 90, pp.1087–1117.

Granger, C.W.J. (1969), "Investigating Causal Relations by Econometric Models and Cross–Spectral Methods", *Econometrica*, 37, pp.424–38.

Granger, C.W.J. (1982), "Generating Mechanisms, Models, and Causality" in W. Hildenbrand (ed.), *Advances in Econometrics*, Cambridge University Press.

Harvey, A.C. (1981), *The Econometric Analysis of Time Series*, Phillip Allan.

Hsiao, C. (1979a), "Autoregressive Modelling of Canadian Money and Income Data", *Journal of the American Statistical Association*, 74, pp.553–60.

Hsiao, C. (1979b), "Causality Tests in Econometrics, *Journal of Economic Dynamics and Control*, 1, pp.321–46.

Hsiao, C. (1981), "Autoregressive Modelling and Money–Income Causality Detection", *Journal of Monetary Economics*, 7, pp.85–106.

Hsiao, C. (1982), "Autoregressive Modelling and Causal Ordering of Economic Variables", *Journal of Economic Dynamics and Control*, 4, pp.243–59.

Huffman, W.E. and J.R. Lothian (1980), "Money in the United Kingdom, 1933–80", *Journal of Money, Credit and Banking*, 12, pp.155–74.

Kiviet, J.F. (1986), "On the Rigour of Some Misspecification Tests for Modelling

Dynamic Relationships", *Review of Economic Studies*, 53, pp.241–61.
Komura, C. (1982), "Money, Income, and Causality: The Japanese Case", *Southern Economic Journal*, 49, pp.19–34.
Komura, C. (1984), "Money, Income, and Causality in Japan – Supplementary Evidence: Reply", *Southern Economic Journal*, 50, pp.1219–23.
Leiderman, L. (1980), "Macroeconometric Testing of the Rational Expectations and Structural Neutrality Hypothesis for the United States", *Journal of Monetary Economics*, 6, pp.69–82.
Ljung, G.M. and G.E.P. Box (1978), "On a Measure of Lack of Fit in Time Series Models", *Biometrika*, 65, pp.297–303.
McGee, R.T. and R.T. Stasiak (1985), "Does Anticipated Monetary Policy Matter?", *Journal of Money, Credit and Banking*, 17, pp.16–27.
Mehra, Y.P. (1978a), "Is Money Exogenous in Money–Demand Equations?", *Journal of Political Economy*, 86, pp.211–28.
Mehra, Y.P. (1978b), "An Empirical Note on Some Monetarist Propositions", *Southern Economic Journal*, 45, pp.154–67.
Mehra, Y.P. and D.E. Spencer (1979), "The St. Louis Equation and Reverse Causation: The Evidence Reexamined", *Southern Economic Journal*, 45, pp.1104–20.
Mishkin, F.S. (1982a), "Does Anticipated Monetary Policy Matter? An Econometric Investigation", *Journal of Political Economy*, 90, pp.22–51.
Mishkin, F.S. (1982b), "Does Anticipated Aggregate Demand Policy Matter? Further Econometric Results", *American Economic Review*, 72, pp.788–802.
Mixon, J.W., L.J. Pratt and M.S. Wallace (1979), "Cross–National Money to Income Causality: U.S. Money to U.K. Income", *Journal of Money, Credit and Banking*, 11, pp.419–26.
Nelson, C.R. and C.I. Plosser (1982), "Trends and Random Walks in Macroeconomic Time Series", *Journal of Monetary Economics*, 10, pp.139–63.
Nerlove, M. and K.F. Wallis (1966), "Use of the Durbin–Watson Statistic in Inappropriate Situations", *Econometrica*, 34, pp.235–38.
Pautler, P.A. and R.J. Rivard (1979), "Choosing a Monetary Aggregate: Causal Relationship as a Criterion", *Review of Business and Economic Research*, 15, pp.1–18.
Pierce, D.A. and L.D. Haugh (1977), "Causality in Temporal Systems. Characterisations and a Survey", *Journal of Econometrics*, 5, pp.265–93.
Ram, R. (1984), "Money, Income and Causality in Japan – Supplementary Evidence: Comment", *Southern Economic Journal*, 50, pp.1214–18.
Ramachandra, V.S. (1983), "Direction of Causality Between Monetary and Real Variables in India – An Empirical Result", *Indian Economic Journal*, 31, pp.65–76.
Rush, M. (1986), "Unexpected Money and Unemployment. 1920 t0 1983", *Journal of Money, Credit and Banking*, 18, pp.259–74.
Sanz, R. (1985), "Trimestralización del PIB por ramas de actividad. 1964–1984", *Servicio de Estudios del Banco de Espana*, Working Paper No. 8514.
Sargent, T.J. (1976), "A Classical Macroeconometric Model for the United States", *Journal of Political Economy*, 84, pp.207–37.
Sarlo, C.A. (1979), "The Role of Money in the Canadian Economy: Fixed Vs. Flexible Exchange Rates", *Canadian Journal of Economics*, 12, pp.89–93.
Sharpe, B.C. and M.B. Miller (1975), "The Role of Money in the Canadian Economy", *Canadian Journal of Economics*, 8, pp.289–90.
Sims, C.A. (1972), "Money, Income and Causality", *American Economic Review*, 62, pp.540–52.

Tjostheim, D. (1981), "Granger–Causality in Multiple Time Series", *Journal of Econometrics*, 17, pp.157–76.

Trivez, F.J. (1986), "Causalidad y modelos econométricos", Ph.D. Dissertation, Department of Econometrics, University of Zaragoza.

Williams, C.A., C.A.E. Goodhart and D.H. Gowland (1976), "Money, Income and Causality: The U.K. Experience", *American Economic Review*, 66, pp.417–23.

APPENDIX

Table A1(a). Data. Variable: GDP*

Year	Q		Year	Q		Year	Q		Year	Q	
1965	1	4.3	1970	1	5.2	1975	1	1.1	1980	1	1.6
	2	5.2		2	4.9		2	1.0		2	1.7
	3	6.5		3	4.6		3	1.4		3	1.6
	4	6.9		4	4.8		4	1.8		4	1.0
1966	1	7.6	1971	1	4.9	1976	1	2.6	1981	1	–0.1
	2	7.8		2	4.8		2	2.8		2	–0.6
	3	7.2		3	5.6		3	3.5		3	–0.4
	4	7.2		4	6.9		4	4.3		4	–0.2
1967	1	6.2	1972	1	8.6	1977	1	4.4	1982	1	0.4
	2	5.6		2	8.8		2	3.6		2	1.3
	3	4.1		3	8.8		3	2.4		3	1.6
	4	3.7		4	8.2		4	2.0		4	1.7
1968	1	4.5	1973	1	8.5	1078	1	2.6	1983	1	2.3
	2	4.9		2	8.2		2	2.8		2	2.2
	3	6.7		3	7.4		3	2.7		3	1.7
	4	8.9		4	8.1		4	1.8		4	2.0
1969	1	9.5	1974	1	7.4	1979	1	0.3	1984	1	2.1
	2	9.9		2	6.9		2	–0.1		2	2.2
	3	9.2		3	6.0		3	–0.1		3	2.7
	4	6.8		4	3.5		4	0.5		4	2.4

* Interannual growth rates in real GDP
Source: R. Sanz (1985), "Trimestralizacion del PIB por ramas actividad. 1964–1984". Banco de España. Servicio de Estudios. Documento de Trabajo no. 8514.

Table A1(b). Data. Variable: M*

Year	Q		Year	Q		Year	Q		Year	Q	
1965	1	20.4	1970	1	17.5	1975	1	18.8	1980	1	17.4
	2	19.6		2	15.5		2	18.1		2	17.0
	3	20.5		3	15.0		3	19.8		3	17.1
	4	19.1		4	14.7		4	19.3		4	16.8
1966	1	17.8	1971	1	16.3	1976	1	18.8	1981	1	15.6
	2	16.2		2	19.5		2	19.3		2	15.2
	3	14.7		3	21.4		3	18.5		3	15.0
	4	14.2		4	23.1		4	19.1		4	15.2
1967	1	14.4	1972	1	23.8	1977	1	19.5	1982	1	16.0
	2	15.4		2	24.2		2	19.5		2	17.2
	3	15.4		3	23.4		3	20.4		3	16.9
	4	15.5		4	23.2		4	18.9		4	16.6
1968	1	15.8	1973	1	24.1	1978	1	18.5	1983	1	15.8
	2	16.8		2	24.4		2	19.4		2	13.8
	3	17.5		3	25.5		3	19.7		3	12.7
	4	18.6		4	25.1		4	19.6		4	12.3
1969	1	19.2	1974	1	23.3	1979	1	17.8	1984	1	11.1
	2	19.1		2	21.9		2	16.5		2	11.0
	3	19.0		3	19.2		3	15.5		3	12.2
	4	18.6		4	18.7		4	14.6		4	11.9

* Interannual growth rates in M3
Source: Bank of Spain, "Boletines Estadisticos".

Table A.2(a). Autocorrelations

Series: M (original); Mean: 17.95; Standard Error: 3.2914

	Lags								
Autocorrelations	1-8	0.921	0.801	0.645	0.493	0.393	0.316	0.266	0.231
Standard Errors		0.112	0.184	0.223	0.245	0.257	0.265	0.269	0.273
Autocorrelations	9-16	0.195	0.167	0.146	0.135	0.139	0.145	0.155	0.141
Standard Errors		0.275	0.277	0.278	0.279	0.280	0.281	0.282	0.283
Autocorrelations	17-24	0.113	0.069	-0.004	-0.071	-0.158	-0.223	-0.256	-0.267
Standard Errors		0.284	0.284	0.284	0.284	0.285	0.286	0.288	0.291

Table A.2(b). Autocorrelations

Series: GDP (original); Mean: 4.1675; Standard Error: 2.8912

	Lags								
Autocorrelations	1-8	0.952	0.852	0.731	0.616	0.534	0.482	0.455	0.450
Standard Errors		0.112	0.188	0.231	0.258	0.276	0.289	0.298	0.307
Autocorrelations	9-16	0.462	0.474	0.480	0.474	0.461	0.440	0.407	0.365
Standard Errors		0.315	0.323	0.332	0.341	0.349	0.356	0.363	0.369
Autocorrelations	17-24	0.320	0.274	0.229	0.183	0.129	0.074	0.030	0.006
Standard Errors		0.373	0.377	0.379	0.381	0.382	0.382	0.383	0.383

Table A.2(c). Autocorrelations

Series: M; Mean: 0; Standard Error: 3.0904

	Lags								
Autocorrelations	1–8	0.927	0.806	0.650	0.495	0.393	0.313	0.257	0.211
Standard Errors		0.112	0.184	0.224	0.247	0.259	0.266	0.271	0.274
Autocorrelations	9–16	0.162	0.123	0.092	0.076	0.080	0.089	0.104	0.094
Standard Errors		0.276	0.277	0.278	0.278	0.278	0.279	0.279	0.279
Autocorrelations	17–24	0.067	0.020	−0.059	−0.133	−0.225	−0.299	−0.342	−0.362
Standard Errors		0.280	0.280	0.280	0.280	0.281	0.283	0.287	0.292

Table A.2(d). Autocorrelations

Series: GDP; Mean: 0; Standard Error: 1.9585

	Lags								
Autocorrelations	1–8	0.875	0.642	0.390	0.156	0.005	−0.070	−0.105	−0.089
Standard Errors		0.112	0.178	0.205	0.214	0.215	0.215	0.216	0.216
Autocorrelations	9–16	−0.042	0.003	0.020	0.020	0.022	0.016	0.009	0.008
Standard Errors		0.217	0.217	0.217	0.217	0.217	0.217	0.217	0.217
Autocorrelations	17–24	−0.004	−0.017	−0.035	−0.080	−0.147	−0.211	−0.252	−0.276
Standard Errors		0.217	0.217	0.217	0.217	0.217	0.219	0.221	0.225

CHAPTER 8

INTEREST RATES AND INFLATION IN ITALY DURING THE SEVENTIES: A CAUSAL ANALYSIS

Enrico D'Elia
Istituto Nazionale per lo Studio della Congiuntura, Rome, Italy

1. INTRODUCTION

In Italy, as in other countries, inflation and nominal interest rates showed a strong positive correlation in the short run during the seventies. Depending on the share of inflation transferred on rates, this empirical evidence has often been regarded as consistent with a causal relation running from inflation to rates, according to the hypothesis that the real rate is substantially constant over time[1].

Really, such a finding is neither necessary nor sufficient for the constancy of real rate. Firstly, as Summers (1983) has recently remarked, in the short run the sign and the direction of the relationships between interest and inflation are allowed to be almost of any kind, also in the standard models implying a constant real rate in the long run, depending on the nature of the shocks affecting the economy.

Secondly, the evidence under examination does not contrast with the hypothesis that the relations between inflation and rates could be spurious and not truly causal. More precisely, some variables could exist which affect independently both prices and interest rates with identical (positive or negative) sign but different intensity and distributed lags, in such a way that inflation and rates appear to be reciprocally related.

To shed some light on the question whether such a set of variables, say x, exists we need to test that 1) x explains inflation rate and interest rates "not worse" than a set including both x and the inflation rate; and 2) the inflation rate

P. Artus and Y. Barroux (eds.), Monetary Policy, 163–177.

explains interest rates "worse" than the larger information set. Moreover, we should discriminate between causal and spurious relations to the end of specifying consistently the set $\boldsymbol{x}$.

Obviously, these hypotheses cannot be supported by studying solely the statistical relations between inflation and rates, but at least a simple model of the relevant economy must be made explicit, and furthermore a concept of "causality" must be defined. The present work starts from the core of the cyclical scheme identified by Carlucci and Giovannini (1984) for the Italian economy in the seventies and is based on the definition of conditional causality due to Granger (1980).

In the paper by Carlucci and Giovannini an increase of the economic activity anticipates both an accelerating inflation after three months, and a worsening in the external trade balance after about one year. The latter is matched by a further increase in the consumer prices index linked to the latest effect of the demand growth; therefore a "spurious" relation between balance and inflation is found.

In our paper some interest rates – quite representative of the monetary market in Italy – are found to follow the dynamics of demand, of domestic and foreign goods, just like inflation does – with compatible signs and distributed lags – and this fact could explain some of the empirical findings without recurring to a direct causal interpretation.

A similar hypothesis was in fact advanced early by Wicksell and Keynes as an explanation of the "Gibson paradox" in the framework of a monetary theory of the business cycle. More generally, it is consistent with a model where the demand for monetary assets is sensitive to the nominal interest rates and to the aggregate demand (both on domestic and foreign goods) and where the monetary authorities look at the variation of trade balance – induced by an increase in national demand – and tries to affect it by controlling liquidity (in so far influencing interest rates).

The nature of the problem requires an identificatiom as exact as possible of the shape of distributed lags in the relations among the variables, rather than the best estimates of the multipliers; therefore arbitrary restrictions on the parameters are not imposed, but we employed a methodology based on the concept of "Granger causality", already suggested by Haugh and Box (1977), that can be articulated in the following steps:

1) the time series of the relevant variables are filtered by univariate ARIMA

models in order to attenuate their inertial movements, which could bias the estimates of correlations between the series;

2) cross–correlograms are computed between each pair of the filtered series to detect dynamic short run relations, which can be causal or not;
3) by using economic theory and verifying the coherence (compatibility) of signs and shapes among the relations detected above, one may advance some preliminary hypotheses about the causal chains linking the examined variables, and about the shape of the distributed lags in the respective equations;
4) finally, these hypotheses are tested by regression techniques.

Consequently to the central role of dynamic features of the estimated equations, monthly data are used in this paper, and two measures of inflation are analysed: the wholesale price index (PW) and the consumer prices index (PC). Inflation is related to the following interest rates: the yield of three months Treasury bills (TB), the official discount rate (DR), the prime rate (PR) and the maximum rate applied to sight interbank deposits (ID). The first two rates can be regarded as partly controlled by the monetary authorities; the last two are formed in the banking environment and seem closer to the free monetary market. Demand is represented by an indicator built on the basis of EEC–ISCO monthly survey on domestic industrial orders (DOL), worked out by the methodology described by Carlucci (1982). Trade balance (B) is evaluated on cash basis.

The analysis is focused on the period January 1973 – December 1979, which is characterised by large fluctuations in the economic activity (both in Italy and in other countries) mainly due to the oil shocks of 1973–74 and 1976–77 and, specifically in Italy, due to repeated financial crises.

2. INTEREST RATES AND INFLATION: A FIRST EMPIRICAL EVIDENCE

First of all, the short run relations between inflation and rates were identified from cross–correlograms on filtered series[2]: Figure 1 shows statistically significant correlations $r(s)$ estimated between two variables, the variable on the left hand side being s months lagged.

Four remarks can be made:

1) each correlation coefficient has positive sign[3]:
2) suggested causal relations do not seem unidirectional (say from inflation to rates), as is generally acknowledged;
3) the relevant causal relations are centred around short lags (less than 8

months at the most, and generally less than a quarter) and do not seem sharply different among the various rates;

4) relations between PW and rates seem shorter than the others.

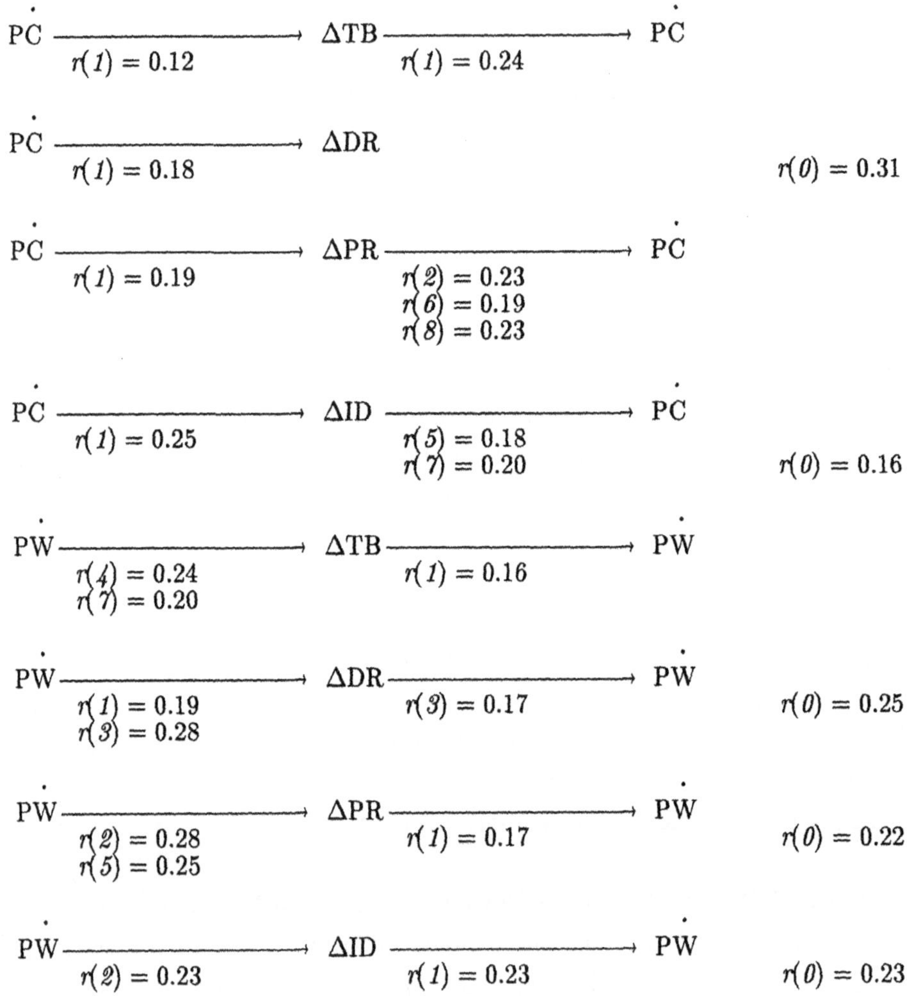

Figure 1: Correlations between interest rates and inflation computed on filtered series (S.E.=0.10). Δ is the first difference operator; a dot above the variables is the logarithmic first difference operator. Instantaneous relations are shown aside.

Remark 1 seems consistent with the common assumptions, and point 2 is not surprising even in a Fisherian world: in fact, if rates incorporate future inflation and if expectations are accurate enough, then a relation between actual rates and future inflation should be expected. Remark 3 is a less standard finding because, under the Fisherian hypothesis, one should suppose that the statistical relations between inflation and rates are likely to appear at lags depending on the average maturity of loans which a certain rate is connected to. Nevertheless, such a result is not unexpected in a standard model with classical long run implications. Finally, the fourth observation seems to agree with the estimated dynamic relation between PW and PC (see equation 2 in Table 1), describing the transmission of the prices from the producers to the market.

3. INTEREST RATES AND INFLATION IN A CYCLICAL SCHEME

In Figure 2 we sketch the main features (relevant here) of the model proposed by Carlucci and Giovannini (1984), briefly summarised in section 1. The aim is to stress the coherence of the dynamic structure of the postulated causal chains and of the respective spurious relationships centred on inflation. The implicit idea is to generalise this scheme inserting some other variables – specifically the interest rates – which show a correlation with inflation and which, at the same time, could be thought as causally related with domestic demand and trade balance.

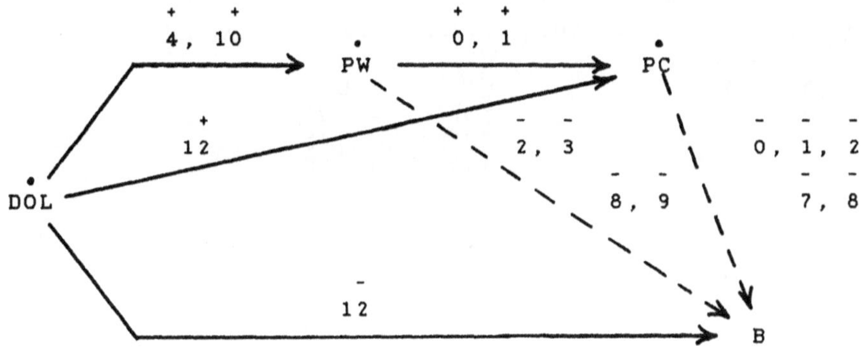

Figure 2: A scheme of the short run relations among domestic demand, inflation, and trade balance

Here, the arrows show the direction of postulated relations; the numbers above the lines point out the lags with which each relation occurs; the symbols above the numbers denote the sign of the influence of a variable on an other; the dashed lines point out the expected relations (the largest part actually observed) that can be considered spurious, i.e. due to the interaction of other variables.

The same relations are estimated by generalised least square method (see equations (1)–(3) in Table 1). For the sake of simplicity, in Figure 2, but not in equation (1), the influence on PW of import prices (PI) – through import of final and intermediate goods – is disregarded, being exogenous in our reasoning.

From a theoretical point of view, interest rates should influence negatively the demand through their effects on consumption and investment plans. Moreover, an increase of the demand is connected with a higher demand for money; if the money demand function is sensitive to the interest rates level, then a positive effect of demand on rates should be expected. Empirical evidence seems to fit these hypotheses well, as is shown in Figure 3.

$\Delta TB \rightarrow \dot{DOL}$		$\dot{DOL} \rightarrow \Delta TB$	
$r(6) = -.18$		$r(3) = 0.17$ $r(10) = 0.29$	
$\Delta DR \rightarrow \dot{DOL}$		$\dot{DOL} \rightarrow \Delta DR$	
$r(3) = -.21$ $r(8) = -.20$		$r(2) = 0.21$ $r(10) = 0.20$ $r(11) = 0.23$ $r(13) = 0.25$	
$\Delta PR \rightarrow \dot{DOL}$		$\dot{DOL} \rightarrow \Delta PR$	
$r(5) = -.18$ $r(6) = -.21$ $r(8) = -.18$		$r(1) = 0.20$ $r(3) = 0.28$ $r(5) = 0.21$ $r(12) = 0.16$ $r(13) = 0.26$	
$\Delta ID \rightarrow \dot{DOL}$		$\dot{DOL} \rightarrow \Delta ID$	
$r(1) = -.14$ $r(8) = -.25$		$r(1) = 0.24$ $r(3) = 0.22$ $r(12) = 0.30$	

Figure 3: Correlations between the interest rates and the level of domestic orders (S.E. = 0.10)

As in the relations between DOL and inflation, the demand seems to affect the rates in two phases: one working out in the first quarter, the other appearing after about one year. If we attribute a "causal" value to these relations, the "coincidence" of distributed lags in the two causal chains could explain some of the statistical correlations between inflation and rates. Generally speaking, the shorter relations in Figure 3 could match relations of the kind "rates → inflation" according to the following scheme:

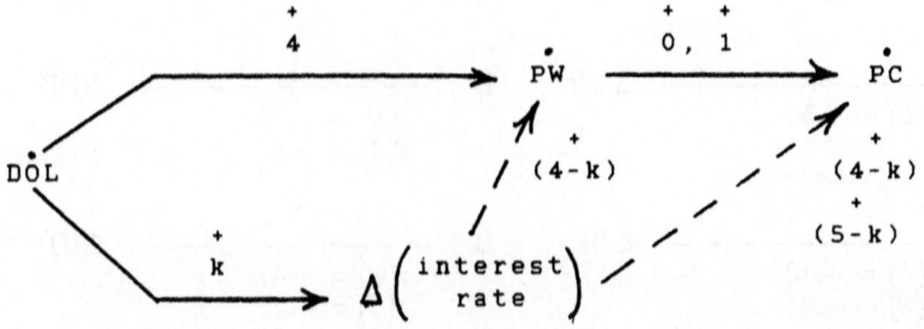

It is easily verified that this explanation cannot be advanced only for the longest relations between PR and ID, on the one hand, and PC, on the other.

The longer relations between DOL and rates could also be associated with other links between inflation and rates according to the following scheme:

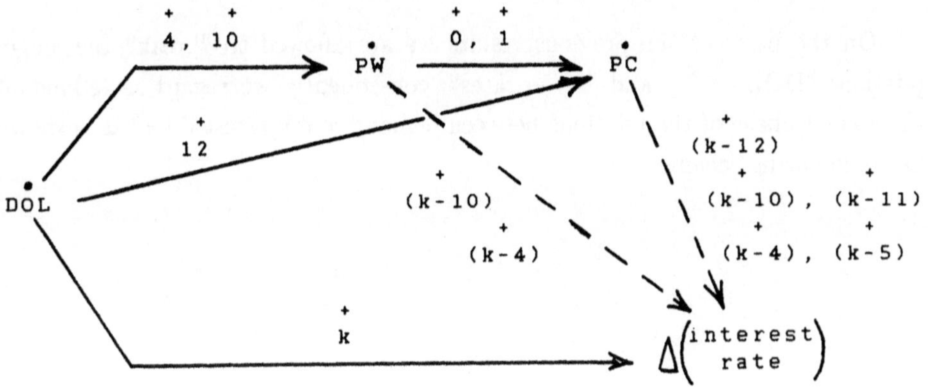

Formally, this scheme could be useful in completing the proposed explanation, but the particular timing of the relationships makes it more reasonable to connect the longer relations between DOL and the rates to the contextual worsening in the trade balance associated with the demand increase (see Figure 2). The worsening implies in fact two main effects: the first is a reduction of the domestic liquidity induced by the external deficit itself, the second is the probable reaction of the monetary authorities trying to cool the demand (directly restricting liquidity) and to draw foreign capitals (and so directly influencing interest rates).

Each of these behaviours contributes in pushing rates in the opposite direction of trade balance, and the empirical findings seem to support this theoretical hypothesis, as is shown in Figure 4.

$B \longrightarrow \Delta TB$: $r(0) = -.56$

$B \longrightarrow \Delta DR$: $r(0) = -.20$, $r(1) = -.47$

$B \longrightarrow \Delta PR$: $r(0) = -.40$, $r(3) = -.24$

$B \longrightarrow \Delta ID$: $r(0) = -.47$, $r(1) = -.25$, $r(3) = -.20$

$\dot{PW} \longrightarrow B$: $r(0) = -.22$, $r(1) = -.26$

$\dot{PC} \longrightarrow B$: $r(0) = -.24$, $r(1) = -.26$

Figure 4: Correlations between the trade balance on the one hand, and the interest rates and inflation on the other (S.E. = 0.10)

On the basis of the previous results we are allowed to "break" the longer relations "DOL $\longrightarrow$ B" and "B $\longrightarrow$ rates"; consequently we regard as redundant the second phase of the relations between demand and interest rates, as is shown in the following scheme:

4. A CAUSALITY TEST

In a recent work, Granger (1980) has specified his previous definition of causality asserting that one can verify a causal relationship only conditional to some information set, including theory and personal believes about the phenomenon under examination.

The nature of the problem analysed here suggests simply to run for each rate a pair of statistical tests jointly conditional on an "a priori" scheme. More specifically we need to test the following hypotheses:

1) DOL and B cause (in the Granger sense) interest rates conditional on an information set including DOL, B, PW, PC, and the past values of interest rates;
2) inflation does not cause interest rates conditional on the same set of variables.

Hypothesis 1 would be contradicted by data if, in the regression of interest rates on the larger information set, distributed lags estimated for DOL and B were jointly insignificant – from the statistical point of view – or did not present the expected sign, and finally, if the explanation based on the smaller information set gave statistically worse results than the general one.

Hypothesis 2 would be rejected if the coefficients of inflation in the regression of the interest rates on the larger set of variables differed significantly from zero, and the explanation based on the inflation only did not work worse than the general one.

One could wish to test these hypotheses allowing for as general as possible distributed lags structure on each variable. The a priori causal scheme advocated here is more precise indeed about the dynamics of the relationships and relays exactly on the coherence of their timing. Moreover, apart from the severe problems of multicollinearity, the overparameterisation implied in a general dynamic formulation would encompass implicitly (and in a shadowing way) a wide set of causal and spurious relationships extraneous to the hypotheses at point. So allowing for a general dynamics would not strengthen such "conditional" causal tests but could introduce an incoherence in the analysis with respect to the specification of the a priori information set.

Consequently here and after we shall make references to both "restricted" and "unrestricted" regressions that actually are each "restricted" with respect to the dynamics. However, the results of an analysis based on a weaker specification of the dynamics are briefly discussed in the below.

The constraints on coefficients implied by the hypotheses 1 and 2 can be tested by running a standard F–test on the unrestricted (derived from regression of interest rates on DOL, B, PW, PC) and restricted (from regression on DOL and B) sum of square of residuals of equations estimated by GLS. To strengthen the tests, the same autocorrelative structure of the residual was preserved in each restricted and unrestricted equation[4]. The results of the tests are summarised in Table 2; the unrestricted estimates are reproduced in Table 1. The degrees of freedom of the F–tests take into account the number of observations actually used in the estimation, after the variables were differenced and lagged. So each test nests a Chow–test for the stability of the model in the period included in the restricted regressions but not in the unrestricted ones.

Hypothesis 1 seems to fit the data well but not for the official discount rate[5]; on the whole, the explanation based on inflation works worse than the general one at 1.5% confidence level at least[6]. Moreover the cross–correlograms of PW and PC against the residuals from the restricted regressions do not suggest that in restricted equations the introduction of any other delay of inflation was significant.

Furthermore, F–tests seem to agree with the hypothesis 2 for each interest rate at 5% confidence level. Moreover in equations (4)–(7) it is evident that only one coefficient of inflation is individually significant (in equation (6) the coefficient of PW 5 months lagged), while the coefficients of DOL and B are almost each statistically different from zero at common confidence level. Finally, no sign of dynamic misspecification was found by cross–correlating the residuals of the equations with lagged explicative variables.

The previous remarks notwithstanding the same testing procedure has been applied to equations in which the distributed lags were not conditioned on the optimal delays search described above. The results[7] do not differ sharply from those summarised in Table 2, including the unsatisfactory explanation of the prime rate. Moreover a test against dynamic misspecification, highly favourable to the proposed equations, can easily be deduced by comparing Table 2 with the table reported in footnote 7. In turn the "general" regressions, not reported here, are flawed by a strong multicollinearity of the estimates, as expected, that darkens the cross relationships among the variables.

Table 1. Unrestricted Transfer Function Models of Variables Utilised in Causality Analysis

---

(1) $$\dot{PW}_t = -\underset{(0.001)}{0.0097} + \underset{(0.031)}{0.268}\,\dot{PI}_t + (\underset{(0.015)}{0.022}\,L^4 + \underset{(0.0149)}{0.0403}\,{}^{10})\dot{DOL}_t + U_t$$

$$R_o^2 = 0.999 \quad R_d^2 = 0.794 \quad S.E. = 0.0092 \quad Q^* = 37.60 \ (35 \text{ d.f.})$$

(2) $$\dot{PC}_t = \underset{(0.0010)}{0.0083} + (\underset{(0.068)}{0.248} + \underset{(0.065)}{0.127}\,L)\dot{PW}_t + \underset{(0.0075)}{0.016}\,\dot{DOL}_{t-12}$$

$$+ (1 + \underset{(0.123)}{0.227}\,L + \underset{(0.116)}{0.264}\,L^2)U_t$$

$$R_o^2 = 0.999 \quad R_d^2 = 0.918 \quad S.E. = 0.0043 \quad Q^* = 39.17 \ (32 \text{ d.f.})$$

(3) $$\ln(B_t + 900) = \underset{(0.155)}{6.688} - \underset{(0.160)}{2.075}\,\dot{DOL}_{t-12} + (1 + \underset{(0.057)}{0.631}\,L + \underset{(0.071)}{0.411}\,L^{12})U_t$$

$$R_o^2 = 0.412 \qquad S.E. = 0.654 \qquad Q^* = 22.20 \ (33 \text{ d.f.})$$

(4) $$\Delta TB_t = \underset{(0.261)}{0.313} - \frac{\underset{(0.101)}{0.737}}{(1 + \underset{(0.143)}{0.727}\,L^{12})} \ln(B_t+900) + (\underset{(7.850)}{4.538}L^4 + \underset{(8.400)}{5.293}L^7)\dot{PW}_t$$

$$+ \underset{(20.300)}{16.096}\,\dot{PC}_{t-1} + U_t$$

$$R_o^2 = 0.929 \quad R_d^2 = 0.441 \quad S.E. = 0.854 \quad Q^* = 20.38 \ (35 \text{ d.f.})$$

(5) $$\Delta DR_t = -\underset{(0.251)}{0.569} - \frac{(\underset{(0.115)}{0.235} + \underset{(0.112)}{0.218}\,L)}{1 + \underset{(0.151)}{0.698}L^{12})} \ln(B_t + 900)$$

$$+ \frac{\underset{(1.220)}{2.340}}{(1 + \underset{(0.142)}{0.813}\,L^4)} \dot{DOL}_{t-2} + (\underset{(11.750)}{13.909} - \underset{(14.195)}{16.119}\,L + \underset{(3.515)}{3.318}\,L^3)\dot{PW}_t$$

$$+ (\underset{(16.501)}{21.846} + \underset{(17.612)}{26.140}\,L)\dot{PC}_t + (1 + \underset{(0.131)}{0.144}\,L^2)U_t$$

$$R_o^2 = 0.950 \quad R_d^2 = 0.467 \quad S.E. = 0.632 \quad Q^* = 23.69 \ (34 \text{ d.f.})$$

$$(6)\quad \Delta PR_t = \underset{(0.235)}{-0.473} - \frac{(\underset{(0.118)}{0.230} + \underset{(0.112)}{0.435}\,L + \underset{(0.114)}{0.104}\,L^3)}{(1 + \underset{(0.087)}{0.781}\,L^{12})} \ln(B_t + 900)$$

$$+ \underset{(1.235)}{2.191}\,\dot{DOL}_{t-1} + (\underset{(7.905)}{12.590} - \underset{(9.356)}{4.468}\,L^2 + \underset{(6.603)}{15.944}\,L^5)\dot{PW}_t$$

$$+ \underset{(17.150)}{17.196}\,\dot{PC}_{t-1} + (1 + \underset{(0.138)}{0.399}\,)U_t$$

$R_o^2 = 0.950 \quad R_d^2 = 0.595 \quad S.E. = 0.672 \quad Q^* = 24.73$ (34 d.f.)

$$(7)\quad \Delta ID_t = \underset{(0.143)}{-0.137} - \frac{(\underset{(0.150)}{0.692} + \underset{(0.143)}{0.252}\,L + \underset{(0.139)}{0.153}\,L^3)}{(1 + \underset{(0.101)}{0.660}\,L^{12})} \ln(B_t + 900)$$

$$+ (\underset{(1.520)}{2.903}\,L + \underset{(1.532)}{1.240}\,L^3)\,\dot{DOL}_t + (\underset{(11.415)}{9.514} + \underset{(8.422)}{5.087}\,L^2)\dot{PW}_t$$

$$- (\underset{(22.370)}{8.790} - \underset{(22.172)}{21.596}\,L)\dot{PC}_t + (1 + \underset{(0.142)}{0.137}\,L)U_t$$

$R_o^2 = 0.936 \quad R_d^2 = 0.614 \quad S.E. = 0.818 \quad Q^* = 30.19$ (34 d.f.)

L is the lag operator; the symbol Δ denotes the first difference operator; and a dot over the variable means that a logarithmic first difference is applied. Standard errors of estimates are shown in parentheses beneath coefficients. R_o is the determination coefficient computed on original (not differenced) dependent variable; R_d is computed on differenced variable. S.E. is the standard error of residuals, and Q* is the Lijung–Box statistic against the null hypothesis that residuals are not autocorrelated until 36th order; related degrees of freedom are shown in parentheses.

Table 2. Tests on the Alternative Causal Hypotheses about Inflation and Interest Rates

	Unrestricted Estimates		Restricted Estimates					
			without PW and PC			without DOL and B		
	RSS	d.f.	RSS	F	d.f.	RSS	F	d.f.
TB	48.15	65	50.08	0.87	3,65	74.14	5.01 (*)	7,65
DR	23.97	59	26.70	1.34	5,59	31.66	1.35	14,59
PR	27.54	60	31.90	2.37 (+)	4,60	41.63	2.56 (*)	12,60
ID	41.18	59	42.29	0.40	4,59	66.58	2.27 (*)	16,59

(*) Significantly different from zero at 1.5% confidence level or less.
(+) Significantly different from zero at 6% confidence level.

5. CONCLUSIVE REMARKS

In this paper we test the hypothesis that the positive relations between interest rates and inflation, observed in Italy during the seventies, were not causal. The test is not led against a "vague" alternative of absolute non–causality as in Granger's and Sims' approach, but exploits the concept of "causality conditional on an information set" more recently suggested by Granger (1980) himself.

Consequently, we propose a simple causal scheme of short run relations among demand, inflation and interest rates and compare it with a direct causal interpretation of the statistical concordance between inflation and interest rates. Our hypothesis is that nominal interest rates are mainly driven by demand level and trade balance, and that those variables are also linked to inflation in such a way that a spurious relationship between rates and inflation is actually observed.

The explanation advanced here is not generally rejected by data, in the period January 1973 – December 1979, for different kinds of interest rates relevant in the Italian monetary market during the seventies, so we are led to conclude that really there was no short run "indexation" of nominal rates in those years, and that the observed behaviour of interest rates was rather a consequence of the reactions of economic operators to the dynamics of aggregate demand.

It is quite surprising that the causal scheme and the distributed lags specified do not differ sharply both for the rates (namely TB and DR) possibly under direct control of the monetary authorities and for the rates linked to the banking system. Apart from the controls on liquidity actuated by the authorities during the seventies, this finding seems to suggest that, in the end, private and public operators acting on the monetary market did not react with strongly hindering behaviours to the movements of aggregate demand and trade balance, although possibly for different reasons.

From the point of view of the monetary authorities, the indexation of nominal interest rates was likely a consequence, possibly not fully unpleasant, of the control on demand and on trade balance. On the other hand, the demand for liquidity of private operators was sensitive to the aggregate demand fluctuations, with evident reflections on the cost of credit; while a trade balance deficit promoted both a destruction of high powered money and the expectation of a stricter monetary policy.

NOTES

(*) I gratefully acknowledge the helpful comments of Francesco Carlucci and an anonymous referee on earlier versions of this paper. The usual caveat applies. Any opinions expressed are those of the author and not of the Istituto per lo Studio della Congiuntura.

1) See, among others, Gibson (1972), Pyle (1972), Cargill (1975), Nelson and Schwert (1977), Tanzi (1980), Carmichael and Stebbing (1983), Gallagher (1986), and Canarella and Garston (1978), the latter on Italian data.
2) Univariate ARIMA models specified for each series are available on request.
3) More precisely, negative relations (statistically significant) were found somewhere for lags of about 15–18 months. They seem to reflect redundant or spurious relations connected to the cycle of k periods and x influences y with a delay of s periods, then a correlation between the two variables is expected to be found at $(s+k/2)$ lags with inverse sign with respect to the first relation. Now, during the seventies in Italy, the length of an average cycle was estimated to be just 32–36 months.
4) This was not found to be a very strong constraint in each case.
5) The partly unsatisfying results of the test performed on this rate could probably be explained by supposing that the monetary authorities move the official discount rate reacting positively to the difference of the actual inflation rate from the planned one.
6) Namely the probability that the coefficients of DOL and B are identically null is less than 1.5%.
7) We estimated equations similar to (4)–(7) allowing for a weaker dynamic specification. To make the computation feasible, lags of each explicative variable are included from zero to the maximum delay revealed by the cross–correlograms (i.e. 1 for PC, 7 for PW, 3 for B, 13 for DOL). A seasonal factor was preserved for B. The correlative structure of the

residuals identified in restricted equations was retained, although it was not found significant quite anywhere. The results of the causality tests are summarised in the table below. Degrees of freedom are specified as above.

	Unrestricted Estimates		Restricted Estimates					
			without PW and PC			without DOL and B		
	RSS	d.f.	RSS	F	d.f.	RSS	F	d.f.
TB	28.21	40	33.93	0.81	10,40	65.00	2.17 (*)	24,40
DR	16.21	39	19.32	0.75	10,39	19.47	1.33	24,39
PR	13.86	39	23.25	2.64 (*)	10,39	35.02	2.48 (*)	24,39
ID	25.88	39	32.71	1.03	10,39	59.94	2.14 (*)	24,39

(*) Significantly different from zero at 1.5% confidence level or less.

REFERENCES

Canarella, G. and N. Garston (1978), "Determination of Nominal Interest Rates: The Case of Italy" in *Rivista Internazionale di Scienze Economiche e Commerciali*, 25, pp.902–15.

Cargill, T. (1975), "The Term Structure of Interest Rates: A Test of the Expectations Hypothesis, *Journal of Finance*, 30, pp.761–71.

Carmichael, J. and P.W. Stebbing (1983), "Fisher's Paradox and the Theory of Interest", *American Economic Review*, 4, pp.619–30.

Carlucci, F. (1982), "La costruzione di una serie mensile di aspettative di inflazione", *Note Economiche*, 2, pp.66–92.

Carlucci, F. and E. Giovannini (1984), "Un'analisi causale della congiuntura italiana negli anni settanta", *Ricerche Economiche*, 2, pp.183–217.

Gallagher, M. (1986), "The Inverted Fisher Hypothesis: Additional Evidence", *American Economic Review*, 76, pp.247–49.

Gibson, W. (1972), "Interest Rates and Inflationary Expectations: New Evidence", *Journal of Finance*, 25, pp.19–34.

Granger, C.W.J. (1980), "Testing for Causality: A Personal View–Point", *Journal of Economic Dynamics and Control*, 2, pp.329–52.

Haugh, L.D. and G.E.P. Box (1977), "Identification of Dynamic Regression (Distributed Lags) Models Connecting Two Time Series, *Journal of American Statistical Association*, 72, pp.121–30.

Nelson, C. and G.W. Schwert (1977), "Short Term Interest Rates as Predictions of Inflation: on Testing the Hypothesis that the Real Rate of Interest is Constant", *American Economic Review*, 67, 478–83.

Pyle, D.H. (1972), "Observed Price Expectations and Interest Rates", *Review of Economics and Statistics*, 54, pp.275–80.

Summers, H.L. (1983), "The Nonadjustment of Nominal Interest Rates: a Study of the Fisher Effect" in J. Tobin (ed.), *Macroeconomics, Prices and Quantities: Essays in Memory of Artur M. Okun*, Basil Blackwell, Oxford.

Tanzi, V. (1980), "Inflationary Expectations, Economic Activity, Taxes and Interest Rates", *American Economic Review*, 70, pp.12–21.

CHAPTER 9

A SHORT TERM DISEQUILIBRIUM MODEL WITH CARRY–OVER, FOR US BUSINESS LOANS

Marcel G. Dagenais, Université de Montréal, Canada

1. INTRODUCTION

Recent studies have applied disequilibrium models to business loans markets. Laffont and Garcia (1977) analysed the supply and demand for business loans by chartered banks in Canada using *monthly* data, and concluded to "the necessity of using disequilibrium methods". Sealey (1979) studied the commercial loan market in the United States with a disequilibrium model, using *quarterly* data. He concluded that "the degree of disequilibrium in the US loans market ... is considerably greater than that found by Laffont and Garcia for the business loan market in Canada".

Ito and Ueda (1981) studied the Japanese and the US business loan markets within a disequilibrium framework, with the express purpose of testing the equilibrium hypothesis in a systematic fashion, based on Bowden's (1978) approach. Using *quarterly* data, they came to the conclusion that, for the US, the "difference between the upward and downward adjustment speeds" of the prime rate is not significant. In addition, the adjustment speed of the prime rate is such that "about 90 percent of the gap between last period's level and the current equilibrium level is adjusted within a quarter". Moreover, "the null hypothesis that the demand is always equal to supply cannot be rejected". Ito and Ueda also point out that their test of the equilibrium hypothesis is based on a more precise statistical argument than that suggested by Sealey.

In line with the above studies, the purpose of the present paper is to introduce carry–over effects of unsatisfied demand in a disequilibrium model of the US business loan market. We have used monthly data, since market

P. Artus and Y. Barroux (eds.), Monetary Policy, 179–199.

disequilibrium and carry–overs are more likely to become manifest when short term periods are considered. The general form of the econometric model used is that suggested in Dagenais (1980).

The results of out study lead us to conclude that, on a *monthly* basis, the US business loan market does behave like a market in disequilibrium; but, the adjustment speed of the prime rate is such that, on a *quarterly* basis, about 90 percent of the equilibrium gap is reduced, which agrees very closely with the findings of Ito and Ueda. However, in our case, the results definitely suggest that, when the analysis is made on a monthly basis, the equilibrium hypothesis can be rejected. Furthermore, when there is excess demand, about one third of the unsatisfied demand does carry over to the next month.

The following section describes the econometric model used. Then, section 3 discusses briefly the estimation procedure. Section 4 analyses the results. In conclusion, section 5 summarises the main findings of the research.

2. THE BUSINESS LOAN MARKET

The actual demand–supply model that we used is very similar to those proposed by Laffont and Garcia (1977), Sealey (1979) and Ito and Ueda (1981), with the exception that our model allows unsatisfied demand to carry over, in part, into the next period. In addition, contrary to Laffont and Garcia (1977), we assume more realistically, we believe, that the price adjustment equation contains a stochastic residual error term. Unlike Sealey and Ito and Ueda, however, our study uses monthly data instead of quarterly data, because we feel that disequilibrium phenomena are likely to be much more easy to detect when monthly rather than quarterly observations are used.

Our model has the following form:

$$\begin{aligned} \ln BL_t^d = {} & \beta_o + \beta_1 \ln IP_t + \beta_2 \ln CUR_{t-1} + \beta_3(\ln PR_t - \ln CBR_t) \\ & + \beta_4(\ln BL_{t-1}^d - \ln BL_{t-1}) + u_{1t}, \end{aligned} \tag{1}$$

$$\begin{aligned} BL_t^s = {} & \psi_o + \psi_1 W_t \ln DMB_t + \psi_2(1 - W_t)\ln DMB_t \\ & + \psi_3(\ln PR_t - FFR_t) + u_{2t}, \end{aligned} \tag{2}$$

$$\ln BL_t = \min(\ln BL_t^d, \ln BL_t^s), \tag{3}$$

$$\Delta \ln PR_t = \gamma(\ln BL^d_{t-1} - \ln BL^s_{t-1}) + u_{3t}. \quad (4)$$

The above symbols are defined as follows:

BL^d_t = demand for business loans, in the US, in constant dollars;

BL^s_t = supply of business loans, in constant dollars;

BL_t = business loans outstanding in US commercial banks, in month t, in constant dollars;

BL_t = BL^*_t/GD^*_t;

BL^*_t business loans outstanding, in current dollars;

GD^*_t = gross national product implicit price deflator (1972=100);

IP_t = US industrial production index;

CUR_t = manufacturing capacity utilisation rate;

PR_t = real return on loans at the prime rate;

PR_t = $(1 + PR^*_t)/GD_t$;

PR^*_t = prime rate;

GD_t = GD^*_t/GD^*_{t-12};

CBR_t = real return on corporate bonds;

CBR_t = $(1 + CBR^*_t)/GD_t$;

CBR^*_t = corporate bonds rate;

DMB_t = $DP_t - BL_t$;

DP_t = bank deposits, in constant dollars;

DP_t = DP^*_t/GD^*_t;

DP^*_t = bank deposits, in current dollars;

W_t = dummy variable
= 1 from January 1959 to August 1968;
= 0 from September 1968 to December 1981;

FFR_t = real return on federal funds
= $(1 + FFR^*_t)/GD_t$;

FFR^*_t = federal funds rate;

u_{1t}, u_{2t}, u_{3t} = residual errors.

Equation (4) can be rewritten alternatively, following Bowden (1978), as:

$$\ln PR_t = \mu \ln PR_{t-1} + (1 + \mu)\ln \tilde{P}R_{t-1} + \mu u_{4t} \quad (5)$$

where $\tilde{P}R_{t-1}$ is the equilibrium value of PR_{t-1} that would have cleared the market in period t−1, u_{4t} is a residual error and

$$\mu = 1 + \gamma(\beta_3 - \psi_3). \quad (6)$$

As $\mu \to 0$, the model becomes a dynamic equilibrium model.

The subscript t refers to the time period and ln stands for the natural logarithm. All monetary variables appearing in equations (1) to (5) are measured in 1972 constant dollars by dividing the current dollar figures by the GNP implicit price deflator[1]. Since the variables are expressed in logarithmic form, the coefficients may be directly interpreted as elasticities. The data used for estimating the parameters contain 264 observations covering the period January 1960 to December 1981. The data and their sources are listed in the Appendix.

In the general theoretical model presented in Dagenais (1980), it was assumed that the error terms of the demand, supply and price equations have a joint normal distribution and that they are contemporaneously correlated but serially uncorrelated. This assumption is replaced here by the more general hypothesis that the error terms are generated by a joint linear stochastic process. This point will be discussed in greater detail in the next section.

Parameters of special interest for the present study are μ and β_4. A value of μ different from zero and comprised between 0 and 1 suggests that the market considered operates under disequilibrium conditions; and a value of β_4 different from zero and lying between 0 and 1 suggests that there is some carry–over of unsatisfied demand into the next period[2].

In the demand equation, the variable IP stands as an index of economic activity. Its coefficient is therefore expected to be positive. The CUR variable can be seen as another index of economic activity or it can alternatively be considered, for the given level of economic activity measured by IP, as an indicator of business profitability. In the former case, one would expect the coefficient of CUR to be positive; if, however, CUR is seen as an index of profitability, one would expect that, as profits increase, the need of firms for short term financing[3] decreases. On these grounds, one would thus expect the coefficient of CUR to be negative. The variable PR_t is the price variable. Its coefficient is expected to be negative in the demand equation. In turn, CBR is a measure of the cost of alternative sources of financing. Clearly, corporate bonds are not the only alternative source of financing for business enterprises, but this rate is undoubtedly very representative of the possible alternative sources. The coefficients of PR_t and CBR_t are constrained to be equal in absolute value, in our demand equation, because it seems reasonable to assume that it is the differential between the two rates that matters. Furthermore, this formulation has the advantage of avoiding severe problems of collinearity. Finally, the term

$(\ln BL^d_{t-1} - \ln BL_{t-1})$ is included to capture the carry–over effect, as mentioned above.

In the supply equation, we have used DMB as the scale variable, instead of DP alone, to minimise possible identification problems, following the suggestion made by Melitz and Pardue (1973). Clearly, the coefficient of this variable is expected to be positive. Given that in September 1968, reserve requirement regulations have changed (Gilbert, 1980) from a contemporaneous reserve accounting (CRA) system to a more flexible lagged reserve accounting (LRA) system, one may anticipate that the coefficient of the deposit variable ln DMB may have changed between the two periods. The dummy variable W has therefore been introduced to take account of this possibility. The price variable PR appears also in the supply equation and its coefficient is clearly expected to be positive. The real return on federal funds, which corresponds to the possible return on a risk free alternative, has been included as a basic measure of the opportunity cost to the banks of lending to corporations. Again, since it is essentially the differential that matters and in order to avoid collinearity problems, the coefficients of ln PR and ln FFR have been assumed to be equal in absolute value[4].

3. PARAMETER ESTIMATION

The parameter estimation procedure used is essentially a nonlinear generalised least squares (NLGLS) procedure applied to the reduced form equation for PR_t. As explained in Dagenais (1980), it is possible, from this reduced form equation, to identify all the structural parameters of the model, except the constant terms. The estimation of the constant terms then requires additional calculations.

If the residual errors u_{1t}, u_{2t} and u_{3t} were assumed to be serially uncorrelated, the residual error of the reduced form equation for PR_t could be assimilated to a stochastic variable following an MA(2) process, since this residual error, say η_t, is equal to:

$$\eta_t = -\gamma u_{2,t-1} - \beta_4 u_{3,t-1} + \gamma u_{1,t-1} + \gamma\beta_4 u_{2,t-2} + u_{3t} \,. \qquad (7)$$

This is the assumption that was originally made in Dagenais (1980). However, actual endeavours (not reported here) to apply the model to several sets of data pertaining to different markets have led us to conclude, from the analysis of the residuals, that in this type of econometric applications, the elements of the η vector do not usually seem to follow such a process. It appears therefore more reasonable to make no specific assumption on the nature of the stochastic process generating the u's but rather to assume directly that the η's were generated by a high order autoregressive process. This type of process is often considered as a satisfactory approximation in econometric applications. In practice, a twelve order autoregressive process, namely:

$$\eta_t = \sum_{i=1}^{12} \rho_i \eta_{t-i} + \epsilon_t , \tag{8}$$

has been considered, where the ϵ_t's are i.i.d. residual errors and the ρ's are the autoregressive coefficients.

The adopted parameter estimation procedure consisted in first obtaining consistent estimates of the η's from the original reduced form equation for PR_t, by an instrumental variable approach. Then, a stepwise regression procedure was applied to the estimated η's to identify the autoregressive process and estimate its coefficients. The variables of the reduced form equation were then transformed so as to eliminate (asymptotically) the serial correlation[5] and consistent estimates of the structural parameters (except the constant terms) were obtained by applying a nonlinear least squares (NLLS) procedure. Finally, the constant terms β_o and ψ_o were estimated by the method suggested in Section 3.2 of Dagenais (1980).

The estimates of ψ_o and β_o obtained by this procedure are possibly biased and inconsistent. Indeed, Monte Carlo experiments designed to represent demand–supply relationships in a wide variety of situations (Dagenais and Laferrière, 1983) confirmed that even if the sample is very large and the values of all the other parameters of the model are known, the estimates of ψ_o and β_o are biased; but these experiments suggested also that the bias is quite negligible, even for small samples and even when the residual errors are serially correlated.

Given that our reduced form equation contained lagged endogenous variables among its explanatory variables (namely PR_{t-1}, PR_{t-2} and BL_{t-2}), an instrumental variable approach had to be used to obtain consistent estimates of the reduced form coefficients and of the η's, in the first step of our procedure. Following the suggestion of Liviatan (1963), consistent estimates of the reduced form coefficients were obtained by applying OLS to the reduced form equation, after having replaced PR_{t-1}, PR_{t-2} and BL_{t-2} by predicted values $\hat{P}R_{t-1}$, $\hat{P}R_{t-2}$ and $\hat{B}L_{t-2}$. These predicted values were obtained by regressing PR_{t-1}, PR_{t-2} and BL_{t-2} on lagged values of the exogenous variables of the model.

From the consistent estimates of reduced form coefficients obtained by the instrumental variable procedure explained above, initial estimates were derived indirectly for β_4 and γ and used to initiate the NLLS procedure for estimating the structural parameters (except the constants). A detailed description of the algorithm used to obtain the NLLS solution can be found in Dagenais (1984).

Under the assumption that the ϵ_t's are normal, uncorrelated and homoscedastic, the asymptotic covariance matrix of our parameter estimates can be evaluated[6] by computing $-\hat{M}^{-1}$, where $\hat{M}$ is the estimated matrix of second derivatives of the log–likelihood with respect to the parameters.

4. THE RESULTS

As explained above, instrumental variable estimates of the parameters of the reduced form were first obtained under the assumption that the η's constituted a white noise series. Then, a twelve order linear autoregressive model was applied to the estimated residual errors and a stepwise regression routine was used. The results suggested that only the autoregressive routine was used. The results suggested that only the autoregressive coefficients of order 1, 3 and 5 ought to be retained. The estimates of these coefficients are shown in Table 1.

Table 1. Autoregressive Coefficients

Coefficient	Estimate	Standard Error	t–Test
ρ_1	0.2618	0.0608	4.3019
ρ_2	0.1266	0.0614	2.0600
ρ_5	0.1404	0.0598	2.3474

The variables of the price reduced form equation were therefore transformed, as explained in section 3, using the estimates obtained for ρ_1, ρ_3 and ρ_5; and the structural parameters (excluding the constant terms) were estimated by the iterative procedure also mentioned in section 3. The examination of the estimated residual errors of the price reduced form equation with the transformed variables then suggested that the ϵ_t's might not be homoscedastic over the whole sample period but that, on the contrary, their variances might be larger near the end of the period. To verify this fact, the series of estimated residuals was split into two subsets, namely those pertaining to the first half of the period (subset 1) and those pertaining to the second half (subset 2), and the following statistic was computed:

$$F = S_2^2/S_1^2 \tag{9}$$

where

S_1^2 = sum of squared residuals of subset 1;

S_2^2 = sum of squared residuals of subset 2.

Since the available sample with the transformed variables contains a large number of observations[7], namely 254, this statistic is approximately distributed as $F_{127,127}$, under the hypothesis of homoskedasticity[8]. Given that F = 2.85 while the critical $F_{127,127}$ value at 99% confidence level is approximately 1.5, it seemed therefore reasonable to conclude to the presence of heteroskedasticity. In order to take account of this situation, the covariance estimates of our parameters were then obtained by applying White's (1980) formula to our linearised equation[9]. The parameter estimates and their estimated standard errors appear in Table 2.[10] Finally, estimates of β_o and ψ_o were obtained by the

Table 2. Parameter Estimates

Variable	Parameter	Estimate	Standard Error	t–Test
1. Reduced Form Equation				
Constant term		0.0440	0.0413	1.0655
2. Demand Equation				
$\ln IP_t$	β_1	0.8795	0.3015	2.9169
$\ln CUR_{t-1}$	β_2	–0.9846	0.3980	–2.4736
$\ln PR_t - \ln CBR_t$	β_3	–2.1806	0.9525	–2.2894
$\ln BL^d_{t-1} - \ln BL_{t-1}$	β_4	0.3325	0.0924	3.6001
3. Supply Equation				
$W_t \ln DMB_t$	ψ_1	0.6381	0.4171	1.6742
$(1-W_t)\ln DMB_t$	ψ_2	0.7443	0.3811	1.7844
$\ln PR_t - \ln FFR_t$	ψ_3	9.0646	3.8634	2.3463
4. Price Equation				
a) Demand–Supply Gap Formulation (equation (4))				
$\ln BL^d_{t-1} - BL^s_{t-1}$	γ	0.0507	0.0218	2.3306
b) Equilibrium Price Gap Formulation (equation (5))				
$\ln PR_{t-1}$	μ	0.4299	0.0799	5.3808

method outlined in Dagenais (1980). The results are shown in Table 3. Except for the coefficient of the ln CUR variable, which could on a priori grounds be either positive or negative, all other coefficients have the expected signs. Furthermore, all t–statistics are relatively high in absolute value, the lowest one being 1.674 which corresponds to the 5% significance level when one–tail tests are considered[11].

Table 3. Constant Terms

Equation	Estimate
Reduced Form	0.0440
Demand	0.3395
Supply	–0.7930

The order of magnitude of the coefficient estimates also appear to reasonable. The coefficient of ln IP represents the elasticity of business loan demand with respect to economic activity. In the long run, one would expect this coefficient to be around one. The coefficient of ln CUR indicates that when the utilisation ratio increases, in relative terms, by one percent, the increase in profits induces firms to resort more intensely to autofinancing and leads to a decrease in business loan demand of 1%. Although it is difficult to have strong priorities on the order of magnitude of this coefficient, the results obtained do not seem unreasonable.

The coefficient attached to the variable ln PR – ln CBR might seem high at first sight. In order to be able to make an appropriate evaluation of this result, one must realise that PR corresponds to the *real return factor* on business loans (that is, PR = *one plus the real interest rate* on business loans), while CBR corresponds to the *real return factor* on corporate bonds. Therefore, a coefficient of –2.18 suggests, for example, that if the real rate of interest on business loans increased from 0.05 to 0.06 while the real rate of interest on corporate bonds stays put at 0.04 – which means that the ratio of these return factors increases from 1.05/1.04 to 1.06/1.04, that is from 1.01 to 1.02 – the demand for business loans will fall by 2.2%. Given that in our sample, which includes a period of very high nominal business loan rates (greater than 20%), the range of PR/CBR extends only between 0.973 and 1.058, with an average value of 1.000, our results indicate that an increase in the value of PR/CBR equal to the difference between the extreme values observed in our sample would induce a reduction of 17% in the real demand for business loans[12]. This effect appears to be rather moderate.

The coefficient of the excess demand variable ($\ln BL^d_{t-1} - \ln BL_{t-1}$) lies between 0 and 1 as anticipated. Its value (0.33) suggests that on average, one third of unsatisfied demand is carried over into the next period.

In our supply equation, the elasticities with respect to unmatched deposits DMB_t appear to be reasonable both for the CRA and LRA periods. The difference between the two coefficients is 0.1063 with a standard error of 0.0564 and a t value of 1.88. Therefore, the distinction between the two periods appear to be warranted. Furthermore, the fact that the elasticity is larger when the more flexible LRA system is enforced is a coherent result.

The coefficient of ln PR – ln FFR in the supply equation must be interpreted in a similar fashion as the coefficient of ln PR – ln CBR in the demand equation. In our sample, the range of PR/FFR extends between 1.004 and 1.057 with an average value of 1.016. Therefore, according to our results, a drop in PR/FFR, equal to the total length of the range observed in our sample for this variable, would induce, ceteris paribus, a decrease of 36% in the real supply of business loans. Although this percentage is much higher than the percentage mentioned above for the demand equation, it is still very plausible.

The γ coefficient of the price equation is difficult to interpret it itself, but the interpretation of the derived value of μ is straightforward. In our case, this coefficient lies between 0 and 1, as anticipated, and is equal to 0.43. This corresponds to an adjustment speed of 0.92 over a three month period. This result is quite similar to the adjustment speed found by Ito and Ueda, namely 0.90[13].

5. CONCLUSION

The results reported in the preceding pages suggest that the disequilibrium model with carry–over suggested in Dagenais (1980) is useful for analysing the US business loan market. These results also suggest that the characteristics of disequilibrium markets become more apparent when shorter time periods are considered. Our findings suggest indeed that when monthly periods are considered, the business loan market does appear as a market in disequilibrium where a non–negligible part of unsatisfied demand is carried over into the next period. Yet, our results are consistent with the findings of Ito and Ueda to the effect that when quarterly periods are considered, about 90% of the gap between equilibrium price and actual price is adjusted within a quarter.

Our research has also permitted to develop an operational algorithm to estimate the structural parameters of our dynamic disequilibrium model. Our results have also demonstrated that, with a sufficiently large sample, meaningful results could be obtained.

NOTES

* This research was financed in major part by the Social Science Research Council of Canada. It was also supported by the Fonds F.C.A.R. of Quebec. Mr. Jean–Francois Fillion made a significant contribution as research assistant. Denis Bolduc and Tran Cong Liem provided advice and assistance on algorithmic design and programming. Monique Bélanger, Alain Fugère and Robert Gosselin also participated in the project at various stages.

1) This deflator is available only on a quarterly basis. Liner interpolation has been used to obtain monthly estimates.
2) Note that when unsatisfied demand in period t–1 carries over into period t, transactions will be made at price P_t and not at price P_{t-1}. Hence, the carry–over of unsatisfied demand, namely $\beta_4(D_{t-1}-Q_{t-1})$, should strictly vary with ΔP_t. We should therefore have $\beta_4=\beta_4(\Delta P_t)$. We have ignored this fact and have assumed, as a first approximation, that β_4 is constant. This is probably not a bad approximation for markets where prices do not vary abruptly, if the time periods considered are short and if purchasing decisions show some rigidity due to technical or institutional constraints.
3) Business loans are essentially short term loans with a maturity of 3 to 6 months.
4) Note that in our supply equation, no inventory variable appears as such, while such a variable was present in the general model presented in Dagenais (1980). In fact, in financial markets the variable DMB plays a role similar to that of the inventory variable in markets for goods.
5) Following the approach suggested by Wallis (1967) for first order serial correlation.
6) Note that these covariance estimates are obtained under the implicit assumption that the autoregressive coefficients (ρ_i, i=1,...,12) of the original residual errors η, are known. The fact that these have to be estimated in the first place introduces an additional element of uncertainty which is not taken into account here.
7) The basic series used, which are reproduced in the Appendix, contained 264 observations; but the presence of lagged variables together with the serial correlation correction procedures adopted reduced the sample available at the final step of the estimation procedure to 254 observations.
8) The residual error estimates are approximately independent for large sample. If the condition of independence is verified, and if all residuals have a common variance σ^2, then S_1^2/σ^2 and S_2^2/σ^2 are independent χ^2_{127} stochastic variables. hence, F is distributed as $F_{127,127}$.
9) An alternative approach would have been to use weighted least squares. However, this approach requires that one can identify the variable or variables that "cause" heteroskedasticity. Our efforts in this direction were unsuccessful.
10) The standard error estimates obtained by applying White's formula were

not very different from those obtained when ignoring the presence of heteroskedasticity.

11) One–tail tests would be appropriate here for all variables except CUR_{t-1} since one has prior expectations on the signs of all other variables.

12) This percentage has been computed in the following way:

$$p = \left[\frac{Y_1 - Y_2}{Y_1}\right] \times 100 = \left[\frac{(X_1^\alpha - X_2^\alpha)}{X_1^\alpha}\right] \times 100 = \left[\left[1 - \left[\frac{X_2}{X_1}\right]^\alpha\right] \times 100\right]$$

where p = percentage of reduction in Y;
Y_1 = original value of Y;
X_1 = original value of X. In our case, $X_1 = 0.973$;
Y_2 = final value of Y;
X_2 = final value of X. Here, $X_2 = 1.058$;
$\alpha = -2.2$.

13) We define here the "adjustment speed" as $1-\mu$.

REFERENCES

Bowden, R.J. (1978), *The Econometrics of Disequilibrium*, North–Holland, Amsterdam.

Dagenais, M.G. (1980), "Specification and Estimation of a Dynamic Dis–equilibrium Model", *Economics Letters*, 5, pp.323–28.

Dagenais, M.G. and M. Dagenais (1982), "Algorithme de sélection sous constraintes d'un sous–ensemble d'éléments homogènes", *Annales des sciences mathématiques du Québec*, VI, 1, pp.43–51.

Dagenais, M.G. and R. Laferrière (1983), "L'évaluation du biais d'estimation des termes constants, dans un modèle de déséquilibre dynamique", Cahier no. 8334, Département de sciences économiques, Université de Montréal.

Dagenais, M.G. (1984), "A Short–Term Disequilibrium Model with Dynamic Spill–Over Effects, for Business Loans", Cahier no. 8436, Département de sciences économiques, Université de Montréal.

Gilbert, A. (1980), "Lagged Reserve Requirements: Implications for Monetary Control and Bank Reserve Management", *Federal Reserve Bank of St. Louis*, pp.7–20.

Ito, T. and K. Ueda (1981), "Tests of the Equilibrium Hypothesis in Disequilibrium Econometrics: An International Comparison of Credit Rationing", *International Economic Review*, 22, 3, pp.691–708.

Laffont, J–J. and R. Garcia (1977), "Disequilibrium Econometrics for Business Loans", *Econometrica*, 54, pp.1187–1204.

Liviatan, N. (1963), "Consistent Estimation of Distributed Lags", *International Economic Review*, 4, pp.44–52.

Melitz, W. and M. Pardue (1973), "The Demand and Supply of Commercial Bank Loans", *Journal of Money, Credit and Banking*, pp.669–92.

Oberhofer, W. and J. Kmenta (1974), "A General Procedure for Obtaining Maximum Likelihood Estimates in Generalized Regression Models", *Econometrica*, 42, pp.579–90.

Sealy, C.W. Jr. (1979), "Credit Rationing in the Commercial Loan Market: Estimates of a Structural Model under Conditions of Disequilibrium", *Journal of Finance*, 34, pp.689–702.

Wallis, K.F. (1967), "Lagged Dependent Variables and Serially Correlated Errors: A Reappraisal of Three–Pass Least–Squares", *Review of*

Economics and Statistics, 49, pp.555–67.
White, H. (1980), "A Heteroskedasticity–Consistent Covariance Matrix Estimator and a Direct Test for Heteroskedasticity", *Econometrica*, 48, 4, pp.817–38.

APPENDIX

1. Description and Sources of Data

All series except the interest rates are seasonally adjusted.

BL* : commercial and industrial loans outstanding, in billions of dollars. January 1973 to December 1981. Source: CITIBASE. CODE: FCLCI. This series is not available before January 1973.
January 1960 to December 1972. Source: CITIBASE. CODE: FCLICX. This series was linked to the FCLCI series by applying the following univariate regression model:

$$FCLCI_t = \xi \, FCLICX_t + v_t$$
$$v_t = rv_{t-1} + s_t$$

Since both the FCLCI and the FCLICX series were available between January 1973 and June 1979, these common observations were used to estimate ζ and r. The estimates are $\hat{\xi} = 1.0593$ and $\hat{r} = 0.8891$.

GD* : GNP implicit price deflator, 1972=100. Source of quarterly series: CITIBASE. CODE: GD. Monthly estimates were obtained by linear interpolation.

IP : industrial production index, 1967=100. Source: CITIBASE. CODE: IP.

CUR : capacity utilisation rate in manufacturing. Source: CITIBASE. CODE: IPXMCA

PR* : prime rate. Source: CITIBASE. CODE: FYPR.

CBR* : average yield on corporate bonds. Source: CITIBASE. CODE FYAVG.

DP* : bank deposits, in billion of dollars =

demand deposits	Source: CITIBASE. Code: FMSD
+ other checkable deposits	Source: CITIBASE. CODE: FMCD
+ saving deposits	Source: CITIBASE. CODE: FMSVC
+ small term deposits	Source: CITIBASE. CODE: FMSTB
+ long term deposits	Source: CITIBASE. CODE: FMLTC

FFR* : federal funds rate. Source: Bank of Canada. CODE: BC4408

2. Actual Data Used in the Statistical Analysis

	BL_t^*	IP_t	CUR_{t-1}	PR_t^*	CBR_t^*	DP_t^*	FFR_t^*	GD_t^*
				1959				
January								66.85
February								67.04
March								67.21
April								67.38
May								67.55
June								67.64
July								67.72
August								67.81
September								67.87
October								67.94
November								68.00
December								68.15
				1960				
January	42.4	68.8	83.6	5.0	4.91	176.5	3.96	68.29
February	42.7	68.2	85.6	5.0	4.88	175.9	3.89	68.44
March	43.0	67.6	84.6	5.0	4.81	176.1	3.82	68.48
April	43.5	67.0	83.2	5.0	4.76	176.2	3.93	68.52
May	43.8	67.0	82.3	5.0	4.80	176.5	3.79	68.56
June	43.9	66.1	81.5	5.0	4.78	177.0	2.71	68.66
July	44.0	65.9	80.2	5.0	4.74	178.2	3.14	68.76
August	44.0	65.8	79.7	4.9	4.61	180.2	2.89	68.86
September	44.3	65.1	79.1	4.5	4.58	180.8	2.64	68.89
October	44.4	65.0	77.9	4.5	4.63	181.3	2.00	68.93
November	44.5	64.1	77.5	4.5	4.64	182.2	1.50	68.96
December	44.6	62.9	75.8	4.5	4.66	183.0	1.89	68.93
				1961				
January	44.6	63.0	74.3	4.5	4.65	183.6	0.66	68.91
February	44.8	62.9	74.1	4.5	4.59	185.4	2.54	68.88
March	45.0	63.3	73.5	4.5	4.54	186.3	1.61	68.99
April	45.0	64.6	73.9	4.5	4.56	187.5	1.14	69.11
May	45.0	65.6	75.4	4.5	4.58	189.0	2.14	69.22
June	44.9	66.5	76.4	4.5	4.63	190.1	1.18	69.33
July	45.2	67.3	77.3	4.5	4.70	190.9	0.86	69.43
August	45.4	67.9	78.1	4.5	4.73	192.0	1.50	69.54
September	45.6	67.8	70.0	4.5	4.74	192.9	1.96	69.58
October	45.8	69.1	78.2	4.5	4.73	193.9	2.36	69.61
November	45.9	70.2	79.6	4.5	4.70	195.2	2.29	69.65
December	46.5	70.8	80.8	4.5	4.71	196.1	2.86	69.84

	BL^*_t	IP_t	CUR_{t-1}	PR^*_t	CBR^*_t	DP^*_t	FFR^*_t	GD^*_t
				1962				
January	46.6	70.2	81.6	4.5	4.70	197.4	2.14	70.04
February	46.7	71.3	80.2	4.5	4.70	199.2	2.47	70.23
March	47.2	71.7	81.4	4.5	4.67	201.3	2.88	70.31
April	47.5	71.9	81.9	4.5	4.63	202.8	2.86	70.40
May	47.9	71.8	81.7	4.5	4.58	203.9	1.71	70.48
June	48.2	71.6	81.3	4.5	4.59	204.7	2.89	70.53
July	48.4	72.3	80.9	4.5	4.63	205.6	2.95	70.57
August	49.0	72.4	81.5	4.5	4.64	206.2	2.93	70.62
September	49.5	72.8	81.4	4.5	4.61	207.2	2.79	70.77
October	49.8	72.9	81.8	4.5	4.57	208.8	2.82	70.93
November	50.2	73.2	81.4	4.5	4.55	210.5	2.89	71.08
December	50.4	73.2	81.8	4.5	4.52	212.4	3.00	71.19
				1963				
January	50.7	73.8	81.7	4.5	4.49	213.8	2.98	71.30
February	51.0	74.6	81.9	4.5	4.48	214.9	3.00	71.41
March	51.3	75.1	82.4	4.5	4.47	216.5	2.98	71.43
April	51.6	75.8	82.6	4.5	4.47	217.8	3.00	71.44
May	51.9	76.7	83.5	4.5	4.48	219.6	3.00	71.46
June	52.3	76.9	84.0	4.5	4.47	220.2	2.96	71.53
July	52.5	76.6	83.9	4.5	4.49	222.1	3.41	71.59
August	52.6	76.8	83.3	4.5	4.50	223.8	3.48	71.66
September	53.1	77.5	83.5	4.5	4.52	224.9	3.48	71.83
October	53.8	78.1	83.8	4.5	4.52	226.5	3.50	72.00
November	54.6	78.4	84.3	4.5	4.54	229.0	3.50	72.17
December	55.2	78.3	84.3	4.5	4.55	229.6	3.50	72.23
				1964				
January	55.5	79.0	84.0	4.5	4.57	231.1	3.48	72.30
February	55.9	79.5	84.5	4.5	4.55	232.4	3.48	72.36
March	56.1	79.5	84.7	4.5	4.56	232.8	3.43	72.43
April	56.7	80.8	84.4	4.5	4.58	233.7	3.47	72.50
May	57.2	81.3	85.6	4.5	4.59	235.4	3.50	72.57
June	57.7	81.5	85.6	4.5	4.59	236.7	3.50	72.70
July	58.2	82.0	85.4	4.5	4.58	238.7	3.42	72.84
August	58.8	82.6	85.9	4.5	4.57	240.8	3.50	72.97
September	59.4	82.9	86.1	4.5	4.57	242.7	3.45	73.03
October	60.0	81.7	86.2	4.5	4.57	244.5	3.36	73.10
November	60.7	84.2	84.6	4.5	4.58	246.4	3.52	73.16
December	61.9	85.2	86.8	4.5	4.58	248.0	4.00	73.36

	BL^*_t	IP_t	CUR_{t-1}	PR^*_t	CBR^*_t	DP^*_t	FFR^*_t	GD^*_t
				1965				
January	63.1	86.2	88.0	4.5	4.57	250.5	4.00	73.57
February	64.3	86.7	88.6	4.5	4.55	252.2	3.93	73.77
March	65.5	87.8	88.7	4.5	4.56	253.8	4.09	73.89
April	66.5	88.2	89.3	4.5	4.56	255.5	4.09	74.01
May	67.4	88.9	89.3	4.5	4.57	256.6	4.07	74.13
June	68.2	89.6	89.4	4.5	4.60	258.4	3.80	74.27
July	69.1	90.4	89.5	4.5	4.64	260.7	4.09	74.42
August	69.8	90.8	90.3	4.5	4.65	263.1	4.13	74.56
September	70.8	91.1	89.9	4.5	4.69	265.8	4.13	74.69
October	71.6	92.0	89.6	4.5	4.72	268.9	4.00	74.83
November	72.5	92.4	89.8	4.5	4.75	270.8	4.11	74.96
December	73.6	93.5	89.6	4.5	4.84	273.2	4.43	75.21
				1966				
January	74.7	94.4	90.5	5.0	4.89	275.2	4.55	75.46
February	75.6	95.0	90.9	5.0	4.89	275.2	4.55	75.46
March	76.5	96.3	90.9	5.4	5.10	278.3	4.68	76.00
April	77.5	96.6	91.6	5.5	5.16	281.2	4.48	76.29
May	78.5	97.4	91.5	5.5	5.18	282.1	4.84	76.58
June	80.2	97.9	91.6	5.5	5.28	282.9	5.43	76.72
July	81.3	98.4	91.5	5.8	5.36	283.5	5.46	76.85
August	82.2	98.5	91.4	5.9	5.50	284.6	5.34	76.99
September	82.8	99.4	91.4	6.0	5.71	286.5	4.50	77.24
October	83.3	100.1	91.2	6.0	5.67	285.5	5.04	77.50
November	83.4	99.4	91.6	6.0	5.65	285.0	5.64	77.75
December	83.3	99.6	90.1	6.0	5.69	286.8	5.57	77.92
				1967				
January	84.2	99.8	90.0	6.0	5.50	289.5	5.18	78.08
February	84.9	99.0	89.5	5.8	5.35	292.8	5.18	78.25
March	85.8	98.5	88.1	5.7	5.43	296.5	4.25	78.34
April	86.3	99.2	87.2	5.5	5.42	297.5	4.00	78.44
May	86.9	98.7	87.5	5.5	5.56	301.0	3.95	78.53
June	87.8	98.4	86.4	5.5	5.75	304.7	4.07	78.78
July	88.6	98.7	86.1	5.5	5.86	307.8	3.93	79.03
August	88.7	100.0	85.3	5.5	6.91	311.1	3.59	79.28
September	89.4	100.3	86.3	5.5	6.00	313.6	4.00	79.56
October	89.5	101.2	85.9	5.5	6.14	315.8	3.50	79.85
November	89.9	102.6	86.2	5.7	6.36	318.0	4.36	80.13
December	91.3	103.5	87.1	6.0	6.51	320.3	4.63	80.47

	BL_t^*	IP_t	CUR_{t-1}	PR_t^*	CBR_t^*	DP_t^*	FFR_t^*	GD_t^*
				1968				
January	91.6	103.7	87.5	6.0	6.45	321.9	4.55	80.81
February	92.2	104.3	87.1	6.0	6.45	321.9	4.55	80.81
March	93.0	104.7	87.3	6.0	6.42	325.5	5.39	81.48
April	94.0	104.9	86.9	6.2	6.53	326.4	5.63	81.81
May	94.5	106.2	86.8	6.5	6.60	328.6	6.02	82.14
June	94.9	106.6	87.6	6.5	6.63	330.9	6.14	82.37
July	96.0	106.5	87.6	6.5	6.57	334.0	6.05	82.61
August	97.0	107.1	87.0	6.5	6.37	337.9	5.93	82.84
September	98.0	107.1	86.8	6.4	6.35	341.0	5.70	83.22
October	98.9	107.4	86.6	6.0	6.43	345.1	5.91	83.61
November	100.8	108.6	86.5	6.2	6.56	349.2	5.73	83.99
December	101.6	108.8	87.3	6.6	6.80	353.0	6.25	84.32
				1969				
January	103.5	109.5	86.7	7.0	6.89	353.1	6.27	84.64
February	104.7	110.2	87.0	7.0	6.93	352.5	6.61	84.97
March	105.7	110.8	87.2	7.2	7.11	352.5	6.87	85.35
April	107.2	110.6	87.3	7.5	7.17	352.9	7.79	85.72
May	108.1	110.3	86.8	7.5	7.10	352.5	8.92	86.10
June	108.7	111.2	86.2	8.2	7.27	352.3	8.34	86.56
July	109.1	111.8	86.5	8.5	7.39	349.6	8.05	87.03
August	109.5	112.3	86.7	8.5	7.37	346.5	8.82	87.49
September	109.9	112.3	86.4	8.5	7.53	346.0	9.61	87.87
October	110.7	112.5	86.2	8.5	7.72	345.3	8.39	88.24
November	111.3	111.4	85.7	8.5	7.76	345.0	8.32	88.62
December	111.9	111.2	84.6	8.5	8.13	345.2	8.71	89.04
				1970				
January	111.6	109.1	84.0	8.5	8.32	345.6	9.30	89.47
February	111.4	108.8	81.8	8.5	8.29	342.9	8.41	89.89
March	111.3	108.8	81.5	8.4	8.18	345.6	7.45	90.28
April	111.5	108.6	81.1	8.0	8.20	350.2	8.43	90.68
May	111.7	108.3	80.7	8.0	8.46	352.1	7.64	91.07
June	112.8	108.1	80.3	8.0	8.77	353.8	7.21	91.31
July	113.8	108.4	79.8	8.0	8.85	360.5	6.89	91.55
August	114.4	108.3	79.8	8.0	8.73	367.3	6.34	91.79
September	115.2	107.6	79.2	7.8	8.68	373.9	6.05	92.20
October	115.4	105.4	78.5	7.5	8.63	378.7	6.11	92.63
November	115.7	104.8	76.4	7.3	8.65	383.0	5.16	93.03
December	116.4	107.2	75.8	6.9	8.35	388.9	4.82	93.49

	BL_t^*	IP_t	CUR_{t-1}	PR_t^*	CBR_t^*	DP_t^*	FFR_t^*	GD_t^*
					1971			
January	116.8	108.1	77.5	6.3	8.04	394.8	4.23	93.94
February	117.8	108.0	78.0	5.9	7.75	401.2	3.46	94.40
March	117.6	108.0	77.9	5.4	7.84	408.4	4.02	94.83
April	117.9	108.5	77.5	5.3	7.86	411.7	4.14	95.27
May	118.9	109.1	77.8	5.5	8.03	415.6	4.68	95.70
June	119.3	109.6	78.4	5.5	8.14	419.5	5.07	95.97
July	120.1	109.8	78.5	5.9	8.14	422.5	5.38	96.25
August	121.3	108.9	78.5	6.0	8.12	424.4	5.48	96.52
September	122.2	110.3	77.4	6.0	7.97	427.8	5.43	96.81
October	122.5	110.9	78.5	5.9	7.88	432.1	5.11	97.10
November	122.7	111.3	79.2	5.5	7.77	435.8	4.86	97.39
December	122.7	112.3	79.3	5.5	7.75	440.7	4.05	97.83
					1972			
January	122.9	114.6	79.7	5.2	7.66	445.8	3.43	98.28
February	123.7	115.3	80.8	4.8	7.68	450.5	3.34	98.72
March	124.8	116.5	81.3	4.8	7.66	454.8	4.09	98.95
April	126.3	117.7	81.8	5.0	7.71	458.1	4.20	99.19
May	127.2	118.1	82.7	5.0	7.71	461.6	4.38	99.42
June	127.9	118.7	82.7	5.0	7.66	465.6	4.49	99.70
July	128.5	119.3	82.9	5.3	7.66	470.8	4.54	99.97
August	129.1	120.7	82.9	5.3	7.61	476.9	4.90	100.25
September	130.1	121.8	83.8	5.5	7.59	482.6	4.99	100.68
October	132.3	123.4	84.4	5.7	7.59	486.5	5.01	101.11
November	134.1	124.4	85.3	5.8	7.52	491.8	5.03	101.54
December	136.3	125.8	85.9	5.8	7.47	497.9	5.34	102.00
					1973			
January	139.3	126.3	86.9	6.0	7.49	503.4	6.35	102.46
February	144.4	127.8	86.5	6.0	7.57	509.1	6.75	102.92
March	149.5	128.5	87.5	6.3	7.62	516.1	7.11	103.51
April	151.8	128.5	87.7	6.6	7.62	520.9	7.14	104.10
May	154.0	129.6	87.4	7.0	7.62	526.1	7.95	104.69
June	156.8	129.9	87.9	7.5	7.69	530.3	8.59	105.27
July	159.6	130.4	87.8	8.3	7.80	535.0	10.58	105.86
August	162.2	130.4	88.0	9.2	8.04	542.7	10.79	106.44
September	163.0	131.1	87.6	9.9	8.06	546.5	10.84	107.18
October	163.5	131.4	87.8	9.9	7.96	547.4	9.90	107.92
November	163.9	131.6	87.7	9.8	8.01	551.7	10.09	108.66
December	165.7	131.3	87.7	9.8	8.05	555.6	9.52	109.31

	BL^*_t	IP_t	CUR_{t-1}	PR^*_t	CBR^*_t	DP^*_t	FFR^*_t	GD^*_t
				1974				
January	167.8	129.9	87.3	9.7	8.12	561.2	9.47	109.95
February	169.5	129.6	85.8	9.2	8.17	566.7	8.81	110.60
March	174.4	130.0	85.3	8.9	8.28	571.4	9.61	111.51
April	180.4	129.9	85.4	10.0	8.54	578.3	10.78	112.42
May	182.8	131.3	85.1	11.3	8.71	584.3	11.54	113.33
June	185.0	131.9	85.6	11.5	8.89	590.3	11.97	114.31
July	189.3	131.8	85.7	12.0	9.15	594.6	12.29	115.28
August	191.6	131.7	85.4	12.0	9.43	597.2	11.84	116.26
September	193.6	131.8	85.1	12.0	9.78	600.4	11.12	117.37
October	194.8	129.5	84.8	11.7	9.92	602.3	9.72	118.48
November	196.0	124.9	82.9	10.8	9.70	604.5	9.46	119.59
December	197.4	119.3	79.5	10.5	9.63	607.0	8.45	120.62
				1975				
January	198.0	115.2	75.1	10.1	9.65	610.4	6.99	121.64
February	196.8	112.7	71.9	9.0	9.43	612.1	6.15	122.67
March	195.2	111.7	70.1	7.9	9.36	615.1	5.53	123.19
April	193.9	112.6	69.0	7.5	9.59	614.6	5.71	123.70
May	192.1	113.7	69.9	7.4	9.66	617.9	5.14	124.22
June	190.2	116.4	70.3	7.1	9.55	624.2	5.72	124.96
July	189.4	118.4	71.9	7.2	9.54	628.9	6.25	125.70
August	188.6	121.0	73.3	7.7	9.61	628.4	6.23	126.44
September	188.7	122.1	74.8	7.9	9.67	632.6	6.29	127.21
October	188.9	122.2	75.7	8.0	9.63	633.8	5.65	127.97
November	189.0	123.5	75.5	7.5	9.55	640.9	5.28	128.74
December	189.9	124.4	76.2	7.3	9.57	643.0	5.18	129.13
				1976				
January	189.4	126.1	76.6	7.0	9.42	645.8	4.80	129.51
February	189.1	128.1	77.5	6.8	9.31	650.2	4.80	129.90
March	186.9	128.7	78.8	6.8	9.26	654.0	4.84	130.29
April	183.7	129.0	79.0	6.8	9.12	658.2	4.93	130.69
May	184.2	130.1	79.1	6.8	9.16	660.9	5.50	131.08
June	184.5	130.7	79.6	7.2	9.16	665.0	5.58	131.61
July	184.5	131.2	79.7	7.3	9.08	669.5	5.28	132.13
August	185.0	132.0	80.1	7.0	8.93	672.7	5.28	132.66
September	186.6	131.3	80.1	7.0	8.79	677.3	5.32	133.36
October	188.2	131.3	79.8	6.8	8.71	682.7	4.99	134.05
November	190.0	132.6	79.5	6.5	8.66	688.5	4.90	134.75
December	191.3	133.6	80.1	6.4	8.47	696.5	4.66	135.38

	BL^*_t	IP_t	CUR_{t-1}	PR^*_t	CBR^*_t	DP^*_t	FFR^*_t	GD^*_t
				1977				
January	191.7	133.7	80.5	6.3	8.41	703.8	4.72	136.01
February	193.5	134.5	80.2	6.3	8.48	709.0	4.74	136.64
March	195.7	136.3	80.4	6.3	8.51	714.9	4.74	137.40
April	196.3	137.1	81.5	6.3	8.49	720.0	4.82	138.15
May	197.5	138.0	81.7	6.4	8.74	723.7	5.45	138.91
June	199.1	138.9	82.1	6.8	8.38	730.5	5.43	139.52
July	200.4	139.0	82.4	6.8	8.33	736.5	5.45	140.14
August	202.7	139.3	82.5	6.8	8.34	742.3	6.02	140.75
September	204.3	139.6	82.4	7.1	8.31	748.0	6.35	141.47
October	207.2	140.1	82.4	7.5	8.42	754.0	6.49	142.19
November	209.6	140.3	82.6	7.8	8.48	761.3	6.55	142.91
December	211.2	140.5	82.5	7.8	8.54	768.0	6.65	143.58
				1978				
January	213.7	140.0	82.6	7.9	8.74	775.9	6.72	144.26
February	217.2	140.3	81.7	8.0	8.78	780.0	6.78	144.93
March	221.1	142.1	81.7	8.0	8.80	787.1	6.82	146.16
April	224.0	144.4	82.7	8.0	8.88	796.0	7.00	147.40
May	227.4	144.8	83.8	8.3	9.02	805.2	7.36	148.63
June	230.3	146.1	83.8	8.6	9.13	812.5	7.78	149.56
July	232.7	147.1	84.3	9.0	9.22	817.4	7.88	150.49
August	234.9	148.0	84.8	9.0	9.08	823.4	8.28	151.42
September	237.3	148.6	85.2	9.4	9.04	831.4	8.62	152.61
October	240.8	149.7	85.5	9.9	9.20	832.6	9.24	153.80
November	244.3	150.6	86.0	10.9	9.40	841.4	9.85	154.99
December	246.1	151.8	86.3	11.6	9.49	846.1	10.25	156.05
				1979				
January	251.3	152.0	86.8	11.8	9.65	849.9	10.12	157.10
February	256.2	152.5	86.6	11.8	9.63	852.0	10.06	158.16
March	259.3	153.5	86.8	11.8	9.76	854.6	10.00	159.16
April	263.6	151.1	87.2	11.8	9.81	860.4	10.09	160.17
May	267.4	152.7	85.3	11.8	9.96	862.1	10.28	161.17
June	270.9	153.0	86.3	11.7	9.81	867.7	10.32	162.19
July	275.0	153.0	86.1	11.5	9.69	874.1	10.63	163.21
August	279.1	152.1	86.0	11.9	9.74	882.3	11.16	164.23
September	285.0	152.7	84.9	12.9	9.93	892.0	11.61	165.31
October	287.9	152.7	85.2	14.4	10.71	897.6	15.61	166.39
November	288.4	152.3	84.8	15.6	11.37	902.0	12.46	167.47
December	291.1	152.5	84.4	15.3	11.35	904.8	13.49	168.72

	BL^*_t	IP_t	CUR_{t-1}	PR^*_t	CBR^*_t	DP^*_t	FFR^*_t	GD^*_t
				1980				
January	296.8	153.0	84.1	15.3	11.74	910.5	13.54	169.98
February	301.7	152.8	84.0	15.6	12.92	919.0	14.62	171.23
March	304.2	152.1	83.6	18.3	13.73	923.5	17.78	172.58
April	303.4	148.2	82.7	19.8	13.21	925.1	15.12	173.93
May	299.1	143.8	80.3	16.6	12.11	927.1	9.46	175.28
June	296.9	141.4	77.6	12.6	11.64	930.4	9.08	176.58
July	298.1	140.3	75.7	11.5	11.77	932.8	8.98	177.88
August	303.4	142.2	74.9	11.1	12.33	943.5	10.03	179.18
September	308.4	144.4	75.8	12.2	12.80	953.5	10.85	180.72
October	313.9	146.6	77.0	13.8	13.07	962.4	13.17	182.27
November	320.7	149.2	78.2	16.1	13.63	978.4	17.43	183.81
December	324.9	150.4	79.3	20.4	14.04	985.5	18.45	185.25
				1981				
January	329.3	151.4	79.8	20.2	13.80	1000.8	18.12	186.70
February	330.8	151.8	80.0	19.4	14.22	1007.8	14.96	188.14
March	330.6	152.1	79.8	18.1	14.26	1011.1	13.48	189.11
April	331.8	151.9	79.8	17.2	14.66	1017.1	16.28	190.09
May	336.0	152.7	79.8	19.6	15.15	1023.0	18.71	191.06
June	340.2	152.9	80.0	20.0	14.76	1032.4	19.20	192.58
July	345.8	153.9	79.6	20.4	15.18	1037.8	18.54	194.09
August	352.3	153.6	79.8	20.5	15.60	1049.6	17.41	195.61
September	357.7	151.6	79.6	20.1	16.18	1053.7	15.00	197.08
October	361.7	149.1	78.3	18.5	16.20	1057.0	14.87	198.54
November	362.4	146.4	76.6	16.8	15.35	1064.5	12.42	200.01
December	358.0	143.4	74.8	15.8	15.38	1071.0	12.54	201.23

PART V

ECONOMETRIC MODELS OF THE FINANCIAL MARKETS: THEIR USE IN ASSESSING THE CROWDING–OUT EFFECTS

CHAPTER 10

REAL AND FINANCIAL LINKAGES IN THE UK ECONOMY

George W. McKenzie and Stephen H. Thomas, *University of Southampton, UK*

1. INTRODUCTION

Over the past fifteen years there has been a steady revolution in attitudes towards the role of monetary policy in the United Kingdom. In the years following the publication of the Radcliffe Commission Report in 1959 there was widespread belief that monetary policy was unlikely to affect economic activity. In part this conclusion stemmed from a view that aggregate expenditure, in particular investment, was not responsive to interest rates. However, a dominant concern was that monetary policy was simply incapable of systematically controlling aggregate liquidity and credit. This viewpoint is most elegantly stated in the famous paragraph 392 of the Radcliffe Report:

> ....If there is less money to go round, in relation to the other assets (both physical and financial), it will be held only by people willing to make a greater sacrifice in order to hold it: that is to say, rates of interest will rise. But they will not, unaided, rise by much, because in a highly developed financial system (such as the United Kingdom system), there are many highly liquid assets which are close substitutes for money, as good to hold and only inferior when the actual moment for a payment arrives.

To a large extent, these views found support in the important academic writings of Gurley and Shaw (1955, 1960) and of the Yale School led by Tobin (1971). However, thinking began to change in the late 1960s. The various quantitative and interest rate controls in use by the Bank of England were thought to reduce the efficiency and competitiveness of the British banking industry. The thrust of the Competition and Credit Control policies inaugurated in 1971 was to improve this situation. The Monetary Control legislation of 1981 carried developments further. In addition policy objectives

P. Artus and Y. Barroux (eds.), Monetary Policy, 203–231.

changed in the late 1970s. The reduction of inflation was now considered to be the prime goal rather than the maintenance of high levels of employment. Monetarists of all hues were both eloquent and persistent in calling attention to their view that well formulated monetary policies were necessary and, to some economists, sufficient for a stable and prosperous global economy.

But what has happened to the Radcliffe view? To some extent is is lurking in the background. In the 1980 Green Paper on Monetary Control and in various statements by Governors of the Bank of England there has been a recurring theme: namely, that competitive de–regulated financial markets and effective monetary control may be incompatible objectives. In a competitive environment any attempt to reduce the rate of growth of the money supply will lead to the growth of near–money assets and hence to an offsetting increase in the velocity of circulation. The relationships between currency and bank deposits and between bank deposits and nominal spending may not be as rigid as required for effective monetary control. Further, the relationship between bank reserves and bank deposits may not be as stable as is necessary if it is highly sensitive to changes in relative interest rates.

The recent dominance of the classical and new classical approach to monetary control can therefore only be explained by some particularly compelling reasons. In our opinion, the key is contained in the perceptive remark made in 1971 by the late Harry Johnson. He argued that the methods of monetarism "offered liberation to the small–scale intellectual, since it freed his mind from dependence on the large–scale research team and the large and expensive computer program." Monetary models, even those involving international linkages, could be reduced to a few equations. Thus their structure can be comprehended easily by students, financial analysts and, importantly, by policy makers. Further, they can be subjected to the panoply of estimation procedures and diagnostic tests developed by time series statisticians, whether or not they are attracted by the structure of rational expectations formulae. Indeed these advantages are even more compelling today with the recent development of portable personal computers and powerful econometric software which enables the execution of research programmes whether it be on a Concorde flight between New York and Paris or on a TGV speeding between Gare de Lyon and Geneva. But surely if our technical skills have reached this level, we should be expending more effort in refining our models so as to reflect the current complex financial environment and its linkages with the real sector.

We believe that this objective can be achieved best by modifying the conventional monetary model to take into account some of the most important conjectures raised in the Radcliffe Report by Tobin and by Gurley and Shaw. In particular, we propose to focus upon three issues:

1) disaggregation of the liquidity demand function into its constituents: notes and coins, current account deposits, time deposits, other retail liquidity and foreign currency deposits. These are treated as functions of wealth, GDP and interest rates.
2) through the balance sheet identity of the UK banking system, the above assets provide banks with a supply of loanable funds. it is conjectured that these funds determine aggregate domestic expenditure.
3) it is assumed that the prices of traded and non–traded goods are generated by aggregate cost equations rather than by a market clearing process. Important explanatory variables in these equations are (i) the exchange rate and (ii) a proxy for the cost of borrowed funds. The latter is influenced by the position of foreigners vis–a–vis the UK banking sector.

The linkages between the real and financial sectors of our model exhibit two distinct differences in comparison to the orthodox monetary approach:

1) the money supply and other liquidity variables do not directly influence nominal expenditure. In our model asset demand decisions together with the policies of the Bank of England determine the supply of credit provided by the banking system. Bank credit is one of the variables explaining nominal expenditure.
2) the effect of interest rates on demand is also indirect, operating through two channels. First, variations in interest rates influence asset demands and hence credit availability. Second, interest rates influence the cost and hence the price of aggregate output. Given nominal expenditure and the price level, output is determined.

The structure of this paper is as follows. In section 2, we set out two model structures. The first case involves a standard text book explanation of the money supply process and is designed to act as a benchmark against which subsequent work can be compared. It also enables us to identify some of the basic concerns expressed in the Green Paper on Monetary Control. The second model includes the additional financial assets thought important to the study of the monetary transmission mechanism. The model is closed with equations explaining nominal expenditure, prices, interest rates and exchange rates. Section 3 discusses our modelling methodology , while in the final section we present the results obtained from estimation of a dynamic version of the model.

2. SOME THEORETICAL CONSIDERATIONS

Case 1. This simple model involves the following variables:

M_0	= monetary base
NC	= notes and coins held by the non–bank private sector
BR	= commercial bank reserves
D	= commercial bank deposits
CRED	= commercial bank credit
M	= money stock
cr	= cash ratio
r_{mlr}	= minimum lending rate (statutory)
r	= market rate of interest

The money base and money supply are defined as follows:

$$M_0 \equiv NC + BR \tag{1}$$

$$M \equiv NC + D \tag{2}$$

We can rearrange (1) as

$$\frac{M_0}{M} \equiv \frac{NC}{M} + \frac{BR}{D} \cdot \frac{D}{M} \tag{3}$$

Anticipating our more general model we assume that the proportion of notes and coins and of deposits relative to money arises from a portfolio decision by private sector agents:

$$\frac{NC}{M} = g(r, Y) \tag{4}$$

$$\frac{D}{M} = 1 - g(r, Y) \tag{5}$$

Similarly, we assume that the ratio of bank reserves to total bank deposits arises from a portfolio decision on the part of bank management

$$\frac{BR}{D} = f(cr, r, r_{mlr}) \tag{6}$$

The relationship between the market rate of interest r and the minimum lending rate determines the extent of excess reserves. That is, the higher is r relative to r_{mlr} the lower will be the ratio BR/D.

Substitution of (4), (5) and (6) into (3) yields the standard textbook money multiplier

$$\frac{M}{M_0} = \frac{1}{g(r,Y) + f(cr,r,r_{mlr})(1-g(r,Y))} \tag{7}$$

The central result to emerge from equation (7) is that the ratio of the money stock to the monetary base is a variable depending upon the level of nominal expenditure, the cash ratio, the market rate of interest and the minimum lending rate. The degree to which these variables are important determines the extent to which the monetary authorities are able to influence the money supply by means of the monetary base. However, it also calls attention to the fact that variation in cr and r_{mlr} may be necessary to achieve this control. To a large extent, this simple model summarises some of the underlying concerns expressed in the 1980 Green Paper on Monetary Control (c.f. chapters 1 and 4).

Before we pass on to discuss our more general model, it is useful to close the system in a simple manner in order to provide a direction flag for subsequent results. For the sake of argument assume (a) a fixed exchange rate regime such that r is equal to the foreign rate of interest r* and (b) that the central bank sterilises all international financial flows in the manner of the Exchange Equalisation Account. Also let us assume that nominal spending is only a function of available credit, viz

$$Y = y(CRED) \tag{8}$$

where

$$CRED = D - BR = D(1-f(cr, r, r_{mlr})) \tag{9}$$

Substitution of (5), (7) and (9) into (8) yields:

$$Y = y\left[\frac{(1-g)(1-f)M_0}{g + f(1-g)}\right] \tag{10}$$

which can be solved to yield a reduced form expression for nominal spending:

$$Y = h[M_0, cr, r^*, r_{mlr}] \tag{11}$$

Thus in this simple world of case 1 we would not expect to observe a fixed ratio between Y and M_0 . These relationships depend not only on M_0 but also on the level of r_{mlr} relative to r*.

Case 2. As noted above, a concern expressed in the Radcliffe Report was the degree to which the existence of near monies could thwart the effectiveness of monetary policies. As Johnson (1962) pointed out in his enduring survey of monetary economics, the central empirical issue is the degree to which various financial assets are substitutable for one another. In this section, we expand the previous model to allow for a broader spectrum of assets. In particular, we adhere to the Gurley and Shaw distinction between (a) deposits at monetary financial intermediaries (banks) which are a medium of exchange and (b) deposits at non–monetary financial intermediaries (denoted hereafter as NMFIs) which are a source of liquidity but cannot be utilised for transactions' purposes. The basic relationships set out in this section will be those actually estimated in dynamic format and presented in the following section. Thus in addition to the financial sector, we also need to provide details concerning interest rate, price and exchange rate sectors.

a. The Financial Sector in a Complex World

Instead of a single aggregate variable called bank deposits we consider four separate categories of financial institution liability:

D_1 = demand deposits
D_2 = time deposits
D_3 = retail liquidity (e.g. building society deposits)
D_4 = foreign currency deposits held by UK residents at UK banks

In this expanded model notes and coins and each of the four above assets will be assumed to depend upon a vector of interest rates (discussed in (b) below); real GDP and financial wealth, where nominal financial wealth FW is defined as the sum of all financial assets considered.

$$FW \equiv NC + D_1 + D_2 + D_3 + D_4 \quad (12)$$

In addition to FW we shall be concerned with explaining the following three financial aggregates:

$$M_1 \equiv NC + D_1 \quad (13)$$
$$M_3 \equiv NC + D_1 + D_2 \quad (14)$$
$$CRED \equiv D_1 + D_2 + D_4 - BR - \text{non–deposit liabilities} \quad (15)$$
$$EL \equiv D_1 + D_2 + \text{bank liabilities to the public sector} \quad (16)$$

where EL represents eligible liabilities. Commercial bank reserve behaviour is now described by the relationship

$$\frac{BR}{EL} = f(cr, r, r_{mlr}) \quad (17)$$

The aggregates above are explained by the portfolio behaviour of the private sector.

$$NC/P = g_0(FW/P, Y/P, r) \quad (18)$$
$$D_1/P = g_1(FW/P, Y/P, r) \quad (19)$$

$$D_2/P = g_2(FW/P, Y/P, r) \quad (20)$$
$$D_3/P = g_3(FW/P, Y/P, r) \quad (21)$$
$$D_4/P = g_4(FW/P, Y/P, r) \quad (22)$$

where r is a vector of interest rates (determined in the next section) and P represents the GDP deflator.

b. Interest Rates, Prices and Exchange Rates

The remaining equations of the model describe the processes whereby events in the United Kingdom as well as abroad work through the economy ultimately affecting the financial sector activity and then feeding back onto real sector expenditure. Three sectors are identified. By and large, all endogenous variables explained in these sectors are determined by mark–up relationships rather than market clearing processes. This reflects our belief that in a world of uncertainty and incomplete information about current events or indeed even the recent past, economic agents adopt rules of thumb or in some instances simply follow market leaders.

i) Interest rate determination

In this section we are concerned with six asset yields:

r_1 = three month euro–dollar yield
r_2 = three month euro–sterling yield
r_3 = UK bank deposit rate
r_4 = three month UK Treasury bill yield
r_5 = Building Society deposit rate
r_6 = yield implied by covered interest rate arbitrage condition

We treat r_1 as an exogenous variable. Cassese and Lothian (1982) present evidence supporting this. The other five yields are determined by the following five behavioural equations:

Covered interest arbitrage condition

$$(1+r_6) \equiv \frac{E1}{EF}(1+r_1) \quad (23)$$

Fisher parity condition

$$(1+r_2) = \frac{E1}{EE1}(1+r_1) \quad (24)$$

Treasury bill rate

$$r_5 = z_1(r_4) \quad (25)$$

Commercial bank deposit rate

$$r_2 = z_2(r_5, r_4) \tag{26}$$

Building Society deposit rate

$$r_3 = z_3(r_5, r_2) \tag{27}$$

Equation (23) generates the UK interest rate, r_6, which is compatible with covered interest rate parity with the euro–dollar rate, where E1 and EF are the spot and three month forward dollar/sterling exchange rates, respectively. In contrast, equation (24) reflects the assumption that the euro–sterling interest rate is generated by the euro–dollar rate and the future expected interest rate, EE1. In addition, it is assumed that arbitrageurs ensure that there is a relationship between the Treasury bill rate r_4 and the euro–sterling rate (i.e. equation (25)). Commercial banks set their deposit rate according to (i) general market conditions, assumed to be reflected in the Treasury bill rate, r_4, and (ii) wholesale market conditions as reflected in r_2. Hence equation (26). Finally, it is assumed that Building Societies not only look at general financial market conditions (r_4), but also at their close competition, the commercial banks. Hence the bank deposit rate is included as an explanatory variable in equation (27).

ii) <u>The price formation sector</u>

This sector is described in detail in a paper by McKenzie and Blofeld (forthcoming). It involves four equations: two aggregate cost functions, one for the manufacturing (traded goods) sector and the other for the non–traded goods sector; a 'spill–over' equation relating wages in the manufacturing sector to (i) wage bargains struck in the non–traded goods sector and (ii) the general price level; and a weighting equation explaining the GDP deflator as a function of prices in the traded and non–traded goods sector. The relationships take the following form:

$$P_w = P_w\left(W_m, P_{NT}, \frac{FWP}{E1}, P_E, r_4\right) \tag{28}$$

$$P_{NT} = P_{NT}(W_{NT}, P_w, P_E, r_4) \tag{29}$$

$$W_M = W_M(W_{NT}, P) \tag{30}$$

$$P = P(P_w, P_{NT}) \tag{31}$$

In equation (28), it is assumed that the wholesale price index P_w, here used as a proxy for the price of traded goods, is a function of the cost of inputs: (i) wages in the manufacturing sector, (ii) the price of goods and/or services obtained from the non–traded sector P_{NT}, (iii) the price of foreign goods expressed in sterling, FWP/E1, (iv) the price of oil, and (v) the cost of borrowed funds proxied by r_4. A similar aggregate cost function is used to explain prices in the non–traded goods sector. Here the wages in that sector W_{NT} play an important role. Equation (30) represents an attempt to link wage bargains in the two sectors. The so–called Scandinavian theory conjectures that the price of traded goods, which affect wage bargains struck in that sector, influence, in turn, the wage bargains struck in the non–traded sector. However, the conjecture made in this paper is that for the case of the United Kingdom, the direction of causality is just the reverse. The non–traded goods sector in the UK essentially involves the public sector and public sector corporations. It accounts for approximately one half of GDP. Given its power and the influence of organised labour in the non–traded goods sector, it is not unreasonable to assume that it is a wage leader. Thus W_{NT} is treated as an exogenous variable to the model and as an explanatory variable for W_M. We assume also that the general price level will influence this variable. Finally, the GDP deflator P is treated as a function of the prices in the two sectors. Equation (31) is thus really no more than a 'weighting' function.

iii) The exchange rate sector

This sector is described in detail in a paper by McKenzie and Thomas (1987) and basically involves two conjectures. First, we assume that the spot exchange rate is determined by variables which reflect the perceptions of market operators and if data was available could be captured by an extended portfolio model. Second, we follow Levich (1987) in the view that notions like market efficiency and the Fisher parity condition are relevant only as long run stationary state concepts. In the short run deviations from these conditions can be expected.

Thus we conjecture that the spot exchange rate is determined as follows

$$E1 = e(L27, A87, Q_{oil}, EE1) \tag{32}$$

where

L27 = the value of UK sterling bank liabilities held by foreigners
A87 = the value of UK sterling bank assets vis–a–vis foreigners
Q_{oil} = the quantity of UK oil production
EE1 = the expected future spot rate here defined by the Fisher parity condition (cf. equation (24))

The inclusion of L27 and A87 (both treated as exogenous) impart a flavour of a portfolio balance type approach to (32). Bond data is generally not satisfactory, and money variables are not significant when added to the equation. The role of banking in exchange rate determination is a seriously neglected area given the predominance of these institutions in carrying out international financial transactions. Thomas and Wickens (1987) provide a formal justification for bank assets and liabilities in exchange rate determination and a discussion of its importance in practice. Note that the potential endogeneity of L27 and A87 should not be a problem since there is little change when they are instrumented out.

Finally, in a long run stationary state we would expect all relevant exchange rates to be equal to each other, i.e.

$$EE1 = E1 \tag{33}$$

$$EE1 = EF \tag{34}$$

However, in the short run we would expect the two equalities to break down as transactors may only respond slowly to new information or perhaps vary their perception of risk premiums in some systematic manner. A test of the dynamic versions of (33) and (34) by McKenzie and Thomas (1987) show that the processes generating the actual forward rate e_f and the forward parity rate implied by the Fisher condition, EE1, are significantly different.

The structure of the model described above is summarised in the flow chart contained in Figure 1.

3. MODELLING METHODOLOGY

The model outlined above offers a coherent vehicle for analysing the possibility for asset substitution in response to interest rate changes, whether emanating from abroad (r_2 and r_6) or domestic monetary policy (r_4), and the implications of such substitution for real and nominal activity. However, we do not subscribe to the view that such a model, in its static or simple partial adjustment form, can really capture the essential dynamic relationships between the variables under discussion: neither would the imposition of rational

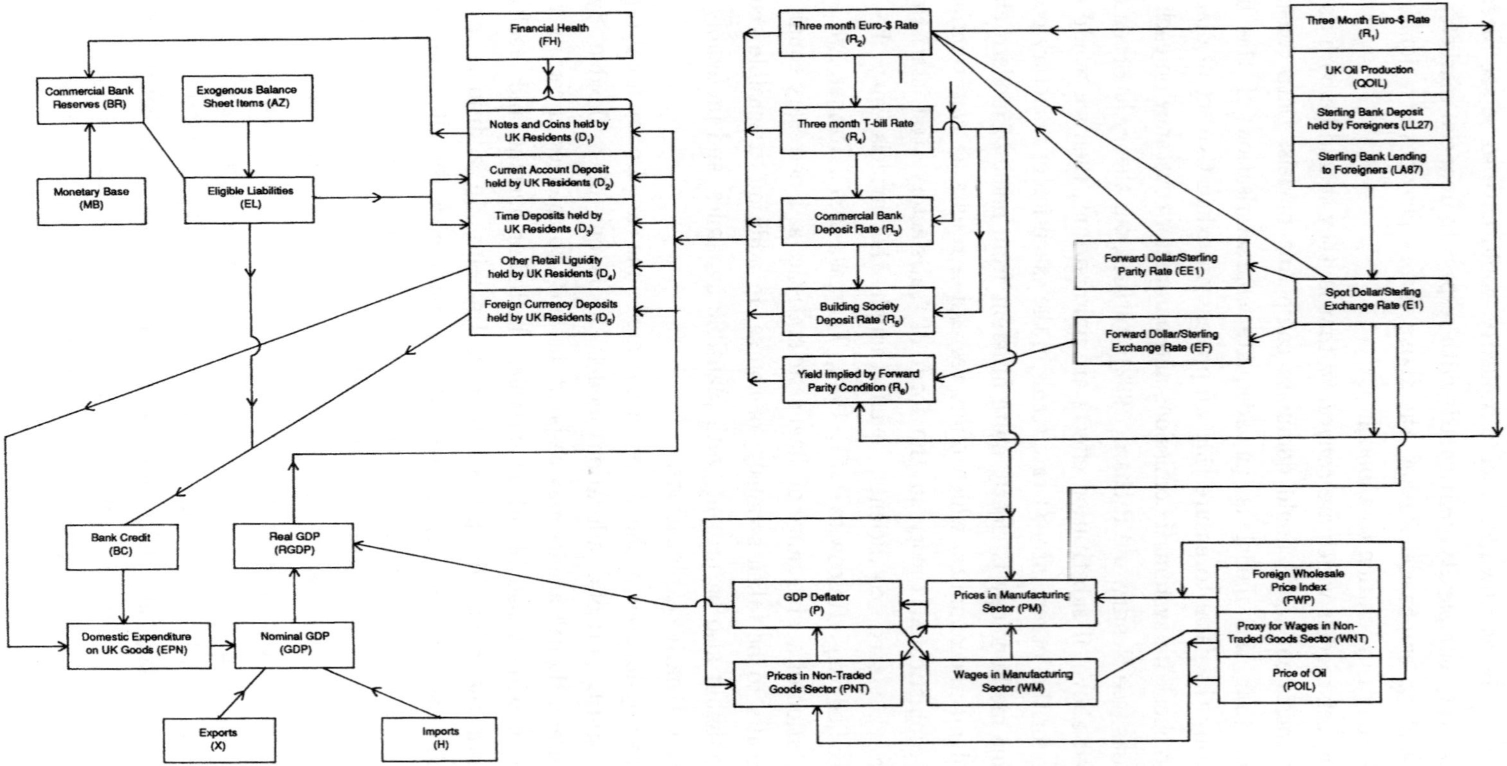
Financial Health
(FH)
Commercial Bank
Reserves (BR)
Exogenous Balance
Sheet Items (AZ)
Monetary Base
(MB)
Eligible Liabilities
(EL)
Notes and Coins held by
UK Residents (D_1)
Current Account Deposit
held by UK Residents (D_2)
Time Deposits held by
UK Residents (D_3)
Other Retail Liguidity
held by UK Residents (D_4)
Foreign Currrency Deposits
held by UK Residents (D_5)
Three month Euro-$ Rate
(R_2)
Three month T-bill Rate
(R_4)
Commercial Bank
Deposit Rate (R_3)
Building Society
Deposit Rate (R_5)
Yield Implied by Forward
Parity Condition (R_6)
Three Month Euro-$ Rate
(R_1)
UK Oil Production
(QOIL)
Sterling Bank Deposit
held by Foreigners (LL27)
Sterling Bank Lending
to Foreigners (LA87)
Forward Dollar/Sterling
Parity Rate (EE1)
Spot Dollar/Sterling
Exchange Rate (E1)
Forward Dollar/Sterling
Exchange Rate (EF)
Bank Credit
(BC)
Real GDP
(RGDP)
Domestic Expenditure
on UK Goods (EPN)
Nominal GDP
(GDP)
Exports
(X)
Imports
(H)
GDP Deflator
(P)
Prices in Manufacturing
Sector (PM)
Prices in Non-Traded
Goods Sector (PNT)
Wages in Manufacturing
Sector (WM)
Foreign Wholesale
Price Index
(FWP)
Proxy for Wages in Non-
Traded Goods Sector (WNT)
Price of Oil
(POIL)

expectations be worthwhile, since complexity would have to be sacrificed, and it is that very complexity, particularly with respect to financial markets, which we so wish to emphasise. Rather, the above theory provides a rationale for a sensible long run solution to a model.

We seek models which are *congruent*: that is, they should be both data and theory consistent, and should dominate competing models. Data consistency requires that the model is an adequate characterisation of the process generating the data: to ensure this we present an exhaustive set of diagnostic tests to check for systematic omissions and parameter constancy on each of our equations (see Hendry and Richard, 1982). Further, our theory has been clearly outlined above: if substitution effects are unimportant, then we would expect no role for the 'other' interest rate terms in the execution of monetary policy.

This methodology is clearly quite different from much of modern classical applied macroeconomics, which offers regression results as *confirmation* of a fairly sophisticated theory in the form of 'satisfactory' test statistics and 'correctly' signed coefficients, even though the models may be badly misspecified (e.g. Hercowitz 1981, 1982, Thomas, 1987). Rather, we see the presentation of a wide range of diagnostic statistics as a necessary condition for *any* results to be taken seriously; of course, in addition, a sensible economic theory should also be present, with plausible dynamics, and preferably tested against alternative explanations.

The implications of the above for our modelling exercise are important. We reject static portfolio allocation models in favour of a flexible dynamic structure: although agents may respond instantly to changes in certain rates of return, a wide range of other variables, including income and wealth may influence the allocation process with a time–lag. In addition, any given portfolio specification may not completely characterise the allocation problem facing agents and included dynamics may act as proxies for any omitted effects. This is in contrast to much of the conventional portfolio allocation literature (e.g. Backus and Purvis, 1980) but is clearly more general.

Similarly, our interest rates are determined as a distributed lag on the policy variable, r_4, (the Treasury Bill rate), and other rates, as markets do not adjust completely within one quarter to external shocks. The data is allowed to 'reveal' such lags, and unless we rule out the existence of market imperfections this is surely quite plausible. The price sector also features distributed lag effects of wages and prices, which is a standard feature of models involving inflexibilities such as goods and labour market contracts and inventories. That we have not sought to introduce rational expectations is seen by many to be a disadvantage. However, with our level of disaggregation the exercise would soon get out of hand. Even the use of substitution approach of Wickens (1982) and McCallum (1976), which introduces MA errors, would prove problematical on standard econometric software. Non–rational expectations may be considered a necessary first step to advance our knowledge, albeit imperfectly, of an important set of issues.

On the other hand, we may believe that certain sectors, for instance, the foreign exchanges, are more likely to be 'nearly rational' than others: to this end our exchange rate equation involves the euro–interest differential forward rate as a predictor of the future spot rate, though even here we do not impose such an assumption on our model, and a flexible dynamic model selection procedure allows market efficiency to be revealed if it is required.

A final word is in order about the recent enthusiasm for cointegration analysis (e.g. Granger, 1981), and indeed the theoretical structure described in section 2 could be couched in terms of the appropriate form the variables in the long run solution should take. However, we feel that when short run dynamics is being investigated, and when no strong preference is revealed for error correction models, then there is no particular advantage to carrying out a rigorous cointegration analysis: omitted dynamics may have serious small sample effects (Banerjee et al, 1986). In addition, the behaviour of variables over certain historical periods of, say, 10 to 20 years, may yield quite inappropriate inferences as to the degree of integration of the underlying series, (e.g. interest rates), and the economist may quite correctly reject such 'short run long run' information. We prefer to search for congruent models within a general dynamic formulation. Gilbert (1986) provides a highly readable account of such a methodology and how it differs from the North American tradition.

4. THE RESULTS

The joint estimation of our theoretical model would clearly violate the Sargan (1975) conditions, which state that in linear models the number of observations should exceed the number of different endogenous and exogenous variables. Rather we turn to two–stage least squares in the belief that if sensible data consistent specifications are obtained by single–equation techniques. It is often the case that subsequent joint estimation has little effect on the parameters (e.g. see Thomas and Weldon, 1987).

The model was estimated using quarterly data for the period 1965–81, with the last eight quarters being used for a Chow test of parameter constancy. It falls naturally into four self–contained blocks, and allows us to use limited information methods within individual blocks. Appendix I contains the equations estimated by within–block 2SLS on RATS, while Table 2 presents the exhaustive diagnostic checks obtained from the program GIVE. The long run solutions to the equation obtained using the Bewley (1979) technique are presented in Table 1.

Table 1. Long Run Elasticities
(the prefix "L" indicates that all variables are expressed in logarithms)

t–values in parentheses

Bank Reserves

$$LBR = \underset{(21.7)}{0.459}\ LL256 + \underset{(6.71)}{0.105}\ LCR$$

Notes and Coins

$$LNC - LP = \underset{(21.7)}{2.24}\ LRFW + \underset{(18.4)}{7.48}\ LRGDP + \underset{(19.4)}{10.5}\ LR_3 - \underset{(-19.6)}{75.7}\ LR_5$$

Time Deposits

$$LD2 - LP = \underset{(6.9)}{1.55}\ LRGDP + \underset{(4.8)}{4.27}\ LR_2 - \underset{(-2.9)}{4.68}\ LR_3 - \underset{(-0.43)}{0.18}\ LR_6$$

Retail Liquidity less M_3

$$LD3 - LP = \underset{(44.1)}{12.3}\ LRFW - \underset{(-12.7)}{0.38}\ LRGDP - \underset{(-43.6)}{26.4}\ LR_3 - \underset{(-45.2)}{46.3}\ LR_5$$

Foreign Currency Deposits

$$LD4 - LP = \underset{(32.6)}{5.38}\ LRGDP + \underset{(16.8)}{13.8}\ LR_2 - \underset{(-20.1)}{33.9}\ LR_3 + \underset{(13.0)}{20.8}\ LR_4 + \underset{(9.7)}{2.9}\ LR_6$$

Nominal Expenditure

$$LEPN = \underset{(14.9)}{0.62}\ LCRED + \underset{(11.95)}{0.55}\ LD$$

Bank Deposit Rate

$$LR_3 = \underset{(17.5)}{1.11}\ LR_4 - \underset{(-3.7)}{0.22}\ LR_2$$

Treasury Bill Rate

$$LR_4 = \underset{(26.6)}{0.91}\, LR_2$$

Building Society Deposit Rate

$$LR_5 = \underset{(20.2)}{0.49}\, LR_3$$

Wholesale Price Index

$$LWPM = \underset{(23.4)}{0.83}\, LWM - \underset{(-9.1)}{0.32}\, LNPT + \underset{(30.2)}{0.49}(LFWP-LE1)$$

$$+ \underset{(16.4)}{0.08}(LPOIL-LE1) + \underset{(4.8)}{0.33}\, LR_4$$

Non–Traded Goods Price Index

$$LRPNT = \underset{(15.9)}{1.04}\, WNT + \underset{(52.1)}{1.22}\, LWPM - \underset{(-9.6)}{0.12}(LPOIL-LE1) + \underset{(14.4)}{1.73}\, LR_4$$

Wages in Manufacturing Sector

$$LWM = \underset{(1.5)}{0.10}\, LWNR + \underset{(172.8)}{0.94}\, LP$$

Spot Exchange Rate

$$LE1 = \underset{(1.69)}{0.10}\, LL27 - \underset{(-1.86)}{0.12}\, LA87 - \underset{(-0.69)}{0.002}\, LQOIL + \underset{(10.2)}{0.79}\, LEE1$$

Expected Exchange Rate (generated by Fisher parity condition)

$$LEE1 = \underset{(212.0)}{1.01}\, LE1$$

Forward Exchange Rate

$$LEF = \underset{(202.0)}{1.00}\, LE1$$

Table 2. Diagnostic Statistics

Variable Name	Symbol	Q(4)	Q(8)	A(1)	Chow
Bank Reserves	BR	1.33	3.51	0.08	0.61
Notes and Coins	NC	1.86	2.60	0.23	2.67
Time Deposits	D2	1.21	1.81	0.93	2.17
Other Retail Liquidity	D3	1.70	3.01	0.68	2.22
Foreign Currency Deposits	D4	4.88	7.21	0.01	1.39
Total Expenditure	EPN	2.22	5.78	0.06	1.43
Spot Exchange Rate	E1	4.45	8.08	0.02	4.00
Forward Parity Rate	EE1	0.52	5.67	0.85	4.66
Forward Rate	EF	3.42	9.54	0.47	6.02
Bank Deposit Rate	R_3	0.97	1.83	0.38	1.05
Treasury Bill Rate	R_4	1.42	5.69	0.46	0.67
Building Society Rate	R_5	3.08	5.39	0.51	1.66
Wholesale Prices	WPM	3.36	6.52	0.82	0.08
GDP Deflator	P	2.51	7.56	0.13	1.12
Manufacturing Wages	WM	1.19	5.77	1.65	0.81
Non–traded Goods Prices	PNP	1.57	3.41	0.53	0.30

Q(4) = fourth order Chi–squared test for autocorrelation
Q(8) = eighth order Chi–squared test for autocorrelation
A(1) = first order Arch test for heteroskedacity (Chi–squared)
Chow = F–test for structural stability, 8 periods 1979:1 to 1981:4

4.1 The Financial Sector

The financial sector involves estimation of the private sector's portfolio allocation decision given by equations (18) to (22) and the rule by which banks hold reserves in response to changes in the reserve ratio, profit opportunities, and the stock of eligible liabilities demanded by agents, equation (17). Together they yield an equation for bank credit (15). Finally, a behavioural equation relates nominal expenditures to credit, both bank and 'retail' credit. The equations contain satisfactory time series' diagnostics and in general sensible long run properties. We present the Box–Pierce statistics as a summary indication of the presence or otherwise of residual autocorrelation, although we feel strongly that economists should investigate the *individual* autocorrelation coefficients for evidence of misspecification since economic explanations are more likely to be suggested with this precise information. We carry out such an analysis and individually significant *autocorrelation* terms are absent from all our regressions.

A number of interesting features arise in the estimation. Several of the rates of return are important for the portfolio allocation process and are indeed highly significant, rejecting unambiguously the charge that multicollinearity among rates may be a problem. The Retail Liquidity variable is highly responsive to changes in financial wealth, which accurately reflects the rapidly growing financial innovations in the non–bank sector. Time deposits, foreign currency deposits and notes and coins are more closely related to GDP, presumably reflecting their transactions' orientation. The foreign currency equation was developed in a different context by McKenzie and Thomas (1983). The coefficient estimates on the rates of return indicate large responses by agents. With the period split at 1978(iv) we believe we have a fairly rigorous check for parameter instability: the UK underwent a change of government, oil prices rose dramatically, and exchange controls were dismantled within a short space of time. The volatile nature of financial markets in the 1970s may be expected to be picked up by significant ARCH (Engle, 1983) effects: there is no evidence of such misspecification. The portfolio allocation decisions feed directly into the nominal activity equation. There has been much work on seeking appropriate measures of liquidity and credit in driving nominal expenditures. Although not based on an explicit optimising theory, the familiar transmission story can be told, involving credit availability or liquidity leading to higher prices and/or real activity. We include L3 as a proxy measure for Retail Credit: clearly we would prefer to use retail deposits directly, but if retail reserves and capital are a fixed proportion of deposits, then L3 should be a fair reflection of the appropriate variable. Nominal expenditure turns out to be a weighted average of bank and non–bank credit in the long run.

4.2 The Interest Rate Sector

The mark–up equations perform well, accounting for a large part of the variation in interest rates, lacking systematic omissions, and revealing constant parameters. The low (<1) coefficient in LR3 in the Building Society Deposit Rate equation presumably reflects the different taxation treatment of the two respective assets: otherwise the various rates are weighted averages of each other in the long run. In the short run adjustment to changes in the rates is not instantaneous due to transactions and information costs, and the distinction between transitory and permanent changes in these variables.

4.3 Wages and Prices

The determination of manufacturing wages, wholesale prices, non–traded goods' prices, and the GDP deflator are considered jointly on a mark–up basis. There is extensive evidence that prices are set this way. Manufacturing wages are a distributed lag of its rate of change and inflation in the GDP deflator. Labour contracts are slow to unwind. The implicit deflator is a distributed lag on wholesale prices and past inflation, wages in manufacturing, foreign wholesale prices, and the sterling price of oil. The cost of borrowing in the form of r_4 is also important. Finally, non–traded goods' prices respond to wages in both traded and non–traded goods' sectors, the sterling price of oil and r_4.

The long run solutions in general reveal sensible and significant parameter estimates, while the dynamic equations are well specified. The only cause for concern is the negative long run influence of non–traded goods' prices on the wholesale price index, though we suggest that this may well be the result of some complicated dynamic relationship which is not yet well understood.

4.4 The Exchange Rate Sector

This sector draws heavily on McKenzie and Thomas (1987). Conventional models of exchange rate determination are notorious for their poor empirical performance (e.g. Backus, 1984). We reject the uncovered interest parity maintained hypothesis and introduce a list of financial assets which may be thought to be mobile internationally. They involve foreign residents' holdings of sterling loans and deposits at UK banks. A more complete list of bank–related financial assets is, as yet, unavailable. Invoking the existence of market imperfections and adjustment lags, we jointly estimate an equation for the spot £/$ rate, the forward premium forward rate, and the forward rate implied by the interest differential. The last two are not identical, and in particular appear to have very different stochastic properties (see Appendix). The Chow tests reveal some instability, but the long run solutions are plausible. Kesselman (1971) and Kindleberger (1980) find separate roles for the forward premium and interest parity forward rate, but the emphasis on small models has led to convenient, but frequently untested, maintained assumptions. It is fair to say that uncovered interest parity is now rejected in almost every empirical application. One characterisation of the risk premium (together with other imperfections) may be present in our exchange rate sector.

The criticism that we have not got a well specified portfolio model is inappropriate. Rather, we suggest that studies which contain a completely inaccurate characterisation of the open–economy portfolio problem (Frankel

(1982)) are inadequate since they contain unreliable, unstable and unlikely estimates within misspecified models: we acknowledge the paucity of suitable data, use that which is accurate and available (e.g. LL37 and LA87) and seek a well specified model with sensible decision variables.

REFERENCES

Backus, D.K. (1984), "Empirical Models of the Exchange Rate: Separating the Wheat from the Chaff", *Canadian Journal of Economics*, 16, No.4, pp.824–25.

Backus. D.K. and D. Purvis (1980), "An Integrated Model of Household Flow of Funds", *Journal of Money, Credit and Banking*, Vol.XII, No.2, pp.400–21.

Banerjee, A., J.J. Dolado, D.F. Hendry and G.W. Smith (1986), "Exploring Equilibrium Relationships through Static Models: Some Monte Carlo Evidence", *Oxford Bulletin of Economics and Statistics*, 48, pp.253–78.

Bewley, R.A. (1979), "The Direct Estimation of the Equilibrium Response in a Linear Model", *Economic Letters*, 3.

Blofeld, M. and G. McKenzie (forthcoming), "Wages, Prices and Non–traded Goods".

Cassese, A. and J.R. Lothian (1982), "The Timing of Monetary and Price Changes and the International Transmission of Inflation", *Journal of Monetary Economics*, 10, No.1, pp.1–24.

Engle, R.F. (1983), "Estimates of the Variance of U.S. Inflation Based upon the ARCH Model", *Journal of Money, Credit and Banking*, No.3, pp.286–301

Frankel, J.A. (1982), "In Search of the Exchange Risk Premium: A Six–Currency Test Assuming Mean–Variance Optimisation", *Journal of International Money and Finance*, 1, pp.255–74.

Gilbert, C.L. (1986), "Professor Hendry's Econometric Methodology", *Oxford Bulletin of Economics and Statistics*, 48, No.3, pp.283–307.

Granger, C.W.J. (1981), "Some Properties of Time Series Data and their Use in Econometric Model Specification", *Journal of Econometrics*, 16, pp.121–30.

Gurley, J.C. and E.S. Shaw (1955), "Financial Aspects of Economic Develop ment", *American Economic Review*, XIV, pp.515–38.

Gurley, J.C. and E.S. Shaw (1960), *Money in a Theory of Finance*, Brookings, Washington D.C.

Hendry, D.F. and J.–F. Richard (1982), "On the Formulation of Empirical Models in Dynamic Econometrics", *Journal of Econometrics*, pp.3–33.

Hercowitz, Z. (1981), "Money and Dispersion of Relative Prices', *JPE*, 89, pp.328–56.

Johnson, H. (1962), "Monetary Theory and Policy", *American Economic Review*, June, pp.335–84.

Johnson, H. (1971), "Revolution and Counter–Revolution in Economics", *Encounter*, April, pp.23–33.

Kesselman, J. (1971), "The Role of Speculation in Forward Rate Determination: The Canadian Dollar, 1953–60", *Canadian Journal of Economics*, 4, No.3, pp.279–98.

Kindleberger, C.P. (1980), "Myths and Realities of Forward Exchange Markets" in C.P. Kindleberger and J.S. Chipman (eds.), *Flexible Exchange Rates and the Balance of Payments*, North–Holland, Amsterdam.

Levich, R.M. (1978), "The Efficiency of Markets for Foreign Exchange: A Review and Extension" in D.R. Lessard (ed.), *International Financial*

Management, Warren, Gorham and Lamont, New York.

McCallum, B.T. (1976), "Rational Expectations and the Estimation of Econo metric Models: An Alternative Procedure", *Econometrica*, 17, pp.484–90.

McKenzie, G.W. and S.H. Thomas (1983), "Liquidity, Credit Creation and International Banking", *Journal of Banking and Finance*, 7, pp.467–80.

McKenzie, G.W. and S.H. Thomas (1987), "Dominant Factors Influencing the Dollar–Sterling Exchange Rates, 1965–81" in A.K. Chrystal and R. Sedgwick (eds.), *Exchange Rates and the Open Economy*, Wheatsheaf, Sussex, U.K.

McKenzie, G.W. and M. Blofeld (forthcoming), "Wages, Prices and Non–Traded Goods" in G.W. McKenzie and S.W. Arndt (eds.), *The Competitiveness of the UK Economy*, Macmillan, London.

Monetary Control (1980), Green Paper Cmnd.7858, HMSO, London.

Radcliffe Report (1959), Committee on the Working of the Monetary System, Cmnd.827, HMSO, London.

Sargan, J.D. (1975), "Asymptotic Theory and Large Models", *International Economic Review*, 16, pp.75–91.

Thomas, S.H. (1987), "Review of 'Inflation, Stagflation, Relative Prices and Imperfect Information' by Alex Cukierman", *Canadian Journal of Economics*, 20, pp.483–87.

Thomas, S.H. and M.R. Wickens (1987), "Vehicle Currencies, Bank Debt and the Asset Market Approach to Exchange Rate Determination", Southampton University Discussion Paper.

Thomas, S.H. and F. Weldon (1987), "Price Variability in Canada", University of Southampton Discussion Paper.

Tobin, J. and W. Brainard (1971), "Financial Intermediaries and the Effective ness of Monetary Controls" in J. Tobin (ed.), *Essays in Economics*, 1, North–Holland, Amsterdam.

Wickens, M.R. (1982), "The Efficient Estimation of Econometric Models with Rational Expectations", *Review of Economic Studies*, 49, pp.55–67.

APPENDIX

STRUCTURAL REGRESSION EQUATIONS AND LIST OF VARIABLES

List of Variables

All variables are expressed in natural logarithms. Thus variable names in the text are preceded by the letter "L". Where a variable appears as a first difference, the additional prefix "D" is added. All data has been taken from various issues of *Economic Trends, Financial Statistics* and the *Bank of England Quarterly Bulletin.*

1. Financial/Expenditure Sector

LBR = commercial bank reserves

LL256 = eligible bank liabilities

LCR = statutory cash reserve ratio

DINT = difference between the minimum lending rate (LMLR) and the Treasury Bill rate (LR4)

LNC = notes and coins

LD2 = time deposits

LD3 = retail liquidity (e.g. building society deposits)

LD4 = foreign currency deposits held by UK residents at UK banks

LRFW = financial wealth divided by the GDP deflator P

EPN = nominal expenditure

CRED = commercial bank credit

2. Interest Rates

LR1 = euro–dollar rate (three month)

LR2 = euro–sterling rate (three month)

LR3 = commercial bank deposit rate

LR4 = UK Treasury bill rate (three month)

LR5 = building society rate

LR6 = yield implied by covered interest rate arbitrage

3. Prices

P = GDP deflator

LWPM = wholesale price of manufactures (traded goods)

LPNT = price of non–traded goods

LWM	=	wages in the manufacturing sector
LWNT	=	wages in the non–traded goods sector
LFWP–LE1	=	foreign wholesale prices (expressed in dollars) divided by the spot dollar/sterling exchange rate
LPOIL–LE1	=	price of oil expressed in sterling

4. Exchange Rates

LE1	=	spot dollar/sterling exchange rate
LL27	=	sterling bank deposits held by foreigners
LA87	=	sterling loans extended to foreigners
LQOIL	=	'expected' exchange rate implied by the Fisher parity condition (LEE1 = LE1 + .25(LR2 – LR1))
LEF	=	actual forward exchange rate (three month)

Dummy Variables

Ones for periods indicated, zeros elsewhere.

1. Pre–Credit and Competition Control

DUM1	1963(1) to 1971(3)

2. Supplementary Reserve Deposit Periods

DC1	1973(4)	1974(2)
DC2	1976(4)	1977(2)
DC3	1978(2)	1978(4)

3. Other Dummies

DUM2	1971(1) (+1)	1971(2) (–1)
DUM3	1981(3)	1981(4)
DUM12	1977(3) (+1)	1977(4) (1)
DUM13	1980(2) (+1)	1980(3) (–1)

Dependent Variable:		LBR	from 1965:1 to 1981:4	
Observations		68	Degrees of Freedom	58
R**2		.94768766	RBAR**2	2.93957022
SSR		.13380478	SEE	.48031021E–01

Label	Lag	Coefficient	Stand. Error	T–Statistic
Constant	0	2.467337	.3255741	7.578420
LBR	3	–.162773	.8720613E–01	–1.866533
LL256	0	.7428541	.2216177	3.351961
LL256	1	–.6651207	.2473588	–2.688890
LL256	4	.4560372	.1390236	3.280286
LCR	0	.1224115	.1665504E–01	7.349815
DINT	0	–2.550711	2.447917	–1.041992
DUM3	0	–.1365320	.5481017E–01	–2.490997
DUM12	0	–.8760399E–01	.3430247E–01	–2.553869
DUM13	0	–.8594031E–01	.3499089E–01	–2.456077

Dependent Variable:		LNC–LP	from 1965:1 to 1981:4	
Observations		68	Degrees of Freedom	51
R**2		.97786744	RBAR**2	.97092390
SSR		.69637186–E02	SEE	.11684344E–01

Label	Lag	Coefficient	Stand. Error	T–Statistic
Constant	0	3.408664	1.438878	2.368973
LNC–LP	1	.7731855	.1162779	6.649464
LNC–LP	2	.1202927	.9036790E–01	1.331033
LNC–LP	3	–.2989875	.8584904E–01	–3.482712
LNC–LP	4	.3890156	.7419874E–01	5.242886
LR3	0	.1729075	.1520564	1.137128
LR5	0	–1.249631	.4724848	–2.644806
LRGDP	0	.2901941	.4984000E–01	5.822514
LRGDP	1	–.1666693	.6525175E–01	–2.554250
LRFW	0	.2757292	.1264132	2.181174
LRFW	1	–.2388404	.1317878	–1.812310
DC2	0	.8917871E–02	.8050288E–02	1.107770
DC3	0	.1910770E–01	.8183561E–02	2.334889

Dependent Variable:	LD2–lp	from 1965:1 to 1981:4	
Observations	68	Degrees of Freedom	58
R**2	.99363659	RBAR**2	.99264917
SSR	.22815580E–01	SEE	.19833610E–01

Label	Lag	Coefficient	Stand. Error	T–Statistic
Constant	0	–5.811101	.9078959	–6.400625
LD2–LP	1	.7023756	.7785608E–01	9.021461
LD2–LP	2	.1456309	.6071916E–01	2.398434
LR2	0	–.1101793	.1672684	–.6586976
LR3	0	.9425818	.2117478	4.451484
LR6	0	–.8078055E–01	.5964020E–01	–1.354465
LRGDP	0	–.1632685	.6706750E–01	–2.434390
LRFW	0	1.964536	.1429125	13.74624
LRFW	1	–1.593634	.1667860	–9.554962
LRGDP	3	.1205962	.6173590E–01	1.953421

Dependent Variable:	LD3–LP	from 1965:1 to 1981:4	
Observations	68	Degrees of Freedom	58
R**2	.99611790	RBAR**2	.99499806
SSR	.16396075E–02	SEE	.56152393E–02

Label	Lag	Coefficient	Stand. Error	T–Statistic
Constant	0	1.507757	.5728029	2.632244
LD3–LP	1	1.129916	.8176239E–01	13.81950
LD3–LP	2	–.3871676	.1109636	–3.489140
LD3–LP	3	.2505140	.5532014E–01	4.528441
LR3	0	–.1777461	.6952130E–01	–2.556714
LR5	0	–.3117029	.1902883	–1.638056
LRGDP	0	–.1204888	.2261946E–01	–5.326778
LRGDP	1	.2033827	.2269564E–01	8.961313
LRFW	0	.1965281	.6171314E–01	3.184542
LRFW	0	–.1991317	.6240610E–01	–3.190901
DC1	0	–.1313306E–01	.4576458E–02	–2.869699
DC2	0	–.3742719E–02	.3699985E–02	–1.011550
DLDEF	0	–.8949927	.9383177E–01	–9.538270
DLDEF	1	.1401920	.1052930	1.331447
DLDEF	3	.1317214	.7134574E–01	1.846241
DUM2	0	–.6572780E–02	.4352913E–02	–1.509973

Dependent Variable:	LD4–LP	from 1965:1 to 1981:4	
Observations	68	Degrees of Freedom	59
R**2	.99235327	RBAR**2	.99131642
SSR	.37216549	SEE	.79422224E–01

Label	Lag	Coefficient	Stand. Error	T–Statistic
Constant	0	–11.15662	3.763959	–2.964067
LD4–LP	1	.8349243	.5248226E–01	15.90870
LR2	0	2.275101	.6190861	3.674935
LR3	0	–5.592867	1.583453	–3.532069
LR4	0	3.430512	1.652401	2.076077
LR6	0	.4737919	.2326805	2.036234
LRDGP	0	.4527329	.2926693	1.546910
LRGDP	5	.4359198	.2862284	1.522979
DSM	0	–.2768360	.5824283E–01	–4.753135

Dependent Variable:	LEPN	from 1965:1 to 1981:4	
Observations	68	Degrees of Freedom	51
R**2	.99942554	RBAR**2	.99924532
SSR	.16009497E–01	SEE	.17717554E–01

Label	Lag	Coefficient	Stand. Error	T–Statistic
Constant	0	–.5808702	.1749715	–3.282282
LEPN	1	.6745934	.1092796	6.173095
LEPN	4	.2174152	.1291674	1.683205
LEON	5	–.2151658	.1205377	–1.785050
LCRED	0	.1752605	.1543388	1.135557
LCRED	1	–.2628012	.1854770	–1.416894
LCRED	3	.1461642	.1281573	1.140506
LCRED	6	.1383035	.8711797E–01	1.587543
LD3	0	.2711641	.1650185	1.643235
LD3	3	.4348791	.4800866	.9058346
LD3	4	–1.175777	.6894220	–1.705453
LD3	5	.6489052	.3596885	1.804075
DLWPM	0	.2799352	.2345631	1.193432
DLWPM	5	–.5701149	.3125509	–1.824070
SEASONS	0	.5401868E–02	.1013399E–01	.5330446
SEASONS	1	–.3102961E–01	.1481747E–01	–2.094124
SEASONS	2	–.9842731E–02	.8609214E–02	–1.143279

Dependent Variable:		LR3	from 1965:1 to 1981:4	
Observations		68	Degrees of Freedom	63
R**2		.89468940	RBAR**2	.88800302
SSR		.62212041E–02	SEE	.99372668E–02

Label	Lag	Coefficient	Stand. Error	T–Statistic
Constant	0	.1946448	.2071307	.9397197
LR3	1	.6249284	.1573744	3.970965
LR4	0	.8479426	.1320813	6.419855
LR4	1	–.4342982	.2181790	–1.990560
LR2	3	–.8138082E–01	.4877626E–01	–1.668451

Dependent Variable:		LR4	from 1965:1 to 1981:4	
Observations		68	Degrees of Freedom	64
R**2		.91921298	RBAR**2	.91542608
SSR		.52691521E–02	SEE	.90736156E–02

Label	Lag	Coefficient	Stand. Error	T–Statistic
Constant	0	.8614294E–01	.1731056	.4976323
LR2	0	.4731093	.5673356E–01	8.339144
LR2	1	–.2853344	.7405837E–01	–3.852831
LR4	1	.7933375	.7682997E–01	10.32589

Dependent Variable:		LR5	from 1965:1 to 1981:4	
Observations		68	Degrees of Freedom	64
R**2		.96098965	RBAR**2	.95916104
SSR		.87090519E–03	SEE	.36888879E–02

Label	Lag	Coefficient	Stand. Error	T–Statistic
Constant	0	.8015798	.2118512	3.783693
LR5	1	.6596941	.5929670E–01	11.12531
LR3	0	.1679291	.2978074E–01	5.638849
DUM8	0	.4237166E–02	.1604457E–02	2.640873

Dependent Variable:		LWPM	from 1965:1 to 1981:4	
Observations		68	Degrees of Freedom	51
R**2		.99991207	RBAR**2	.99988449
SSR		.17896544E–02	SEE	.59237879E–02

Label	Lag	Coefficient	Stand. Error	T–Statistic
Constant	0	–2.697042	.3985040	–6.767919
DLWPM	0	–3.600229	.1923634	–18.71577
DLWPM	1	2.377242	.1519833	15.64146
DLWPM	2	–1.044099	.9808227E–01	–10.64513
DLWPM	4	1.029331	.1200230	8.576115
DLWPM	5	–1.502269	.1163166	–12.91534
DLWPM	7	–1.129416	.7722402E–01	–14.62519
DLWM	1	–.2466083	.4311676E–01	–5.719546
DLFWP–LE1	1	–.3376309	.2215722E–01	–15.23796
DLFWP–LE1	3	–.2297467	.2571215E–01	–8.935336
DLPOIL–LE1	1	.1192515	.1216375E–01	9.803838
DLPOIL–LE2	2	–.1205755	.1071325E–01	–11.25480
LWM	1	.8258616	.3524052E–01	23.43500
LPNT	1	–.3236686	.3565530E–01	–9.077713
LFWP–LE1	1	.4854444	.1606473E–01	30.21802
LPOIL–LE1	1	.8007865E–01	.4862667E–02	16.46805
LR4	1	.3379687	.7044833	–4.797398

Dependent Variable:		LPNT	from 1965:1 to 1981:4	
Observations		68	Degrees of Freedom	56
R**2		.99954268	RBAR**2	.99945285
SSR		.12045508E–01	SEE	.14666232E–01

Label	Lag	Coefficient	Stand. Error	T–Statistic
Constant	0	–13.02519	.5628820	–23.14018
DLPNT	0	–7.116795	.4433710	–16.05156
DLPNT	2	2.354216	.1749010	13.46028
DLPNT	4	1.970727	.1340564	14.70073
DWNT	2	–1.830853	.1627253	–11.25119
DWNT	3	–.9160362	.1256058	–7.292948
DLWPM	1	3.889864	.3082515	12.61912
DLPOIL–LE1	3	.4137163	.2880371E–01	14.36330
LWNT	1	1.039104	.6529028E–01	15.91514
LWPM	1	1.218783	.2339983E–01	52.08514
LPOIL–LE1	1	–.1224315	.1271978E–01	–9.625287
LR4	1	1.729850	.1200812	14.40566

Dependent Variable:	LP	from 1965:1 to 1981:4	
Observations	68	Degrees of Freedom	59
R**2	.99978877	RBAR**2	.99976012
SSR	.42767477E–02	SEE	.85139444E–02

Label	Lag	Coefficient	Stand. Error	T–Statistic
Constant	0	–1.552113	.1232551	–12.59269
DLP	0	–2.519634	.2750330	–9.161203
DLP	5	–.5768096	.1055249	–5.466098
DLP	7	–1.090500	.1147577	–9.502636
DLWPM	1	1.742787	.2050379	8.499829
DLWPM	2	–.8748623	.1170461	–7.474513
DLPNT	2	.6447596	.8365462E–01	7.707400
LWPM	1	.3632051	.2591848E–01	14.01336
LPNT	1	.6133182	.2446643E–01	25.06774

Dependent Variable:	LE1	from 1965:1 to 1981:4	
Observations	68	Degrees of Freedom	55
R**2	.94697232	RBAR**2	.93540264
SSR	.73263086E–01	SEE	.36497344E–01

Label	Lag	Coefficient	Stand. Error	T–Statistic
Constant	0	.3105469	.2250387	1.379971
LL27	0	.2519482	.8144055E–01	3.093646
LL27	1	–.1493475	.8914525E–01	–1.675327
LA87	0	–.4020291	.1117652	–3.597088
LA87	1	.5149371	.1643656	3.132877
LA87	2	–.4081334	.1734548	–2.352967
LA87	3	.1745108	.1212318	1.439481
LQOIL	0	.1005180E–01	.6132698E–02	1.639050
LQOIL	1	–.1286734E–01	.6279194E–02	–2.049203
LEE1	1	1.183529	.1311464	9.024484
LEE1	2	–.6047533	.2021492	–2.991618
LEE1	3	.3732725	.2061102	1.811033
LEE1	4	–.1539033	.1283230	–1.199343

Dependent Variable:	LEE1	from 1965:1 to 1981:4	
Observations	68	Degrees of Freedom	64
R**2	.99860637	RBAR**2	.99854104
SSR	.19805246E–02	SEE	.55628856E–02

Label	Lag	Coefficient	Stand. Error	T–Statistic
Constant	0	–.6611037E–02	.4319952E–02	–1.530350
LEE1	1	.6144929	.9815156E–01	6.260654
LE1	0	1.006899	.1593157E–01	63.20150
LE1	1	–.6157759	.1009249	–6.101329

Dependent Variable:	LEF	from 1965:1 to 1981:4	
Observations	68	Degrees of Freedom	63
R**2	.99862002	RBAR**2	.99853240
SSR	.18658988E–02	SEE	.54421908E–02

Label	Lag	Coefficient	Stand. Error	T–Statistic
Constant	0	.2408002E–02	.4384683E–02	.5491850
LEF	1	.5866721	.9156946E–01	6.406853
LEF	2	.6241185E–01	.1663804E–01	3.751154
LE1	0	1.011720	.1616601E–01	62.58315
LE1	1	–.6615602	.9283357E–01	–7.126303

CHAPTER 11

CROWDING–OUT, REAGANOMICS AND MONETARY POLICY

J.C. Siebrand and J. Swank, *Erasmus University, Rotterdam, The Netherlands*

1. INTRODUCTION

The size of the collective sector and its impact on the market sector are still crucial issues in the design of economic policy in industrial countries. Rapid growth of the collective sector is held responsible for a decrease in private activity in the past and hopes exist that a reduction of the burden of collective activity will revitalise market development. Crowding–out of private activity used to be mainly associated with interest rate increases caused by government borrowing, but with less high interest rates in the last years the discussion tends to shift to the impact of average and especially marginal tax rates. In as far as economic agents do not identify current taxation, and see the latter as equivalent to current borrowing with future taxation, the direct impact of additional government spending obviously depends on the way it is financed. Therefore both crowding–out through increased borrowing and crowding–out through increased taxation are potentially interesting. A similar conclusion holds for the reverse case of "crowding–in". The way of financing identifies only the major impact channels however, as both borrowing and taxation can take different forms, and financial and other conditions that accompany changes in government activity may also differ. From a macroeconomic point of view two types of mechanisms are of particular importance with respect to crowding–out: the way monetary policy reacts to financial and other conditions and the endogenous component of the collective sector, in particular the response of social security benefits and premiums to changes in private activity and their ultimate burden. The present paper focuses on the effects of different kinds of budgetary policy that affect the size of the collective sector and the role of monetary conditions. The US economy

P. Artus and Y. Barroux (eds.), Monetary Policy, 233–250.

is taken as an example and the measures taken by the Reagan administration and the Federal Reserve Board are analysed with respect to their impact on private activity and economic conditions in general. Computations are based on the RASMUS–model of the US economy, which integrates Keynesian, neoclassical and financial arguments with respect to the effectiveness of economic policy. Section 2 discusses the structure of the model and potential crowding–out mechanisms. Section 3 elaborates the consequences of different types of fiscal policy. The actual policies pursued under president Reagan and by the Fed under Mr. Volcker are studied in section 4. Conclusions are drawn in the final section.

2. THE STRUCTURE OF THE MODEL

The size of the RASMUS–2c model precludes a detailed description in the context of the present paper. Therefore we discuss only its main characteristics and refer the reader to other publications for more details (Swank and Siebrand (1986), Swank (1986)).

Model RASMUS–2c is an annual macroeconometric model of the US economy, based on an integrated set of national and financial accounts. It contains 43 stochastic equations and 192 endogenous variables. The overall structure of the model is highly comparable to its predecessors, models RASMUS–2a and 2b.[1] Those models and a similar one covering a block of 6 members of the EC were designed as parts of a three–block world model, to be used for the evaluation of the options for national economic policy in an international setting and in particular the gains from international coordination or cooperation. The RASMUS models are intended to cover a wide range of theoretical notions with respect to the effectiveness of economic policy. Therefore, rival arguments are simultaneously modelled in (virtually) uniform systems. The RASMUS models contain the determination of real variables, like product demand and supply, labour demand and supply, as well as a rather detailed monetary sector describing the main financial relations between the central bank, commercial banks, government and the private and foreign sector. The traditional Keynesian type of argument is represented in the present model by elements like the multiplier–accelerator mechanism, mark–up pricing, the Phillips curve, expansion–induced short–term productivity gains, dependence of international trade flows on relative prices, as well as on pressure of demand in different countries. Relevant for supply conditions are the CES production structure, factor demand based on relative prices, capital costs based on endogenous interest rates, and the encouraging effect of shorter labour time on labour supply. These elements are reinforced by financial feedbacks, such as the impact of the financial position of government and of firms on their borrowing behaviour and therefore on interest rates and on debt service. As a result of this combination of Keynesian, neo–classical and financial elements the multipliers of RASMUS–2c show features of quite different lines of reasoning.

The model can be divided into seven interdependent equation blocks. The first block represents the supply side of the US economy. It is based on a CES–type production function with an estimated elasticity of substitution of about 0.5, which constrains the cost–minimisation problem from which the factor–demand equations, as well as the determination of the output deflator, are derived. These equations were estimated simultaneously in order to assure their mutual consistency. Capacity utilisation follows from the confrontation of aggregate demand with the short–run CES function. The utilisation rate of labour is captured by an index of average working–hours, which depends on both secular and cyclical influences. Imports of goods and services are the foreign contributions to aggregate supply. Their main determinants are total sales, relative prices and utilisation rates.

The main components of aggregate demand are determined in the second block. Private consumption depends on both current and past income streams, real interest rates and private liquidity. Disposable income and interest rates also play a part in the determination of residential construction, next to prices and capacity utilisation. The equation for non–residential business investment describes the gradual adjustment of the actual capital stock to its planned level, which is a function of planned capacity and real capital costs. The speed of adjustment depends on the rate of capacity utilisation and on private liquidity. Capital costs are determined by the price of investment goods, the long–term interest rate, the rate of physical decay and a number of parameters representing the influence of corporate taxes, the investment tax credit and depreciation deduction. Inventory formation is related to sales according to a flexible–accelerator approach in which allowance is made for the existence of unplanned inventories. Besides, the unemployment rate represents the precautionary motive for stock–building. Exports follow from world trade, relative prices and utilisation rates.

Wages and prices are determined in the third block. Wages are discerned in those paid by companies and those paid by the government and social security funds. The hourly wage rate of companies strongly depends on the state of the labour market, represented by the conventional Phillips–Lipsey effects. Moreover, wage earners are assumed to be compensated for changes in consumer prices and labour productivity. Forward shifting of taxes and social security contributions – potentially a major crowding–out mechanism – was not found to be significant in combination with the explanatory variables included in the present equation. The wage rate in the public sector follows the private wage rate, apart from an additional Phillips–curve effect.

The equation explaining the output deflator is based on the assumption of mark–up pricing, but also includes as explanatory variables the price of imports, allowing for the pricing behaviour of foreign competitors in domestic markets, and the rate of capacity utilisation, capturing the pressure of demand. Sectoral price deflators are essentially determined by the output deflator and, barring the price of residential construction, also by import prices. Moreover, the prices of commodity exports and exports of services are further related to the relevant foreign competitors' price.

The fourth block contains private labour demand and labour supply. Labour demand refers to man–hours and is related to planned capacity and real labour costs. The adjustment of actual towards desired labour inputs is assumed to vary with the rate of capacity utilisation. Labour supply is based on an endogenous participation rate, which is negatively affected by real disposable wages and average hours and positively by the tension in the labour market as represented by the rate of employment.

Block five describes the social security sector. Social benefits are explained by the private wage rate, unemployment and the excess–savings of social security funds, next to a trend term representing the secular growth of the number of beneficiaries. The government share in social benefits mainly depends on the level of unemployment. Total contributions are linked to total benefits. The shares of the contributions paid by employers and employees vary with the unemployment rate.

The government sector (block six) is relatively simple. Taxes are endogenous. The expenditures in constant prices and government employment are exogenous. Interest payments are endogenous and split up in payments to residents and payments to foreigners.

The financial surpluses resulting from the real transactions of the private sector, the foreign sector and the government are the major inputs for the monetary sector (block seven). This sector is divided into four subsectors: the central bank, commercial banks, the private and the foreign sector. For each of these the balance sheets are specified. Portfolio considerations are the main determinants of the demand for currency, demand deposits, net loans of the private sector and commercial banks to abroad, and private borrowing from banks. The distribution of government borrowing over the private sector and commercial banks depends on the ratio of short–term and long–term interest rates. Debts and interest rates determine net capital income transfers to abroad and the commercial banks' financial surplus. The other balance–sheet items are either explained by definitions or are exogenous. Interest rates are explained by the ratios of assets and liabilities of the private sector and of commercial banks, the discount rate and relevant foreign interest rates. The equation explaining the short–term interest rate includes relative inflation rates as a proxy for expected exchange–rate adjustments; these expectations also affect long–term interest rates.

Some major elements of monetary policy are also integrated in this block. In fact, the determination of the official discount rate, open–market policy and intervention on foreign exchange markets are all endogenised. In each case, the reactions of monetary authorities to changes in some potential target variables are assumed to conform to their normal behaviour as revealed by their rather stable conduct in the sample period. The details of the relevant reaction functions are described in the appendix. Exchange–rate changes and inflation affect the official discount rate, which appears to undergo a temporary relaxation if unemployment increases. Its reaction to the liquidity ratio as a monetary target shows a pronounced upward shift in 1979, when Volcker took office as chairman of the Fed[2]. The rate of change of the exchange rate of the US dollar vis–a–vis a basket of six major European currencies in the sample period 1971–1983 can be explained largely as a reaction to the changes in net foreign assets (official and those held by commercial banks) of the countries concerned, scaled on the respective national incomes. This measure of the (ex–post) relative scarcity of the US dollar directly reflects the extent to which the national monetary authorities allowed the exchange rate to be influenced by market forces. Open–market policy is governed by the ratio between long–term and short–term interest rates.

The major spillovers between the real and the monetary sector are the financial surpluses and interest rates. Any action in one sector has an impact in both the real and the financial system. For example, an increase in government spending not only induces "real" effects, such as production growth, an increase in utilization rates, price changes and wage changes, etc., but also financial effects. All ways of financing additional spending induce monetary feedbacks which dampen the initial "real" effects, at least after some time. Induced net capital imports and exchange–rate adjustment tend to relax but not to mitigate these monetary feedbacks.

It will be clear from this survey of the main characteristics of the RASMUS model that it has much in common with e.g. the Federal Reserve Board's MPS model, at least conceptually. There are however several major differences. The interaction between the monetary and the real sector is an example. In principle, this interaction is more intense in the RASMUS model. For one thing, the full integration of national and monetary accounts implies that any real transaction has financial repercussions. Moreover, the tension in commodity markets, as expressed in the rate of capacity utilization, has a direct impact on some financial transactions. On the other hand, not only interest rates affect transactions in real markets, but also portfolio elements such as the liquidity ratio. However, with respect to the implementation and interpretation of policy simulations the most important difference concerns the treatment of monetary policy. As explained above, the behaviour of monetary authorities is based on their normal reactions to changes in potential target variables, as revealed by their conduct in the sample period.

In our view the approach to monetary policy adopted in the RASMUS model has some distinct advantages over the modelling of monetary policy by the (alternative) fixation of specific target variables, as e.g. in the MPS model. The foundation on average behaviour in the past is likely to contribute to the realism of policy measures considered, whereas plausible deviations from conventional reactions can always be introduced. Moreover, the design and implementation of any change in policy takes time, as does the adjustment of the behaviour of the agents affected by the new measures. In reality, monetary authorities are not likely to be so well informed and so flexible that they can preclude fluctuations in the variables they intend to stabilise. Our policy–reaction functions incidentally suggest the relevance of major policy changes, as in the case of the increased sensitivity of the discount rate to overall liquidity associated with the installation of Volcker as chairman of the Fed. But on the whole they are fairly stable and they appear to describe policy adjustment rather well. Therefore we are inclined to assume that in particular the dynamics of the RASMUS model benefit from our focus on instrument variables rather than on target variables.

Overviewing the model, the major potential crowding–out mechanisms of increased government spending are, in the case of capital market financing, the interest effects on private consumption and investment, particularly those on residential construction, and liquidity effects on private consumption and on the speed of investment adjustment. Taxes on corporate income can also increase the user cost of capital and will also affect domestic activity negatively through their effects on private liquidity. Increases in corporate and income tax rates however decrease the interest sensitivity of money demand as after–tax interest rates are relevant. Decreases in disposable family income tend to *increase* labour supply, as income effects were found to dominate substitution effects, and to decrease consumption demand. As the empirical results did not produce convincing evidence for the opposite case, the wage equation of the model excludes shifting of either direct or indirect taxation of wage–earners to firms. The model therefore lacks these potentially important crowding–out devices.

3. FISCAL POLICY AND CROWDING–OUT.

The dynamic properties of the present model depend on the value of some 200 parameters. In practice, not all parameters turn out to be of equal importance, however. In fact, a few crucial mechanisms, depending on a very limited set of parameters, appear to dominate the simulations. The simulation of different fiscal policy measures to be discussed next will illustrate this point. The measures studied stimulate private activity, at least in the short run. They are scaled in such a way that their direct impact amounts to about 0.5% of GNP.

The first three columns of Table 1 describe the results of a once and for all increase in government expenditure on goods and services, financed by increased borrowing in the capital market. Initially the multiplier/accelerator effects dominate and a general rise in activity can be noted, which generates some extra tax income and reduces the government share in social benefits, so that the ex post burden on the government budget is slightly less than that of the impulse. The unemployment rate falls and capacity utilisation increases, resulting in higher wages and prices. After a few years, the effects of accumulating government borrowing make themselves felt, however, through persistent increases in interest rates, which first affect residential construction and later decelerate the expansion–fed investment process. The rise in capital costs also

Table 1. Accumulated Effects of Some Fiscal Policy Measures
(all financed in the capital market and amounting to 0.5% of GNP)

	increase in government purchases			decrease in personal income taxes			increase in investment/tax credit		
Year	1	5	10	1	5	10	1	5	10
Percentage Changes a)									
Volume of:									
1. Private Consumption	0.0	0.3	0.6	0.3	1.0	1.3	0.2	1.3	1.4
2. Business Fixed Investment	1.4	0.9	0.8	0.4	-0.1	0.6	2.4	5.2	1.0
3. Residential Construction	0.0	-3.0	-2.8	0.0	-1.2	-2.3	0.0	-4.7	5.1
4. Exports of Goods	-0.6	-0.4	-0.2	-0.2	-0.3	-0.2	-0.2	1.2	0.7
5. Imports of Goods	2.4	2.8	4.6	0.8	2.5	4.7	1.5	3.5	2.5
6. Private GDP	0.8	0.6	0.6	0.3	0.4	0.5	0.4	1.2	1.2
7. Price of Production	0.3	1.2	2.8	0.1	1.1	3.0	-0.1	-1.0	0.1
8. Private Wage Rate	0.5	1.7	3.6	0.2	1.5	3.8	0.1	0.1	1.8
9. Employment of Companies	0.3	0.3	0.3	0.2	0.3	0.2	0.2	0.5	0.6
10. Exchange Rate ($/ECU6)	0.2	1.6	5.6	0.0	1.3	5.7	0.3	2.7	3.1
Levels b)									
11. Unemployment Rate (%)	-0.2	-0.2	-0.2	-0.1	-0.2	-0.2	-0.1	-0.2	-0.3
12. Utilisation Rate (%)	1.4	0.8	0.8	0.4	0.7	0.9	0.8	0.0	-0.2
13. Current Account *	-0.1	-0.2	-0.2	-0.1	-0.2	-0.2	-0.1	-0.1	-0.1
14. Government Budget Deficit *	0.4	0.6	0.8	0.5	0.5	0.7	0.5	0.7	0.9
15. Government Debt to Private Sector *	0.5	2.4	4.2	0.5	2.3	3.9	0.5	2.5	4.7
16. Liquidity Ratio *	-0.3	-0.4	-0.5	-0.1	-0.3	-0.5	0.0	-0.1	-0.3
17. Unborrowed Reserves *	0.0	-0.1	-0.5	0.0	-0.1	-0.5	0.0	-0.2	-0.2
18. Official Reserves *	0.0	-0.1	-0.3	0.0	0.0	-0.3	0.0	-0.2	-0.1
19. Long Term Interest Rate	0.1	0.5	0.9	0.1	0.4	1.0	0.0	0.3	0.6
20. Short Term Interest Rate	0.3	0.6	0.9	0.1	0.5	1.1	0.0	0.2	0.5

a) Calculated according to $(X_i^S - X_i)/(0.01X_{i-1})$, where X_i^S and X_i are level variables, referring to the shocked solution and the control solution respectively (i=1,...,10).

b) $X_i^S - X_i$.

* As a percentage of net national income.

boosts inflation, for which wage earners are compensated. The extra net capital imports, due to decreased domestic saving and higher interest rates to some extent compensates the deterioration of the current account, but a loss in official reserves occurs, together with a depreciation of the US dollar. This causes international substitution effects which renders some support for the current account. Nevertheless, in the longer run the increase in government spending consumes a substantial part of the official reserves, and the induced interest payments makes the government budget deficit much larger than the initial impulse. Though the measure would lead to serious imbalances, that eventually would require policies that reduce private activity, in itself the crowding–out effects of government spending are moderate: after some years only residential construction suffers considerably, as a result of its high interest sensitivity.

The second case is that of lower taxes on personal income, also involving the same amount of money. The price effects of the change in tax–tariffs are so small that the results – presented in the columns 4, 5 and 6 of Table 1 – are not essentially different from those of higher government purchases.

The results of a third exercise in which the government borrows the same amount of money in order to increase investment tax credit rather than for additional spending are shown in the last three columns of Table 1. This policy not only improves corporate income, but also makes investment less costly. Therefore the positive effects on private activity are bigger. Nevertheless, the boost in investment is relatively short–lived, not so much because of a deceleration of product demand, but as a consequence of a moderate rise in nominal interest rates together with a decrease in the utilisation rate caused by the adjustment of the capital stock to the relatively lower cost of capital. The decreases in capital costs are passed on to customers. The resulting downward pressure on prices supports the current account, that nevertheless deteriorates slightly because of the high domestic demand elasticity of imports. On a five–years horizon the US dollar depreciates somewhat more than in the former exercise, as the smaller rise in interest rates generates less net capital imports, but after ten years the dollar value falls less, because the lower inflation rates make future depreciation less likely.

So far we found that tax cuts do not pay their own way and that increases in government demand do not necessarily lead to an overall decrease of private activity in the medium term, but that both measures tend to create serious imbalances that call for compensating actions in a later stage. These imbalances confuse the discussion as the nature and timing of reverse policies are far from obvious. In order to avoid this confusion, we may study the results of a simultaneous tax and spending operation, which is ex–ante neutral with respect to the government budget. If the model were linear we could determine the results of such an operation by linear combinations of the corresponding columns. In fact, the model is not linear, but these additions are fairly indicative of what such simultaneous operations would amount to. We therefore abstain from a separate presentation and confine ourselves to a comment on the results.

A decrease in government purchases in order to make room for additional private spending through a cut in taxes on personal income does not have any major macroeconomic effects, apart from the corresponding shift in spending. This was to be expected, as the effects of tariffs on (average) private behaviour were found to be small. There is however an important net gain in activity if the freed funds are used to stimulate investment. In that case the deflationary effects of the cut in spending are reinforced by a decrease in capital costs. Prices and wages fall, which improves the US competitive position. The improvement in the current account of the balance of payments is small however, due to the firm growth of imports induced by higher domestic activity. Interest rates fall with the upward pressure on the value of the dollar. This of course has a negative impact on net capital imports. Nevertheless, the impact on the total balance of payments is positive, so that the US dollar slightly appreciates. The government budget benefits considerably from the decreases in unemployment and interest rates. Summarising, the implied package would be very beneficial in terms of all conventional targets of macroeconomic policy: growth, inflation, unemployment, the government budget, the balance of payments, while also real wages and the value of the US dollar would rise. In the next section we will demonstrate that these findings cast serious doubt on the wisdom of the economic measures taken by the Reagan administration.

4. THE MAJOR MEASURES TAKEN BY THE REAGAN ADMINISTRATION

Partly the measures of Reaganomics can be seen as inspired by the wish to reduce government activity in order to make room for tax cuts. The tax cuts were large, but contrary to the potential effectiveness suggested by the former macro–economic analysis, income–tax reductions were much larger than the reductions in corporate taxes. According to our computations *ex–ante* net revenue losses due to the Economic Recovery Tax Act (ERTA) of 1981 and the Tax Equity and Fiscal Responsibility Act (TEFRA) of 1982 were in the neighbourhood of 1.6% of Gross National Product; the corresponding figure for the increased deductability of investment outlays operating from 1983 was about 0.7%. These measures could be financed for about 40% by a decrease in social security payments, but remained uncovered for the rest. In fact, other government spending did increase. Defense outlays were largely responsible for this increase. If we take the average outlays as a percentage of GNP in the period 1978–1980 as a norm, defense outlays rose from 5% in that period to about 5.5% in 1981, 6.1% in 1982 and so on to about 6.6% in 1985. In the light of the previous section, the combination of these measures can be expected to be expansive but very destabilising. This is confirmed by our simulation of the *redress* of the policy changes since 1981. The results of this simulation are presented in Table 2, columns 1, 2 and 3.

The overall–activity level of the US economy would have been much lower (about 3% in 1985), unemployment would have been higher (about 1% in 1985), and imports would have been lower (about 10% in 1985). But the government budget would not have shown a substantial deficit and also the current account of the balance of payments would have looked much brighter, in spite of a higher value of the dollar. We noted before that in the 1980s the US economy was not only confronted with a change in budgetary policy, which can be associated with the Reagan administration, but also with a change in monetary policy coinciding with the installation of Volcker as chairman of the Federal Reserve Board. The stronger reaction of the official discount rate to a change in the national liquidity ratio will have had its impact on the US economy both by itself and through the change in the monetary environment in which the fiscal measures were taken. We investigated these influences by first studying the question what would have been the consequences of a maintenance of the Volcker conditions – the results of which are presented in the columns 4, 5 and 6 of Table 2 – and after that the combined results of a redress of both the Reagan and the Volcker policies in the last three columns of this table.

The impact of undoing the partial Volcker effect on business fixed investment would have been practically the opposite of redressing the Reagan effect. Apart from residential construction, which reacts anticyclically to changes in the utilisation rate of capital, all spending categories show the opposite sign with generally lower absolute effects. The activity gains are clearly due to lower interest rates, in particular for short–term loans. The boost of activity would not

Table 2. Accumulated Effects of a Redress of Policy Changes in the 1980s

	Undoing Reagan's fiscal measures			Undoing Volcker's tighter monetary policy			Undoing the measures of Reagan and Volcker		
Year	1982	1985	1988	1982	1985	1988	1982	1985	1988
Percentage Changes [a]									
Volume of:									
1. Private Consumption	-0.1	-1.7	-3.3	1.1	1.7	1.5	0.9	0.0	-1.7
2. Business Fixed Investment	-2.8	-8.0	-6.7	2.9	7.4	6.1	0.1	-0.4	-0.2
3. Residential Construction	1.8	4.7	-0.2	10.3	5.4	12.7	12.2	10.9	13.8
4. Export of Goods	0.4	-1.0	-1.9	0.2	2.1	2.3	0.6	1.1	0.4
5. Imports of Goods	-4.2	-9.5	-12.9	3.8	5.7	7.2	-0.4	-4.0	-6.1
6. Private GDP	-1.5	-3.1	-3.7	1.5	2.0	1.8	0.0	-1.0	-1.7
7. Price of Production	-0.5	-1.3	-3.8	0.6	2.0	3.2	0.0	0.5	-1.1
8. Private Wage Rate	-1.0	-3.1	-6.2	1.1	3.3	4.9	0.0	-0.1	-2.0
9. Employment of Companies	-0.8	-1.7	-2.1	0.7	1.1	0.9	-0.1	-0.5	-1.0
10. Exchange Rate ($/ECU6)	-2.0	-8.7	-13.8	7.8	11.7	13.6	5.6	2.3	-1.7
Levels [b)]									
11. Unemployment Rate (%)	0.4	1.0	1.1	-0.4	-0.5	-0.4	0.0	0.4	0.6
12. Utilisation Rate (%)	-2.2	-2.9	-2.1	2.2	1.0	-0.6	0.0	-1.8	-2.6
13. Current Account *	0.5	0.9	1.1	-0.2	0.0	0.1	0.3	0.9	1.2
14. Government Budget Deficit *	-1.8	-3.6	-4.5	-0.6	-0.8	-0.8	-2.5	-4.4	-5.1
15. Government Debt to Private Sector *	-1.8	-8.4	-16.0	-1.3	-2.7	-3.9	-3.2	-11.2	-19.9
16. Liquidity Ratio *	-0.2	-0.4	-0.7	-0.3	-0.9	-1.7	-0.2	-0.2	-0.6
17. Unborrowed Reserves *	0.2	0.7	1.3	-1.6	-1.9	-1.8	-1.5	-1.3	-0.7
18. Official Reserves *	0.2	0.6	0.9	-1.4	-1.5	-1.4	-1.2	-1.0	-0.6
19. Long Term Interest Rate	-0.4	-1.4	-2.4	-0.8	-0.6	-0.5	-1.2	-2.0	-2.9
20. Short Term Interest Rate	-0.5	-1.1	-1.6	-2.7	-2.7	-1.9	-3.2	-3.9	-3.8

a) Calculated according to $(X_i^S - X_i)/(0.01X_{i-1})$, where X_i^S and X_i are level variables, referring to the shocked solution and the control solution respectively (i=1,...,10).

b) $X_i^S - X_i$.

* As a percentage of net national income.

so much have affected the current account. This is the result of the substitution effects induced by a sharp drop in the value of the dollar. The lack of support for the capital account in terms of high interest rates would have resulted however in substantial net capital exports and a dramatic fall in official reserves, which ultimately would have forced the Fed either to pursue more restrictive policies or to accept a sharp decline in the external value of the dollar. (It should of course be kept in mind that the simulation starts from the actual situation with increasing government budget deficits). Meanwhile, easier money would have led to a lower burden of interest payments: the combination of these effects would have reduced the government budget deficit considerably. The last three columns of Table 2 present what would have happened if the policy changes initiated both by the fiscal authorities and the Fed hat not taken place. The results come close to the sum of the partial results shown in the preceding columns. Easier money would of course have resulted in lower interest rates, this would have led to net capital exports which would more than offset the improvement in the official reserves due to more budgetary discipline. The redress of the stimulating fiscal policy would to a large extent have been compensated by a stimulating monetary policy: the loss in private activity would have been small. This is partly due to the fact that lower capital costs would have resulted in lower prices, which would have improved US competitiveness. As these substitution effects take time, the improvement in the current account would increase over time. Initially, the dollar would have become weaker, but this development would have been gradually reversed.

5. CONCLUDING REMARKS

The present paper investigates the relevance of the crowding–out problem in the context of a macroeconomic model of the United States. The setting has both drawbacks and advantages. The framework does no justice to refined macro-economic considerations related to distributions within aggregates and differences in marginal conditions between households and firms. The average reactions to average conditions is at best a crude approximation of marginal reactions to marginal conditions. Nevertheless, the treatment of business fixed investment in particular has a relatively firm neo–classical foundation, which renders its reaction to supply conditions easily interpretable. In the context of that model subsidising investment by increasing its fiscal deductability pays off in terms of a higher activity level which can be sustained if the government provides the financial room for this measure by cutting its own spending. The stimulating effects from tax concessions to households did hardly differ from those of extra government spending: average US labour supply tends to fall slightly with increasing real wages.

Given the fact that tax reductions initiated by the Reagan administration were directed towards families more than towards firms, and were only partly compensated for by a decrease in social outlays, no sustainable positive effects could be expected from these measures. As the fiscal scene was further disturbed by a sharp increase in defense spending, not properly covered by additional current income, the deficits in both the government budget and the current account were unavoidable. The model, which takes the rest of the world as exogenous does not well explain the sharp increase in the value of the dollar in recent years. The current much lower value is more in line with its (partial) predictions. Given the size of the US economy a full investigation of the measures studied would require a multi–country model. The US model suggests that the more restrictive monetary policies pursued by the Fed since Volcker took office were a necessity given the lack of fiscal discipline demonstrated by the Reagan administration as a safeguard against either a drastic loss of official reserves or a sharp drop in the value of the dollar, or both.

NOTES

1) See Van der Windt et al. (1984) and Swank and Siebrand (1986).
2) See also Fair (1984).

REFERENCES

Brayton, F., and E. Mauskopf (1985), "The Federal Reserve Board MPS Quarterly Econometric Model of the U.S. Economy", *Economic Modelling,* Vol 2, pp. 170–292.

Fair, R.C. (1984), *Specification, Estimation and Analysis of Macroeconometric Models,* Harvard University Press, Cambridge, Massachusetts.

Swank, J. and J.C. Siebrand (1986), "RASMUS–2b, An Annual Model of the U.S. Economy, 2nd Revised Edition", Discussion Paper 8608/G, Institute for Economic Research, Erasmus University Rotterdam.

Swank, J. (1986), "A Financial Submodel of the U.S. Economy with Endogenous Discount–Rate Policy and Exchange Rate Determination", Discussion Paper 8615/G/M, Institute for Economic Research, Erasmus University Rotterdam.

Van der Windt, N., J.C. Siebrand, J. Swank and J.R. Pijpers (1984a), "RASMUS–2a, An Annual Model of the U.S. Economy", Discussion Paper 8408/G, Institute for Economic Research, Erasmus University Rotterdam.

APPENDIX. Policy Reaction Functions*

(1) Official discount rate

$$r_{CB} = \underset{(2.6)}{0.055}\,\overset{o}{ER}_{-1} + \underset{(4.2)}{0.399}\,\overset{o}{py} - \underset{(5.7)}{0.765}\,\Delta UR_{-\frac{1}{2}} + \underset{(3.5)}{0.042}\left[\frac{SCHP + SDDP}{0.01\ Y}\right]_{-1}$$

$$+ \underset{(4.2)}{0.182}\,DUMVOL\left[\frac{SCHP + SDDP}{0.01\ Y}\right]_{-1} + \underset{(3.5)}{0.478}\,r_{CB_{-1}}$$

Sample period: 1958–1983

Statistics: $\bar{R}^2 = 0.98$; $\bar{S}_e = 0.436$; DW = 2.19

The Fed's discount rate policy is assumed to be aimed at stabilising the exchange rate, depressing the rate of inflation, reducing unemployment and stabilising money supply (M1). The latter target is represented by the liquidity ratio, which is multiplied by a dummy variable for the period in which Volcker was chairman of the Fed. Apparently the impact of the liquidity ratio more than quintupled when Volcker took office (mid 1979), a finding that confirms that of Fair (1984, pp. 146–48). Foreign interest rates were not found to have any significant impact on the US official discount rate, at least when allowance was made for possible simultaneous equations bias.

(2) Exchange rate

$$\overset{o}{ER} = \underset{(6.9)}{-9.591}\left[\frac{LBF + MRC - CPI}{0.01\ Y_{-1}}\right]_{-1} - \underset{(3.3)}{3.615}\,\Delta\left[\frac{LBF + MRC - CPI}{0.01\ Y_{-1}}\right]$$

$$+ \underset{(6.0)}{4.702}\left[\frac{LBF_{EC} + MRC_{EC} - CPI_{EC}}{0.01\ Y_{EC_{-1}}}\right]_{-1}$$

$$+ \underset{(5.0)}{3.205}\,\Delta\left[\frac{LBF_{EC} + MRC_{EC} - CPI_{EC}}{0.01\ Y_{EC_{-1}}}\right]$$

Sample period: 1971–1983

Statistics: $\bar{R}^2 = 0.88$; $\bar{S}_e = 3.466$; DW = 2.20

The exchange rate refers to a weighted average of the spot values of six European currencies in terms of US dollars, where the weights have been determined on the basis of the respective countries' total trade values (imports plus exports). Thus, an *increase* in ER implies a *depreciation* of the US dollar with respect to some kind of ECU. The European countries concerned are the United Kingdom, Germany, France, Italy, The Netherlands and Belgium.

The equation merely relates the percentage change in the exchange rate to some terms which represent (ex post) imbalances in exchange markets, viz. the surpluses of the non–monetary sectors in the US and the EC, relative to the respective lagged values of GDP. As the (changes in the) monetary reserves figure in these surpluses, the monetary authorities are implicitly assumed to intervene in exchange markets to bring about the exchange rate they are willing to accept. So the estimated equation can be said to reflect the extent to which the monetary authorities (in the US and the EC) allowed the market forces to determine the exchange rate during the sample period; possible effects from different types of intervention policies can be studied by simulating the appropriate changes in official reserves.

The fit of the equation is quite acceptable, as is shown by the figure below.

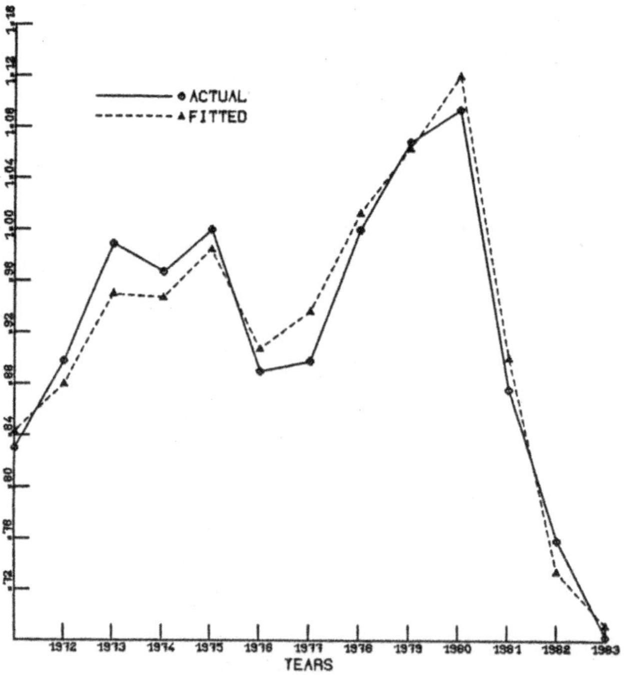

Actual and fitted values of the exchange rate

Fitted values were calculated according to

$$\hat{ER}_t = ER_{1970} * \prod_{i=1971}^{t} (1 + 0.01\, \hat{\overset{o}{ER}}_i)$$

(3) Loans private sector to government

$$\frac{LPG}{0.01\ Y} = \underset{(21.5)}{0.805} \left[\frac{NBG}{0.01\,Y}\right] - \underset{(11.2)}{1.614}\, \Delta\, (r_L/r_K)$$

Sample period: 1958–1981

Statistics: $\bar{R}^2 = 0.94$; $\bar{S}_e = 0.293$; DW = 2.47

Government borrowing behaviour is assumed to respond to market conditions: with relatively rising long–term interest rates the government is more and more inclined to finance its debt (shortly) with commercial banks. This policy tends to stabilise the term structure of interest rates, and obviously may also reflect the government's striving to economise on its interest payments.

Description of variables

CPI	counterpart items
CPI_{EC}	counterpart items EC, converted into US dollars at current exchange rates
DUMVOL	dummy capturing the Volcker period (0.5 for 1979; 1 for 1980 and thereafter; 0 otherwise)
ER	exchange rate, US dollars per unit of EC currency
LBF	loans private banks to abroad (flow)
LBF_{EC}	loans private banks to abroad EC (flow), converted into US dollars at current exchange rates
LPG	loans private sector to government (flow)
MRC	monetary reserves central bank (flow)
MRC_{EC}	monetary reserves central bank EC (flow), converted into US dollars at current exchange rates
NBG	net borrowing by the government (flow)
py	price gross domestic product (1975=1)
r_{CB}	discount rate Fed

r_K	short term interest rate
r_L	long term interest rate
SCHP	stock of currency
SDDP	stock of demand deposits
UR	unemployment rate
Y	gross domestic product (current prices)
Y_{EC}	gross domestic product EC (current dollar prices)

$\overset{o}{z} \equiv 100\,(z - z_{-1})/z_{-1}$

$\hat{}$	refers to estimate

Advanced Studies in Theoretical and Applied Econometrics

---

1. Paelinck, J.H.P. (ed.): *Qualitative and Quantitative Mathematical Economics.* 1982 ISBN 90-247-2623-9
2. Ancot, J.P. (ed.): *Analysing the Structure of Econometric Models.* 1984 ISBN 90-247-2894-0
3. Hughes Hallet, A.J. (ed.): *Applied Decision Analysis and Economic Behaviour.* 1984 ISBN 90-247-2968-8
4. Sengupta, J.K.: *Information and Efficiency in Economic Decision.* 1985 ISBN 90-247-3072-4
5. Artus, P. and Guvenen, O. (eds.), in collaboration with Gagey, F.: *International Macroeconomic Modelling for Policy Decisions.* 1986 ISBN 90-247-3201-8
6. Vilares, M.J.: *Structural Change in Macroeconomic Models.* Theory and Estimation. 1986 ISBN 90-247-3277-8
7. Carraro, C. and Sartore, D. (eds.): *Development of Control Theory for Economic Analysis.* 1987 ISBN 90-247-3345-6
8. Broer, D.P.: *Neoclassical Theory and Empirical Models of Aggregate Firm Behaviour.* 1987 ISBN 90-247-3412-6
9. Italianer, A.: *Theory and Practice of International Trade Linkage Models.* 1986 ISBN 90-247-3407-X
10. Kendrick, D.A.: *Feedback, A New Framework for Macroeconomic Policy.* 1988 ISBN Hb: 90-247-3593-9; Pb: 90-247-3650-1
11. Sengupta, J.K. and Kadekodi, G.K. (eds.): *Econometrics of Planning and Efficiency.* 1988 ISBN 90-247-3602-1
12. Griffith, D.A.: *Advanced Spatial Statistics.* Special Topics in the Exploration of Quantitative Spatial Data Series. 1988 ISBN 90-247-3627-7
13. Guvenen, O. (ed.): *International Commodity Market Models and Policy Analysis.* 1988 ISBN 90-247-3768-0
14. Arbia, G.: *Spatial Data Configuration in Statistical Analysis of Regional Economic and Related Problems.* 1989 ISBN 0-7923-0284-2
15. Raj, B. (ed.): *Advances in Econometrics and Modelling.* 1989 ISBN 0-7923-0299-0
16. Aznar Grasa, A.: *Econometric Model Selection.* A New Approach. 1989 ISBN 0-7923-0321-0
17. Klein, L. and Marquez, J. (eds.): *Economics in Theory and Practice.* An Eclectic Approach. Essays in Honor of F. Gerard Adams. 1989 ISBN 0-7923-0410-1
18. Kendrick, D. A.: *Models for Analyzing Comparative Advantage.* 1990. ISBN 0-7923-0528-0
19. Artus, P. and Barroux, Y. (eds.): *Monetary Policy.* A Theoretical and Econometric Approach. 1990. ISBN 0-7923-0626-0

GPSR Compliance

The European Union's (EU) General Product Safety Regulation (GPSR) is a set of rules that requires consumer products to be safe and our obligations to ensure this.

If you have any concerns about our products, you can contact us on ProductSafety@springernature.com

In case Publisher is established outside the EU, the EU authorized representative is:

Springer Nature Customer Service Center GmbH
Europaplatz 3
69115 Heidelberg, Germany

Batch number: 10761599

Printed by Printforce, the Netherlands